TO MY HUSBAND

Acknowledgements

I would like to thank Jill Gooding for giving me the impetus to begin, Ruth Anderson Katz for her impeccable teaching, and Shepherd Mead for urging me to write about the people I knew in Arabia rather than just the customs and traditions.

My husband was a constant source of encouragement. He was my sounding board throughout the weeks and years of writing and held a steadfast belief in the book and its purpose. Indeed all the family have been unfailingly supportive. I owe them more than I can ever say.

Finally and most especially, I thank with all my heart the Sheikha, the Sheikh, their sons, daughters and friends, without whose courtesy, generosity of spirit, hospitality and constant patience in answering my questions, this book could never have been written. Indeed, this is their book, for their words and life are here. My hope is that it will bring a greater understanding of a people who have a unique culture with its own elegance of manner and mind, rooted in the need to survive.

أشكركم من كل قلبي يا أختي ، وأبنائي ، وبناتي ، وأصدقائي في أبو ظبي .

CONTENTS

Part One

1	The Beginning	1
2	The First Visit	8
3	Al Hareem	17
4	A Jack-of -all-Trades and a Slave	26
5	At Home in Al Ain	37
6	At Home in Park Lane	46

Part Two

7	Changes in the Desert	59
8	Walking to the Island	67
9	The Djinn and the Slave of the Devil	73
10	The Mercy Plane with Gold Taps	85

Part Three

11	Words and Music	99
12	The Woman from Oman	105
13	One Morning and the Man in the Moon	113
14	Sand Storms and Desert Ice	121

Part Four

15	A Bride for a Prince	131
16	Fasting and Feasting in the Tide of Heat	144
17	The Dower House and the Dower	149
18	The Stage is Set	158
19	Of Fantasy, Waltzing and Drums	166
20	A Henna Party and a Declaration of Allegiance	175
21	Parades, Parties and a Gold Cap	180
22	The Bride Comes Home	190
23	Palaces are Planned	193

Part Five

24 Excursion out of Time   199
25 Baby   209
26 Beating the Devil and the Waters of Zam Zam   220

Part Six

27 New Dreams for Old   231
28 The King Who Listened Too Much   241
29 Halcyon Days   247

Epilogue: In Limbo   257

Postscript   276

Glossary   277

Reflection, 2004

I sat on Battery Rocks and watched the helicopter fly in from the Scilly Isles, that splattering of islands dropped carelessly off the coast of Cornwall. A blue September sky. A ship lay off Penzance in the quiet waters of Mount's Bay and an old man was swimming in the deep pool at the foot of the rocks, a pool formed by the tide. An old man? Old? I'm probably older than he is, I thought. Strange. It's strange how I never think about it. Sometimes, when I catch a glimpse of my reflection in a window or mirror, I wonder if that's me, that person with the white hair. It can't be. It's some stranger and I walk on, bewildered by the years.

Three weeks later I sat in a French coffee shop on a narrow back street in a city. The street was caught between high-rise office buildings. Outside two lorries faced each other, their drivers shouting expletives while other drivers in a variety of cars pounded their horns trying to get by, trying to pass or park, trying to push on with their day. Where am I, I asked myself? What city is this? Paris? Rome? Is this Abu Dhabi? No, surely not. It can't be. It's some strange city. Then I turned and watched an Arab coming toward me. There he was. The Second Son of my Arab family. The same face. Older, of course, but the same smile, his kandora whiter than white, his beard perfectly trimmed.

'I know you like good coffee and hot croissants. This is a small place. No view, but the coffee is good.' He smiled his welcome.

Places change. How they change. Beyond imagining. Unrecognisable. But people? The shell changes inevitably, but the centre is always there.

I was back on the Arabian Gulf, back with 'my family' after more than a dozen years. We had kept in touch. I had seen them in London on warm

summer days. There was always the phone, but I couldn't leave my wondrous husband whose long illness had damaged his body but couldn't damage his brightly burning spirit. My Arab family had called regularly.

'How are you? How are you both?'

My answer was always, 'Fine. We are well, thanks be to God,' for I'd learned long ago from the Sheikha that all must always be well, for all is in God's hands.

Now he has gone and after months, years of coming to terms with grief, I am back in Abu Dhabi and I really don't know where I am until I get to the Corniche, which is also unrecognisable because it's no longer a corniche. It's a busy beach by a big, big, big, massive, miles-long pool, a basin all but enclosed by rocks, huge, man-made breakwaters topped with a wide, tree-lined road leading to a restaurant, passing a shopping mall so large that it has a children's amusement park. Inside. Merry-go-round and all.

Abu Dhabi? Where is Abu Dhabi? Where is that island with its salt flats? It's buried somewhere under twenty-first century steel and glass. This is New Abu Dhabi, like New York or New Orleans. Croesus wealth has touched those salt flats and turned them into a city planner's dream of tall buildings facing a turquoise sea, wide, tree-lined streets with rose-covered traffic islands and the accoutrements of traffic and traffic lights and shopping malls and oil terminals and container terminals and more and more and more hotels. It is certainly not the Abu Dhabi I first knew when I became a 'mother without a mask.'

Am I still that 'mother'? No, indeed. I am a 'grandmother' and there aren't so many masks anymore. The grandchildren won't wear them, that's for sure, but the veils are there, the incense, the cardamom-scented coffee in tiny cups, the mint tea, the soft evening air, the silks rustling, the manners, the welcome. Such a welcome. I was enfolded. I was home again.

In past years I would have stayed at the home of one of my 'sons', but now there are so many children that the sons are all pushing their houses out to accommodate their ever-increasing progeny. A variety of extensions face the sea and I am welcomed into the women's majlis guest room where every possible comfort has been thought of for me. From perfumes to plates of dates, from scented soap to that prerequisite for a Western visitor, toilet paper. My room has been aired, hoovered, dusted, sprayed with fly-spray, then with perfumes. The vast, round bed has been given new pink sheets and pink duvet cover, the TV fixed, a kettle provided and a fridge with milk and bottles and bottles of water and butter in little pats. Every small remembrance of my life cared for, and this after all those years away.

One of my 'daughters' rushed about directing a bevy of servants.

'Is it all right? Is it all right? You will be all right? Have I forgotten anything?' Her dear face with her glasses slipping down her nose, her anxious eyes questioning.

'It is perfect, *habibti*, perfect. Very beautiful.'

'You will like your little rug and pillow on the porch in the morning to write?'

I will and I do and in the morning after a dreamless sleep I wake to the muezzin's dawn call, shower, pull on one of my long dresses and walk out onto the long, marble porch that stretches in front of the women's majlis. There it is. A small carpet with a large, hard cushion in its old-fashioned white case with its heavy gold embroidery. I settle myself with my books and papers and watch the day begin. In front of me the mango trees, whose roots were covered in small lakes of water yesterday, defy the already blistering heat of the morning sun. A rare dead leaf dares to fall on the immaculately swept path. Birds chatter. Here is peace, an island of peace in a chaotic world.

All the notes for this book were made as I sat on just such a carpet watching the dawn break. Those notes were eventually gathered together with one purpose in mind: to bring some measure of understanding, to reveal some measure of truth about a culture which had so expanded my own horizons. My hope was and is that that understanding might bring an appreciation of the beauty, grace and manners of a rare society which grew out of the need to survive. Any seed of truth in the stereotype is so buried under layers of prejudice as to be invisible.

Today we live in a dangerous, dark age. Our planet is plagued by demons of fear. Whirling in cyberspace, we cannot catch up with ourselves and the sub-demons of oppression, aggression, ignorance and greed spin us round and round in ever decreasing circles into ever deeper fear. The Middle East is the vortex of this whirlpool. Its pain will inevitably drag us all down unless we can find the lifelines of wisdom and understanding.

'Get wisdom, get understanding…for understanding is a wellspring of life,' wrote Solomon, or Suliman, who is recorded in both the Bible and the Qu'ran. And this must remain the purpose of this book, for surely our true substance and our only future is in understanding.

There is, however, an added dividend, an unexpected bonus which I now treasure. Quite unbeknown to me, during my years away, this book has independently adopted a second – and to me a surprising – path. It was the Youngest Son's wife who explained after she had handed me her own copy to sign. I said that I was surprised but delighted that she had read it.

'But don't you realise this, Mrs Teacup?' she answered, smiling shyly as she poured me a cup of English tea from her Wedgwood teapot, which she then placed carefully on a perfectly set tea tray. 'Don't you understand? We all read this book because it is our history.'

Their history? In the blinking of an eye, from yesterday to today, as my hair has grown white, this story, this tale of events has become their history. I am now caught between amazement, gratitude and hope, the hope that *Mother Without a Mask* will continue to contribute in some measure to understanding, and gratitude for the added, treasured bonus that somehow, in some way, it reflects a small part of their history.

Part One

1

The Beginning

A YOUNG ARAB SAT comfortably on the drawing room couch in our London home drinking English tea and eating chocolate cake.

'Our women are our flowers,' he said as he forked up the chocolate icing.

His jeans were new. His T-shirt was new. He was tall and gangling, an overgrown schoolboy. There wasn't a sign on his cheeks of the soft down that prefigures manhood, but in spite of his adolescence he kept a certain grace of movement. His hands had long, fine fingers which he used constantly when talking. His black, intelligent eyes had the downcast slant of his own falcons. He had thick black hair which was cut too long in the fashion of the day, the mid-1970s. I knew that he spent too much money with the barber at the London Hilton trying to keep it straight.

'Our women are our flowers,' repeated this son of the Gulf, as he stirred four spoonsful of sugar into his tea with my sugar spoon.

'Then why do you shut them up?' I asked.

'Shut them up?' he exclaimed in alarm. 'We don't shut them up.'

'But they are behind masks, under veils, inside walls,' I said.

'It is their custom, their way. It is different. I cannot explain. You must talk to my mother.'

'How can I talk to your mother?' I asked. 'She is in the desert.'

He turned to look at me. It was the blank stare of the Arab who is weighing and balancing before speaking. Expressionless, poker-faced, he was for that moment an adult. Then he turned back to his tea and drank the sickly sweet stuff in two or three gulps.

'You want to meet my mother? This is sure?' he asked, placing his cup and saucer carefully on the table.

'Of course. It is sure.' I repeated his English.

'Then my father will arrange it.'

I don't know whether I believed him or not. There were far too many ifs and buts that could get in the way of my ever meeting his mother. The Arab had that time-worn phrase to cover all contingencies: 'God willing'. Maybe God would be willing and maybe He would not.

So I pushed the conversation well to the back of my mind and concentrated on the problems of the day, most of which centred on what to do with this boy.

The Arab world, or rather that part of the Arab world which borders the Mediterranean, was not strange to me. Ever since our family had become interested in the Middle East, I had travelled both with my husband and occasionally alone to places with such ancient histories as Byblos and Leptis Magna, or other places with the modern comfort and charm Beirut had before it began to tear itself to pieces.

The Arab adventure began quietly, politely and with the best foot forward. It began at a dinner in Berkeley Square, one of those business dinners which occasionally need to be attended. At this particular affair there was an attractive, courteous and forward thinking Sultan from a province in what was then Aden. He had a problem. A simple sort of problem which needed only the knowledge of whom to contact in the echelons of Whitehall, when to contact them and where. My husband had unravelled many such knots for all sorts of people, from students to foreign government ministers. In a lifetime of work he had gathered friends in industry, finance, politics and publishing. The Sultan's tangle was not difficult.

This was the beginning, the first Arab friendship. What we did not know then was that once you come into contact with the Arabian touchstone, an almost irresistible path lies before you. Gate after gate waits to be unlocked. When the Sultan opened the first gate and the lock was sprung, a slow trickle of incidents became a flood and we were tossed willy-nilly down the Arabian road into another world with all its cares, responsibilities and delights.

Nothing had pointed in that direction. Nothing whatever. We had spent our married years in watching our three children grow strong and independent; in keeping our links with my husband's West Cornwall family and my own American one; in building our business in the most unlikely of places, a Welsh valley; and in maintaining friendships which seemed to

be stretching farther and farther around the globe. It was a good life, a busy life, but without the slightest flavour of the Middle East.

Our son was already a partner in the family business when we began to visit peoples whose lands were as distant, forbidding and beautiful as the moon. He often went with one or the other of us on our ever more frequent travels. Even our two young daughters came as often as their lessons or newly chosen careers would allow.

We met Berbers and bedu, sophisticated Egyptians, Tripolitaneans and Lebanese. We travelled into the deep Sahara, sailed on the Nile and explored Crusader's castles.

In those early years, the great Faisal was King of Saudi Arabia, Gaddafi was a golden boy surrounded by twelve companion colonels and the Lebanon was still a nation beating with one heart. On the Gulf, Sultan Qaboos had just taken the reins of power in Oman and north of his borders a new nation was being formed. It would be a collective of Sheikhdoms, a federacy, the near impossible dream of one charismatic Arab leader, Sheikh Zayed bin Sultan Al Nahyan. It was to be the United Arab Emirates, as wealthy a little confederation as any in the world.

Both my husband and our son had visited the Gulf often. They had watched that new nation begin to grow, but I had never been there. I had never seen that turquoise sea, never seen the camels race or the dhows sailing. To me the Gulf remained remote. Isolated. A mystery.

Then this boy arrived.

I shall never forget my first sight of him. He arrived on our doorstep wearing a jacket with a loud, bold check. His escort, an open-faced, educated man, stood smiling in his well-tailored Western clothes as he twiddled his prayer beads with one hand and held the boy with the other. All I could think of at that moment was that the jacket would have to go. Then they were in the house, sitting nervously in the living room. The boy looked as though he might bolt at any moment.

It was his first visit to London, his first visit beyond the Gulf. He was the son of an Abu Dhabi Sheikh, a man who had become an enthusiastic supporter of my husband's work and a good friend. The Sheikh's constant concern for his three sons had brought an invitation for the two younger boys to stay with us for the summer. This boy was the elder of the two. The Second Son.

At first he was unbelievably homesick. He wouldn't leave the room our daughters had vacated for him. He spent his time in long prayers. He wouldn't eat, couldn't sleep. The kind escort came every day for two weeks to talk with him.

Finally I lured him to the kitchen table with a combination of cornflakes and yoghurt, a dish which I was to learn was a bit like that given to Gulf Arab children during Ramadan, the month of fasting: crushed Arabic bread and yoghurt. A few hamburgers and chips and Heinz tomato ketchup followed and at long last he settled in.

His younger brother was sent for and a strange combination of languages began to bounce off our walls as they struggled diligently with books and tutor to learn to speak reasonable English. I became known as Mrs Tea Cup and, for reasons of his own, the boy became Mr Melon while his more formal younger brother adopted the English name of Anthony.

Their questions and my questions never ceased. We had an insatiable curiosity about each other. An insatiable desire to know coupled with something more. A recognition? We knew nothing about each other but we knew each other. We were safe together.

At first the two boys sat in our small Westminster garden under one of two pear trees which yielded a small crop of hard, sickle pears. It is an old walled garden which traps the sun and if the day is still you can hear Big Ben chiming out the hours. We lifted a table on to the patch of lawn and the boys brought out the books which I had found for them at Foyles. English language books for foreign students. Their handwriting was appalling but they made copious notes in Arabic about newly discovered English words and in this way expanded their vocabulary rapidly.

I couldn't keep them cooped up in house and garden, so I eventually found a small English school near Goodge Street underground station. Mastering the underground was a high point. The trains were a delight and they were soon off on their own each morning, returning home in time for a late lunch.

It was a long, hot summer and we had never had such strange strangers in the house before. It was a one-off experiment, a test both for them and for us. Our daughters referred to them as the Sheikhlets and proceeded with their own lives, refusing to alter an inch of skirt or yield the bathroom a second earlier than necessary. Our son accepted the role of elder brother, having never had any younger brothers to guide. With his wide smile and few words of Arabic gleaned from his trips to the Middle East, he soon became their favourite.

The usual bevy of young people drifted in and out of the house, bewildering the two boys with their casual attitudes, for the manners of the young Arabs were impeccable. Both of them were on their feet the moment either my husband or I approached. They greeted us formally each morning and each afternoon on returning from school. They seemed to be innately

courteous, taking pleasure in making our tea and entering into the conversation only when asked.

As the weeks passed and they learned to laugh with us, to tease and to joke, more and more of their separate characters were revealed.

The younger boy was self-contained, charming and had the confidence of an adult. He suffered none of his elder brother's homesickness and balked only at the food. If confused or in a situation unknown to him, he would settle his frame and face into a stillness and passivity that was extraordinary in one so young - he was barely thirteen at the time. His age didn't much matter for he was already an adult in his own mind and it was a brilliant mind that soaked up knowledge, particularly of the sciences. Literature was not his forte. He was bored by any poetry other than that of his own people and barely suffered history. His eyes were squarely set on a technological future.

As for his opinion of the West, this Youngest Son regarded us with the slight disdain we all have for foreign cultures, but he decided within weeks that he could and would conquer Western ways and use them to his own advantage. He overlaid his lack of experience and lack of know-how by walking tall. He was the son of a Sheikh. That was enough. How he could have achieved this total self-awareness in thirteen years intrigued me.

The Second Son, the older boy, the one who had arrived first, was entirely different. Sensitive, quiet, his adolescent eyes never missed a trick. Although he had had the greater difficulty in settling in, he would in the end outrun his younger brother in understanding the West. He was the classic observer. Like the wild falcon, he sat in some eyrie of his own, watching and waiting. 'Why' was the word always in his eyes and frequently in his mouth. Why do you think like this? Why does he act like this? Why does she go this way? Why does he speak that way? And as he learned each answer, a slow smile would rise up from somewhere inside him, a smile so delightful that I'd find myself working to release it.

The Second Son had an air of separateness which I'd seen in other desert people. Something in their spirit kept them apart. Patience, physical endurance and a spiritual stillness gave them the ability to survive in the most desperate conditions in the most desperate climates. Had he been homesick because the human pressure of a great city had almost squeezed the life out of him? Perhaps. Whatever the reason, he worked his way out of his own dilemmas. I could do nothing to help him and could only watch and wait. As he began to understand us, to understand the whys and the wherefores, he began to relax, and other challenges occupied his mind.

Beside the challenge of learning, there was the challenge of foraging in

this wilderness of a city. The two of them began to take longer and longer walks together, peering into small shops or buying some small token in the street markets of Strutton Ground or Tachbrook Street. They were very separate individuals yet wholly attached to each other by that same invisible bond of affection which our own family had. I recognised it and was ever more curious to know who had instilled the bond, and the courtly grace which both of them had.

In late August they announced that their father was coming to fetch them.

'He will be here. He is coming,' said the elder of the two, scarcely covering his relief. I think some corner of his mind believed he'd been abandoned to the city forever.

'And you will tell him how bad we have been?' said the Youngest Son in that strange way Arabs have of hedging their statements as a question or vice versa. Though his mouth was smiling, his eyes were expressionless. I was beginning to understand them a little.

'Do you mean the picture?' I asked, for while sham-fighting they had driven two holes through a nineteenth century oil painting my parents had given us.

'Or the food? Or the bathroom?' The carpet in the bathroom had to be renewed after they left. They were not used to carpeted bathrooms and when they showered water went everywhere.

Both were silent. Then I laughed. 'No, I'll not tell him. I'll tell him how good you are. But,' I added bargaining like an Arab, 'you must tell him how safe you have been even on the underground.' I knew their father had worried about their underground excursions. They agreed. Our bargain was struck.

Father arrived and invited me to meet him at the London hotel where he had booked a suite of rooms for his private visit. I was impressed both by his air of authority and by the absolute stillness of his face. It was a handsome face with an immaculately cut beard, but it revealed absolutely nothing.

'Tell me about my sons,' he said through his secretary. His English was scant. My Arabic was nil.

I looked directly into his eyes. This much I had learned. They do not trust people who shift about with their head, eyes, bodies or attitudes of mind.

Then he added, 'They are your sons now.' It was an expression I had heard all over the Arab world. 'She is your daughter.' 'They are your sons.' It was a remark of respect, of trust.

6

I thanked him and told him as much as I could of their lives in our home. His black-brown eyes occasionally broke into laughter and the laughter itself would follow quickly. Then they would become dark again. The cut-off was total. Nothing of the person inside could be seen. His clothes were Western. He sat easily in the hotel's lobby chair. One felt that it wouldn't have mattered where he was for his self-assurance was complete.

I told him how his sons had graduated from cornflakes to hamburgers, from rhymes to sonnets, from walking with an escort to riding on the underground alone.

'Alone they are not safe,' he said.

'They are here. They are, as you say, my sons. Would I let my sons go in danger?'

He accepted the argument and the boys backed me up. I did not know then that no Sheikh or Sheikh's son moved without an escort. There was good reason for the caution even in those comparatively peaceful times. Young Arabs were a constant prey to the politics of their area and the thieves of ours.

Within a few days they had all left London. I didn't know when or if I'd ever see them again, and I settled back into normal family life. Our daughters stretched out into their two bedrooms, having been squashed into one, and the house settled back into its Englishness. Arab voices, Arab music and boyish high jinks had disappeared into the great desert sands of Arabia.

Echoes remained. There were the things they had left behind. The odd note book. A small, delicately crocheted skull cap. A sarong or, as they called it, a *wezaar*. 'These are our peejahmah Mrs Tea Cup. Our skirt for under the long white.' The long white. Their Arab dress. '*Kandora*, Mrs Tea Cup. *Kandora*.'

Then there were the other echoes. The way their eyes lit slowly from behind when they spoke of their mother, their home, the desert, their family, the sea. Although they had given up trying to explain their way of life to me, the little they did say had tantalised my curiosity, my own desire to know, to see, to understand.

'My father will arrange it,' the boy had said, but could I afford to believe him? Could I afford the dreams which might lead to disappointment? He was so young, so unable to manipulate events. It couldn't happen, I told myself, more as a discipline against dreaming than a belief. It was too difficult. They didn't invite women. It was a closed place. Besides, he would forget. Yes. He would forget. The long, hot summer was over.

2

The First Visit

OCTOBER ARRIVED AND the leaves began to fall. The pears in our London garden were picked and packed into jars with cinnamon and spice. November followed and then December with its plans and preparations for our annual Christmas excursion to Cornwall. We always kept Christmas in Cornwall, relishing the wood fires inside and the blustering gales outside.

We were still in London, parcels wrapped and stacked ready for transport, a wreath on the door and the house heavy with the smell of evergreen when the telex arrived. A ticket was being sent. I was to come to Abu Dhabi for a visit in late January. All was arranged. Hospitality would return hospitality. A hotel was booked. I was not to be concerned. Simply telex time of arrival.

Was it the answer to the boy's promise? Would I meet his mother? Would I meet those strange masked women? Or would I be entertained courteously and generously in a newly built hotel and discover nothing of their real lives? I had no idea. I only knew that I was going.

Throughout that Cornish Christmas I planned and planned again. I read all I could find about the Gulf in our rapidly expanding collection of Middle Eastern books. I searched for pamphlets and government hand-outs. There wasn't much. It didn't take long.

When the two boys telephoned to wish us a happy Christmas their voices were warm and welcoming.

'What should I bring to wear?' I asked the Second Son.

'Clothes for summer and a sweater for winter. And I think, if you can, a long skirt to be more comfortable,' he answered. My hopes rose.

'Will I meet your mother?' I asked.

'God willing,' came the reply and I was as much in the dark as ever.

I packed and repacked, hoped and tried not to hope too much. Then it was time to leave and time to arrive and the first visit began.

I remember well that first journey when all was new and strange. The plane slipped down out of the sky towards a small collection of lights in a black nothingness. It was as though the sky had tipped upside down and a few stars had huddled together for protection.

We landed and as I stepped out into the night I remember my surprise at the gentle heat. The air was soft, kind, enveloping. I had expected something harsher but it was their winter, too.

I remember that the two young sons, my 'sons', rode out in the airport bus to meet me at the foot of the plane's steps. I scarcely recognised them in their Arab dress. They seemed taller, older, full of laughter and enthusiasm for all the plans they'd made. Then quite suddenly, a group of young men surrounded us. There were so many of them. With a wide sweep of hands they introduced a half dozen or so, saying, 'These are our friends.'

These friends cut through the few formalities of the airport like a hot knife through butter. I was escorted to a new Mercedes which stood at the head of a group of Mercedes. One of the friends slipped into the driver's seat, the sons and I settled into the back and we drove in cavalcade down a tarmac road through flat desert toward the sea. There was a town there. A new town spreading over the sand. It was Abu Dhabi.

We drove along the sea front to a new Hilton Hotel which stood in lonely splendour at one end of a narrow road that would eventually become a four-laned parkway known as 'The Corniche'. The hotel looked like a fort standing strong and tall in the desert night. Inside, its lobby was cool and broad with a few white couches. The space seemed right for the white-robed Arab men and the long, full skirts of the European, Indian and Mediterranean women who dressed in the evening.

The boys showed me to my room with its sitting room. A suite. Delight was in every movement, as though they had built the place themselves.

'It is lovely, eh?'

'It is very beautiful,' I answered.

I went to bed that night feeling cossetted but bewildered, slept fitfully and woke with the light from a blue Arabian sky.

There it was. There was the turquoise Arabian Gulf with its borders of

near white sand. I could see it at last.

Along the coast the new town stretched and grew in the sun. I watched as lorries and bulldozers wound up the narrow coast road and massive tankers lying low on the water line worked their way down to the ocean. I watched amazed knowing that oil had first been sucked out of this desert place little more than a dozen years ago; that this town which now boasted a Hilton Hotel had been a small collection of flat-roofed houses dominated by an Arab fort less than a decade earlier.

I knew that when the first oil began to flow down the pipes to the ships, the Bani Yas, the Awamir, the Manasir, the Dhawahir, and the Afar, those tribal collectives under whose banners rode some thirty sovereign tribes numbered less than 15,000 souls in an area of thousands of square miles. Now this new mushrooming town alone had a population of 45,000 including British, American, French, German, Japanese, Indian, Pakistani, Armenian, Sudanese, Iraqi, Egyptian, Palestinian, Uncle Tom Cobley and all. It was a gold rush. A black gold rush and they, those Arabian knights with their black-swathed ladies and their camels and caravans and fine-boned horses were in imminent danger of being drowned.

I turned away from the bright light of the window, picked up the telephone, dialled room service and ordered a breakfast of orange juice, coffee and rolls. I drew a bath, emptying in the vial of bath essence provided courtesy of the hotel, and laid out my clothes for the day. A summer dress with long sleeves. My long skirts were hanging in the closet. Would I ever wear them?

Two hours later there was a knock on the door. The two sons in immaculate white kandoras, their smiles full of affection, had come for me.

They were perfect hosts. That morning and every morning they arrived with a plan. There was lunch in the hotel coffee shop, a swim in the hotel pool, a drive through the town, a rest, dinner with their friends in the darkened hotel restaurant, candles on the tables. There was a visit to the ADNOC (Abu Dhabi National Oil Company) exhibition with its film of life before oil and life after oil. There was a trip to an island to see acres of young vegetables growing in plastic domes under the watchful eyes of young Americans.

There was a visit to the new market with its 'Sport Palace'. 'Hollywood Store' and 'Shaah's Supermarket'. Already the wind and sand and dust and lethargy had invaded and it was beginning to look and smell like an old market, with aromas of roasting coffee, of cinnamon, cardamom and cloves mixing with exhaust fumes, jasmine blossom, Chanel No 5 and Brut. A waft of sandalwood hung in the air as a black-shrouded figure walked by; I

wondered who she was and whether I would ever meet any of them and my heart slipped around in disappointment.

Three days passed. Then four and finally I braved the question.

'But where is your mother?'

The Second Son smiled his slow wide smile. 'You will meet her,' he said.

'Truly? She will come here? Or may I visit her?' I could not hide my hope and seeing it the Youngest Son could no longer contain himself.

'She is in the desert, waiting for you,' he said laughing.

The carefully laid surprise was out. This was the long mid-year school holiday. This was the time to camp by the sea again. The whole extended family was together far down the coast on an inlet, and I was to visit them there. That was why I had had to come at this time and no other.

When the two sons left me that evening, they were convulsed with laughter at my delight, but the elder took me aside, away from his brother and their friends.

'You have your long skirt?'

'Yes.'

'Then wear it. You will be more comfortable. You will be like them.'

'Is there anything I should do or anything I should know?' I asked tentatively.

Again the slow smile. 'No. No. You will see it all. My mother, she has asked for you. She invites you. I have told her about you. She knows of you.'

He took my hand and I walked with him to the car.

'Tomorrow, then.'

'Yes, tomorrow.'

The following day they came in a Range Rover. I climbed into the front seat, gathering my long skirt around me. I'm wearing it at last, I thought, as I felt the silk against my ankles. A strange mixture of eagerness and apprehension, excitement and shyness filled my heart. I'd known these mixtures before but never more so than at that moment.

We drove along the shore and back up the airport road. About half a mile from the town we joined three other Range Rovers. The Sheikh was in the driver's seat of the lead car. He stepped out to greet me formally, his face now full of welcome. A group of men stood around the other cars, some carrying rifles and one with a small sub-machine gun. All were laughing, talking and gesticulating as they talked. Suitcases and stores of various kinds were piled into the cars from a waiting lorry. Cases of Pepsi Cola and chicken soup, sacks of grain, boxes of fruit. Finally all was ready and we set

off down the tarmac road out of Abu Dhabi, leaving the city and then the airport behind.

After an hour's driving the lead car swung off the road past a small cluster of dusty houses and a mosque. The hard packed sand sprayed up clouds of dust as we groaned and bounced over the desert and I began to realise the skill it took to wind in and out of the soft and hard sand, to negotiate dunes and bypass sinking sands, to know where you were. There were no land-marks. Nothing surrounded us but emptiness.

More time passed. Then in the distance, a group of tents began to take shape against the sand. We swung up a small rise and arrived.

The tents were pitched near a narrow, shallow inlet. Camels were hobbled nearby. Goats and sheep grazed on rough tufts of sand grass. A great fire was burning and it was kept going throughout the day and most of the night. There was a water truck standing by. Another pick-up held a generator for the electric lights strung around and in the tents. It was a strange mixture of old ways and new convenience.

The scene was a living mosaic of people and colour. Men tended the fire in long white kandoras, their heads bare or covered with the little white crocheted hats. Other men carried boxes of fish, their checked head-dresses wound into turbans. Naked to the waist, they wore a loin cloth wound around their hips, pulled up through their legs and tucked into the waist.

Children raced about, little girls in brightly coloured long dresses, boys in small white kandoras which exactly matched those of the men. Women servants carried coffee thermoses and fruit on trays, their long dresses whipping about their legs, their heads covered in thin, short, black veils. Slowly the ladies of the family emerged, their own brilliant silks showing beneath knee-length black veils, their faces masked.

'Come, come. This is my mother,' said the Youngest Son. His thin brown hand caught mine and helped me from the car. I felt the sand pour in and out of my sandals as I walked the few yards toward the women. I felt the shyness rise in my throat. One of the women moved toward me, releasing two little girls whom she had been holding by the hand. They leapt toward the Sheikh and he caught them both up in a great sweep of his arms. His wife greeted him formally yet affectionately, placing one hand on his as he held the children. Then she reached out her hand to greet me with a strong, firm grip.

'*Marhaba, Marhaba,*' she said. 'Welcome, welcome.' And with those first words of greeting I was drawn into the life of that remote, disparate place with what now seems to be a strange inevitability, a destiny.

I can remember to this day what she wore. It was a long dress of sky-blue Indian silk with little embroidered gold squares. Her eyes smiled behind her stiff, black burnished gold canvas mask. She stood quietly, unperturbed by the busy scene around her.

I think it was the combination of dignity and innocence which I found so immediately attractive. She was short compared to Western women, but gave an impression of height. Not thin, but lithe and strong with a straight back. She walked with a measured light step, her silks and black veils rustling about her. It would have been impossible to imagine her running or darting about. Her hair was thick, black and strong. She wore it like a child in one long, heavy plait down her back but there were to be days when I would see her twist it into a complicated bun, securing it with a few heavy pins and combs.

Turning, she called to a man-servant to bring my case and then beckoned me to come beside her. We walked together toward a large tent which was pitched slightly apart from the others and close to the water. As we walked she kept up a constant flow of words which sounded welcoming, but which I couldn't understand. Her voice was soft and low, rather throaty though I had just heard that it could be quick and firm when giving an order. She expected to be obeyed. She was a Sheikha.

She was a Sheikha not because she was the wife of a Sheikh, but because she was the daughter of a Sheikh. As with all married women in the Muslim world, she kept the name of her father all her life, a mark of her ultimate independence. She wore no wedding ring.

We reached the tent and she opened the flap and led me inside. I remember being surprised at the comfort of it. It was large - about twenty feet by fifteen. The floor was completely carpeted with Persian rugs and there were several solid, heavy cushions against the sides, cushions that were covered in white cotton cases which had colourful touches of embroidery in the centre. In one corner were three bed rolls and my case was stowed near one of these. I wondered who my companions were to be.

The Sheikha sat on the carpet and gestured that I was to sit beside her. Children seemed to arrive from nowhere along with several women all heavily veiled and with the same black harlequin masks. The two sons had settled near their mother who plied them with questions about my comfort, what we had done in Abu Dhabi, who had been with them, who had driven us, and whether the journey had been easy.

A small handleless cup with a few swallows of coffee in it was put into my hand. The coffee was hot, light and pungent. I looked up to see a maid standing with a thermos pouring cup after cup skilfully and quickly for all

the women there. My cup was refilled and I drank again, quickly and appreciatively. It was good. In fact it was delicious.

Each time the Sheikha turned to me she began her quiet stream of welcoming blessings, queries as to my health, the health of my family. She asked for each of my children by name, checking with her sons as she wrapped her tongue around the unfamiliar English words and laughing at her own efforts.

I couldn't keep my eyes off her. The little mask was wholly strange and yet she wore it with such familiarity and ease that I found myself accepting it. It was entirely unobtrusive.

Her sons adored her. That was obvious. They held her hand, nudged against her, joked with her.

'Now you see my mother,' said the Second Son. 'Now you see her at last. You didn't believe, did you? You never believe, Mrs Tea Cup.' He smiled and motioned me to drink more coffee.

A small tray of fruit arrived and the Sheikha began to peel and cut the apples and pears and bananas, offering me small pieces to eat.

'Eat, eat,' she said, adding words of blessing.

Her hands were exceptionally beautiful with long, strong, supple fingers. She used them continually in speech, sometimes holding up the thumb and third finger in a circle together to accent a point, the palm open and raised. Her finger-nails were painted with henna, as were the soles of her feet where the henna had gone a dark purple.

Her eyes behind her mask were brown, dark brown but as we looked at each other and I smiled, I know that she smiled for her eyes seemed to grow lighter, almost to change colour. In time I would see them lightening to hazel when she was excited or darkening to black with concealed anger. Her eyelashes were thick and dark with *kohl*, the original mascara.

For a moment we looked at each other in a wordless greeting. Then the moment was over, but it was enough to establish a link, a beginning to a friendship which would have to cross chasms of time and tradition. This was the woman I had come so far to meet. Mine had been a journey of miles, thousands of miles. She had had to travel through centuries. We were both aware of the challenge that life had put in front of us. We were both willing to accept it.

'She is the director of the company, eh? The light which draws all the butterflies,' said the Second Son.

'She is the honey for the bees to eat,' shouted the Youngest Son and, grabbing her, kissed her again and again until she pushed him away, laughing and straightening her veils.

Director of the company. Director of the establishment. Arbiter of fashion. Upholder of custom and moral law. A devout Muslim. Manager of the affairs of her husband's home and their family. As the 'home' which I was soon to visit had been described to me as a small village in itself, I imagined that she would need to be mayor, town clerk, farm supervisor, hotel manager and all.

It was an extraordinary thought that this modest, almost shy woman with her veils and mask and, indeed, lack of any formal education, could fulfil all these roles. And yet I was to watch her in them all, always moving quietly, always self-effacing and with good humour. A paragon? Perhaps, for I knew that she, like all Sheikhas, had had to learn early in life to subdue the petty jealousies and ambitions which plague us all. What I didn't know then was that she was a perfectionist, worrying over each detail of life, identifying with the world's tragedies as well as its joys. It was a massive mental and emotional burden which she masked almost as skilfully as she masked her face.

Her sons had told me that she had been married at the age of thirteen, possibly younger. They told me that she had walked to the home of her husband followed by two of her father's black servants who carried an ornately decorated chest filled with all her possessions: her clothes, jewels, masks, perfumes, incense, kohl and prayer mat. The servants had never left her.

I knew too that her husband was the centre but not the circumference of her world. Before the time explosion triggered by oil, he had been always near her. Always home. Now he spent the greater part of his days away in Rome, in Paris, in Delhi or Karachi.

In time I would learn that he telephoned her once a day or more asking, 'Is all well?' and she would invariably answer, 'Yes, all is well.'

This was knowledge I would gain with the years. Now I only knew that the graceful, masked Sheikha beside me was not what I had expected. Charming and hospitable, yes. But also completely in command. She had seen the problems facing her world and knew that she would have to find firm footsteps for her children to cross into the new world in front of them. Had I been chosen as a footstep? Was I to act as a bridge over which they could safely cross? Was this why I had been invited into her world?

That first night in the desert I lay wrapped in a thick blanket on a quilted palliasse. Two Pakistani hand-maids had been assigned to sleep with me as companions, protectors and servants. They lay a few yards away, breathing slowly and steadily in deep sleep. The wind rose and the bamboo tent poles creaked and groaned like a ship sailing on close tack. The water lapped

hard in the inlet. The generator hummed, giving its protective ring of light.

'What am I doing here?' I thought. 'However did I manage to get here?'

I rose, opened the laced tent flap and looked out into the black night. Sand was curling up in little eddies. It was intensely cold. The carpet which covered my tent felt warm and comforting beneath my feet. I laced the flap down again and went back to my palliasse. I felt safe and at peace.

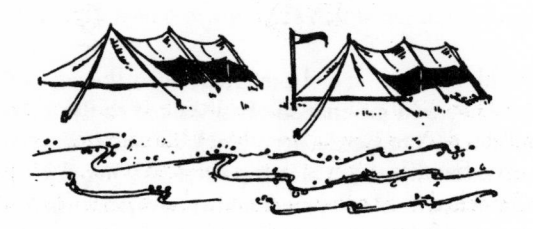

3

Al Hareem

THE FOLLOWING MORNING I woke late after a long, deep sleep. The clean air had acted like a drug on my city-polluted lungs. I knew it was late as the two little hand-maids had both risen and gone, their palliasses neatly rolled and stacked in a corner. I stretched and buried myself deeper in my blankets waiting for the courage to get out and dress. In winter the temperature of a desert can drop sharply at night, reaching a low point in the pre-dawn hours and staying cold until the sun is well risen.

In the centre of the tent was a small, low, sand-filled brazier. Brought in the night before, its modest fire of glowing charcoal had burned itself out in the night. Now there was nothing but ashes. It had been a cold, a very cold night.

Beside my palliasse was a round tin tray about two feet in diameter. On it were two pyrex cups, one with a saucer, one filled with sugar. There were two metal spoons, a piece of silver baco-foil holding some tea bags and a tin of 'Rainbow' condensed milk. A plate of hard-boiled eggs had been brought in by the maids the night before. They had eaten their share at once, placing two on the tray for my breakfast.

There was a rustling and the pad of sandals on sand. Then soft conversation. The tent-flaps opened and one of my sleeping companions came in, followed by a tall, smiling man-servant who carried a shovel full of burning coals. He poured the fire on to the brazier. One of the coals dropped red hot on the carpet. He picked it up and tossed it on to the brazier without a thought and without a burn, nodded his good mornings and padded out.

17

The maid squatted beside me, grinning broadly, and began to make tea from a tall blue thermos which she had brought with her. I sat up and drew my black Burberry cape around me while the little maid peeled the eggs and chattered away in an amalgam of Urdu, Arabic and English. Her name was Selma. Servants in the Gulf generally come from the Muslim populations of Pakistan, Sri Lanka or the Philippines. Selma was from Pakistan. Her voice was low and rich and her eyes full of humour. She had a lively wit. She would one day become a sort of major-domo, presiding over house and kitchen at the right hand of the Sheikha and walking through the family compound in silks and gold necklaces. Now it was cotton hand-me-downs.

We communicated one way or another and I learned that the sons had already breakfasted and were waiting for me. I must hurry and dress, she said. I had slept late. All were up and about. After seeing that I ate both eggs, she picked up the tray and left me to dress.

I washed in the pan of water that had been brought for me and dressed as rapidly as possible. It was still cold. The long skirt felt comfortable and dropped easily into place and I blessed the young son who had told me to bring it. Pulling a shawl around my shoulders, I walked into the now brilliant sun.

The Second Son was standing talking to one of the many young Arabs who always seemed to surround these boys. When he saw me, he turned toward me, his thin young face suddenly smiling.

'Good morning. You sleep well?' he asked.

'Yes, well,' I answered.

'Then come, we will walk,' he said and we started towards the inlet.

It was a short few yards to the water. Kicking off our sandals, we began to wade, crunching myriads of tiny molluscs in their conical shells with every step. The air was clean and fresh, the sun warm and gentle. It was the sort of day we long for through the bone-damp days of an English winter.

'Who are all the women with your mother?' I asked.

'*Al hareem,*' he said with a broad grin.

'The harem!' I exclaimed.

'*Al hareem,*' he nodded and threw back his head laughing. He caught my hand. 'You think they are all my father's wives or concubines. You think that, don't you?' And he danced about me, doubling up with laughter, splashing water at me with his feet. I leapt on to the dry sand to protect my long skirt from getting any wetter.

Suddenly he stopped and looked at me quite seriously. 'Listen, Mrs Tea Cup,' he said, 'I told you my father had only one wife. This is the truth.'

We sat down together on the shore, backs to the sun and feet in the water. It was the start of one of the many lessons I was to be taught by these and other young sons and daughters of the Gulf.

The harem. *Al hareem*. All the mysteries of the East seem bound in that tantalising word. All that is unknown, hidden, forbidden. Over the centuries, we in the West have managed to conjure up extraordinary ideas of this forbidden fruit. Imagination has run riot. From tales of Turkish pashas to the inevitable Hollywood films, we have been conditioned to envisage a vast number of semi-nude ladies with see-through bits of veil across their nose and mouth, languishing beside secret pools, within sealed tents or behind imprisoning walls waiting for their master.

Is there any truth in the travellers' tales which have conditioned our thinking? Of course. From Robert Wither's seventeenth century description of the Egyptian Grand Seignior marching up and down ranks of carefully prepared 'gift' virgins, down to Nawal el Saadawi's passionate recommendation of the new French organisation *Sentinelle* which rescues girls intended for 'honour murder', the evidence is there.

But this patch of sand on the edge of the Gulf where the boy and I cooled our feet was neither Egypt nor Algeria. These women were and are separated by thousands of miles of bitter desert. Their heritage is as different to that of Cairo or Morocco as a Parisienne's is from a Muscovite's. The distance is about the same.

Is their harem - *hareem* - a place full of subservient females, wives and concubines having nothing to do all day but gossip and perfume themselves waiting for the night and the master's selection? Hardly, but that was a discovery I had to make and the first lesson to learn there on the shore of the Gulf was the meaning of the word *hareem* or harem. Soberly and quietly he tried to explain.

'*Hareem* is Arabic for women. It is plural. *Hormah* is woman. *Al hareem* - or the way you say it which you must not - the harem - is the women of the house.'

'That is all?' I queried.

'That is all,' he answered.

But that was not all. There was more. Much more.

I kept questioning. He kept answering.

The word *hormah* - woman - comes from the Arabic root word *haram* - forbidden, holy, sacrosanct, sanctuary. An amazing word full of secrecy and spiritual commitment. *Haram* today is used almost entirely in its meaning of forbidden, not allowed. I began to realise that women of Arabia and the Gulf are cloaked in this word.

'You are a member of the hareem here, Mrs Tea Cup,' said the boy, again doubling over in a convulsion of laughter at the expression on my face. It was a shock to realise that I was included in this sweeping phrase, but I was there and had to be accounted for so I suppose it was inevitable.

On that first visit we were a group which numbered some thirteen or fourteen women. The boy listed them, ticking them off on his fingers for me. First his Grandmother, the Sheikh's mother and her 'lady-in-waiting', an elderly widow; then his mother and her 'lady-in-waiting', a divorcee whose widowed mother was also part of the entourage; another friend who was both the wife and the daughter of one of their tribe and had once been a wet nurse to the Sheikha's children as she had children of her own of about the same age; and finally the occasional visitor, such as myself. This was the immediate hareem, but when travelling all the women would be included in the word, so one would add the young daughter's nurse, the nurse of two small foster daughters and four or five women body-servants or hand-maids who were usually Pakistani or Sri Lankan.

How easy it is for the West to misunderstand this group of women living and moving together, to see something strange and mysterious in these shrouded figures travelling together.

'But your father could have many wives,' I probed. Though our feet were cool in the water, our backs felt an increasingly hot sun.

'Only four, Mrs Tea Cup,' he answered, 'only four.'

'But some have many more,' I insisted.

'Some divorce and marry another one. But it all gets difficult. You have to look after all of them the same. That's the law and that could be very difficult,' he laughed. 'Besides, one is better. The Prophet said so.'

I knew what was written in the Qur'an. I had read it.

> '... Marry women of your choice,
> Two, or three, or four;
> But if ye fear that ye shall not
> Be able to deal justly (with them)
> Then only one, or (a captive)
> That your right hands possess.
> That will be more suitable,
> To prevent you
> From doing injustice.'

It had always seemed obvious to me that the message to the Prophet was that one wife was better all around and I said as much to the boy.

'This is what I said,' he answered, having exclaimed in amazement that I'd read the Qur'an. They are always so delighted if we read their holy book but are rarely willing to look at ours.

His explanation about multiple marriages for Sheikhs was memorable.

'For us,' he said, 'for the Sheikhs you have to be very rich to have more wives. Very rich and very fair. It is easy to be rich but difficult to be fair. One woman is better.'

His was an old head on young shoulders. We talked of Sheikhs he knew who had two or three wives. Some he admired, some he didn't, but he excused them all though he admitted that the emotional traumas were often acute. There seemed to be the same bitter situation that arose in the West when a man takes a mistress and his wife can do nothing about it. The same options are open. Nine times out of ten the same solution is adopted. The wife sticks it out and swallows her pride rather than opt for divorce. What's more, as the boy explained, there is the overriding factor that if a woman remains married she keeps the children. If she is divorced, the children might be allowed to remain with her but if the father wished, he could demand that they be brought up by his own family.

We talked about jealousy, anger and frustration - emotions allotted to his culture as well as mine. A Gulf woman was not trained out of human reactions to a broken family. What is different is the face she puts on. No tears, no traumas.

'This is shameful, Mrs Tea Cup,' said the Second Son. 'We have a saying. 'It is shameful for tears to fall, but tears in the eyes are like pearls.'

I realised how much learning there was ahead of me if I were to begin even to understand something of their lives.

He rose, helped me to my feet and we began to walk slowly back to the camp. I decided that in order to learn I would have to melt as unobtrusively as possible into the background of the hareem, to accept the hospitality of the house without stumbling too much, to settle in quietly. This would be about as easy as a crow settling down in a dovecote. The only common factor was that we were all birds.

A few mornings later, I found the two sons standing by the Range Rover with four of their friends.

'You will come with us?' they asked me. It was scarcely a question.

'Yes, I will come,' I answered. 'Where do we go?'

'You will see,' they laughed.

The engine was revved and we started off, skidding and skating across the sand.

The sons were too young to drive along the highway. There were already regulations about minimum age, so they cut their driving teeth in the desert. Their father, a stern taskmaster, demanded a high degree of proficiency in handling motors of all sorts, whether cars, trucks or boats, as he himself was a master. I had already watched him ease out a truck which one of his drivers had managed to bury hub deep in soft sand. It had seemed almost effortless.

By the time his sons were ready to take to the road, they were able to drive their cars with the same assurance with which they rode their horses and for this Arabian family the ability to ride was as important as the ability to drive. All the men rode. They rode with saddles or without, their legs and hands controlling the powerful Arabian mounts. Riding together, over the desert, robes flying, horses straining, they looked like a painting coming alive.

But these were sights for times to come. Now it was early days and the desert was waiting. To me it was a broad expanse of nothing. To them it was an easily read map. The car whirred and struggled over dunes and the boys joked and laughed, their taped Arabic music singsonging into the empty atmosphere.

Eventually we slid over yet another hillock of sand just large enough to conceal a small encampment beside yet another inlet. There were a few tents, a pick-up truck, some sheep and goats and another brightly burning fire. Beside the fire was a small woman, her black veils drifting over her masked face. She stood quietly watching us as we drove up. Then calling to a man near the truck, she waited for him to join her and the two of them moved toward us as we stopped and stepped out of the car.

It was a greeting of great warmth and welcome. Hearing the man's name, I knew that he was one of the senior Sheikhs of the area. I had heard his name mentioned many times in London.

The slim, small woman by the fire was his daughter-in-law. We stood for a moment while the boys explained who I was, which was unnecessary as they already knew. News travels fast in the desert and at that moment, in that place, I was the news.

The little Sheikha took me by the hand and led me to the women's tent. It was new and white with a pale green lining. Inside was a bevy of women of all shapes, sizes and ages, all masked except for a few young girls and a few serving women. They were chatting and talking in obvious good humour. I was settled down next to a young girl of exceptional beauty. Her meticulous schoolgirl English was a godsend.

Within minutes steaming basins of food on trays were carried in on the

heads of the maids and placed around the tent at various intervals. I didn't know it then but this was the morning visiting time. Each visiting time has its own name, traditions and customs and the more you know about the manners and customs of each one, the higher in the social echelon you are. The courtesies of Al Dhoha embraced a sort of midmorning breakfast and to me it became a kind of baptism.

Until that moment I had taken all my meals in my tent with one or other of the children who could speak English. It was usually the boys' young sister, a wide-eyed child with a generous mouth who had a superb sense of humour under her impeccable manners and modesty. We would sit cross-legged on the carpet, I with a spoon, knife and fork, provided by the Sheikha. I shall never forget my little set of implements. They were quite small, as though made for a child, and had beautifully carved black ebony handles in the shapes of birds' heads. My companion was always served her meals in a large enamel soup bowl into which she dipped her right hand and efficiently scooped up and devoured the meat, rice, fish or salad. I used my bird-handled knife, fork and spoon.

That morning however I was on my own. The girl beside me realised my confusion and began carefully to explain what was in each dish. *Harees* - a kind of glutinous porridge of lamb and cracked wheat; *bilaleet* - a sweet vermicelli with a thin omelette on top; and *khabees* - a strange combination of flour, oil and sugar which looked and tasted something like a sweet couscous. It too was served with an omelette on top.

The girl showed me how to dip into the bowl with the thumb and first and second fingers, how to make a kind of ball and push it off the fingers into the mouth with the thumb.

'Try the harees. It is the easiest,' she said.

So began my first meal 'bedu' style. The harees proved to be delicious and I stuck to that in spite of the urging by the others to try each dish.

'You do well,' said the girl as I struggled.

'Tell me your name,' I answered, half-preoccupied with harees-glued fingers.

'Shamsa,' she smiled. 'It means the sun, but all say Shamza or Shamooz.'

'Your english is very good. Is it from school?'

'Yes,' she answered. 'But it is not good. Not good.'

As she gently urged me on, apologising for their customs, she translated all my remarks to the company in general who would comment, laugh and encourage her to urge me on again. I noticed, however, that the women themselves ate very little: a few mouthfuls of this and a few mouthfuls of that. It was a sort of coffee morning and the most important facet was the

hospitality offered and received.

I was fascinated by the way the women managed to lift their masks and pop the food into their mouths all in one gesture with one hand. The right hand. Using the left hand was ill-mannered, not the done thing. The right hand for eating, the left for washing after going to the toilet. Oh yes. I had many things to learn.

We talked and Shamza translated as the others asked me all the usual questions. Where was my husband, how many children did I have, where were they, what were they doing, the same questions we all hear at any Western women's party. It must have been as extraordinary a morning to them as it was to me.

As we were sitting engrossed in our entertainment of each other, the Youngest Son slowly put his head around the corner of the tent opening and with a wide grin said his greeting, '*Salaam alaikum.*' Peace be with you.

With a shriek Shamza flung herself on the ground behind me, pulling her veils around her. With more shouts all the young girls copied her, hiding behind the nearest ample back.

Women laughed and scolded, girls shouted. A young fox had entered the chicken coop and the young fox was delighted with the impression he had made. Laughing, he beckoned me to come and made his escape.

Shamza rose when she knew he had gone and kissing me on both cheeks, 'English style', she asked me to come again. 'Our house is yours,' she said, translating her mother's words. The little Sheikha then walked with me to our Range Rover. Other women followed, their bright dresses billowing in the winter wind.

As we drove off I saw the little Sheikha bending over the stores of food which had been stacked by the fire. The scene was encapsulated in my mind. The tents, the goats, the camels, the fire, the truck, the children playing by the inlet, and the gentle, hospitable lady already at her work.

I was to see her again in less than a year ensconced in a London hotel with her daughter and other children, commanding cars, porters, drivers and waiters in the same quiet manner. We were to become great friends, but neither of us ever forgot our first meeting.

On the way home, I asked about the wild scene in the tent, the girls' frantic hiding. 'This is nonsense,' said one young boy. 'It is not nonsense, it is written,' said another. 'It is politeness,' said the Second Son, who was driving rapidly over the sand.

There are constant debates about customs on the Gulf and in the Arab world as a whole, but in this area there was no great hurry to change them. Certainly at that time the established practices prevailed. Girls were not

to be seen except by their own immediate family once they passed puberty. In fact, only in a desert camp would the young girls be allowed to show their faces when their mother entertained guests. Probably not even then. Probably, being English, I didn't matter and the rules were bent that day as someone had to translate.

When I look back now, I wonder if it all was arranged. I know I was a curiosity. No doubt I am still a curiosity, but a friendly one. Harmless and sometimes useful.

I thought about Shamza - the sun - the beautiful child-woman who translated for me. She would not be allowed to be seen until she was married, and then only her husband and children would see her face. Tradition dictated. That lovely, calm, intelligent face would be in one sort of purdah or another for the rest of her life and yet this was as natural to her as breathing. Any change in the custom would break some part of her moral code. Once married she would put on the mask and learn to manage it as though it were part of her face.

Purdah is a strange thing to us. Strange, restrictive and even abhorrent. But in these burgeoning, moving families of the desert, this self-imposed purdah seemed more a dance of the sexes, a wildly exaggerated Victorianism. Behind those masks and veils they could see without being seen. Undisturbed, they became classic observers.

When we returned to our own camp, I went back to my tent to change, to rest for an hour and wait for my lunch tray to arrive. This time there was no tray. Selma stood in the sun, beckoning me with a broad grin.

'Come. Sheikha says come.' She looked at me with her bright black eyes and added, 'You can eat bedu style now.'

We walked to the women's tent. I went in, blinded momentarily by the sun. Then the figures took shape. They sat around a square linoleum cloth. A round aluminium tray in the centre was piled with rice and surrounded by bowls of soup, yoghurt, dishes of salad, dates and platters of barbecued fish which had been caught that morning.

'*Marhaba, marhaba*. Welcome, welcome.' The eyes of my hostess smiled. She motioned me to sit beside her where she had placed my bird-handled knife, fork and spoon. 'You ate breakfast like the bedu,' she laughed. 'Rice is more difficult so keep your spoon.' More laughter from the groups of masked figures. Then 'Start, start.' I picked up my spoon feeling like a child who had just been allowed to join the grown-ups' table.

4

A Jack-of-all-Trades
and a Slave

THE DAYS DRIFTED in a timeless haze, each one melting into the next. They had no urgency, no immediacy, no sense of some future mark. It was always now. Tomorrow would come. Yesterday had been. Why concern yourself with any time other than now? There were no sharp edges to time in that place. People came and went, each in their own orbits, circling round about each other. Plans were either dreams of the mind or were executed with immediacy, each one of us dropping neatly into the pattern or dropping out without accusation.

There were special moments which punctuate my memory. A rare ride in one of the Sheikh's power boats, his chief boatman naked to the waist, head bound in a turban, sitting cross-legged on the bow. Like a human compass he lifted a long, thin arm to point out the directions, reading the shadows of the waves like the pages of a book.

Another time, after a wind storm, there was a frenetic drive around the inlet to a windward beach of the great Gulf. Father and sons drove the Range Rovers which were packed with women and children. We skidded over the dunes to find a vast litter of ancient and modern flotsam and jetsam belched up by the sea. Big plastic containers with tops still screwed in place, rusting Pepsi tins, shattered wooden spars, torn fishing nets, broken, water-silvered old masts and booms from drowned and forgotten ships.

The children shouted and ran about collecting treasure. The women in black *abaya* and veils gathered shells and bits of flotsam and called to each other with some remembered story of another time. The sand was very

white, the sea very blue, the coffee, hot and aromatic, was poured again and again into the tiny handleless cups. We went home laden with precious pickings.

Inevitably, the holidays ended. They had been in the desert nearly two weeks and the children had to return to their classes in the newly built schools. Men had to return to their newly built offices and women to their usual rounds of home keeping. Their home was in Al Ain, a village in the Buraimi Oasis over one hundred miles inland from the camp. I was invited to accompany them to Al Ain, an unexpected invitation which I accepted with joy.

Once the decision to go had been made, we moved with an alacrity which would make an army commander envious, yet there was no feeling of haste. Cases were packed and loaded, carpets rolled and stacked, bed rolls bound, tents struck and we were on our way. About five cars and two trucks.

Our modern caravan moved slowly across the unmarked desert. One after another the cars strained through the sand, the drivers competing in dune climbing. Eventually we met the Al Ain-Abu Dhabi highway, its two lanes of tarmac lying in front of us like black ribbon draped over sand. It was not an easy road to drive. The weight of lorries hauling supplies had pushed the sun-heated macadam into ridges and humps, and there was the constant danger of plowing into a stray camel. As we drove, the rolling sands on either side became ever more beautiful, sometimes a warm, rose colour, sometimes yellow, buff or orange and the sky its eternal blue. This was a route which had once taken a week or more to cover by camel, or two to three days by Land Rover. It took us half a day on the new road.

We stopped twice. Once at a desert station which boasted a ramshackle shop with corrugated zinc walls plastered with advertisements for Pepsi Cola and 7-Up. Tins of Pepsi were bought for everyone, but the sweet, lukewarm, bubbly stuff only made us more thirsty.

When we reached a small oasis called Estirahat Khalifa, the road suddenly spanned out to frame an island of flowering shrubs. Tall palms stretched up next to thorn trees and hibiscus bushes to make a sheltered area of unexpected shade and green. The relief to the eyes was immediate. Our car swung to the left through the island of trees but the others went steadily on down the highway. This was to be the second stop.

'I'm thirsty and you must see this place,' said the Second Son, who was with me. We drove up to a large, ultra-modern rest house which stood like a cement and metal box on the edge of the stark desert beyond. Inside, the rooms had an inevitable air of dustiness, but the big armchairs and cool

glasses of mineral water followed by orange juice were welcoming.

'Who built this? What is it for?' I asked.

'The ruler's son. Just to rest on the journey or to come and enjoy.'

'Why didn't your mother and the women and children stop with us?'

'They don't want to,' was the diffident answer. I found that hard to believe, but was to learn later how difficult such a stop would have been for them. They would have had to sit shrouded in their black veils, unable to eat or drink in front of strangers. As for using the toilet - unthinkable. They would never use a public toilet.

In the old days in Abu Dhabi they could not go to the toilet at all in the day time. They all waited till dark and then went down to the sea. The lady who eventually confided this extreme act of modesty saw my pained expression and laughed uproariously.

'We didn't have so much to drink then, either,' she added.

It was here, in this rest house, that the Second Son explained to me that arrangements had been made for me to stay in a hotel in Al Ain.

'There is a Hilton just like in Abu Dhabi,' he said enthusiastically, 'and my mother thinks you are more comfortable there.'

My face fell, as I had looked forward to being with them in their house. Seeing my disappointment he added, 'Believe me, it is better for you. It is a lovely hotel. Truly. And you will visit us and we will visit you.'

It was not until years later that I realised the problems I might have caused. Indeed, I would never have been invited to Al Ain at that time unless there had been a hotel. The relaxed family relationship that I was to be blessed with had barely begun. Camping in the desert was one thing. They were on home ground, so to speak. In Al Ain their life was different. It was in transition. Comparisons could be made. Old houses had given way to new bungalows but old traditions had not yet given way to new methods. There were the physical problems of the lack of guest rooms for Western ladies, to say nothing of the lack of beds. Arab lady visitors slept on palliasses on the dining *majlis* floor in those days. The Sheikha was a perfectionist. With her great heart of hospitality, the Hilton was the only answer. She could not imagine that someone like me would prefer being with them. In her eyes, she was offering me the best they had. It was for me to accept graciously. Perversely, I suddenly found myself looking forward to a hot bath.

After resting half an hour or so in the cool house, the Second Son and I drove on to Al Ain, which was then a sprawling, half-old, half-new overgrown village with one principal street. New blocks of shops with flats above were being built. They bore down on an old general store as if to

squash forever both it and its magnificent shade tree under which men gathered to talk and to trade.

The village was centred among date farms whose green-topped palms rose high above the houses. These date farms and the water which fed them made the whole Buraimi Oasis a precious prize. It is famous in the history of those Sheikhdoms once known as the Trucial States and straddles the border between the United Arab Emirates and Oman.

Originally some four to five miles long and half as wide, it doubled in size as arable farming was introduced through the mighty riches of oil. I first saw it when this farming was still being planned. Al Ain lies toward the south-western end of the oasis.

Standing sentinel over the oasis was a great rock of a mountain, the Jebel Hafeet. It stood quite alone in the sand as though some careless hand had dropped it by accident when piling up the Oman ridge which lay beyond.

The air was so clear, the sun so high that every tree, every house, stood out sharply against the sky.

'A dimension has been lost,' I thought. 'Someone will blow it all down like a paper cut-out.'

We crossed a small bridge over a dry gully and turned sharp left. Suddenly the most incongruous of all sights was in front of us. Another Hilton hotel. It was so unexpected in that place at that time, it could have been a mirage.

The new portico faced a new, painstakingly cultivated garden. Flowers were already growing everywhere. Birds flew in and out of the newly planted bushes. Inside all was cool marble and warm welcome. There weren't many guests in those days. Was I the only one in the hotel? Perhaps.

'You will be all right here, eh?' smiled my escort.

'Very all right indeed.'

'We will come to see you tomorrow.'

'Good.'

I settled into my room and the luxury of a bath. There was a short-lived sense of relief at being in an environment I understood, but almost immediately mind pictures of the quiet, veiled figures surrounded me. I felt alone and with a strange bewilderment I realised I missed them.

That evening as I sat in my room sorting my notes I had a phone call from a young Palestinian who was working at the museum. He had been told by the Sheikh that I was staying in the hotel and offered his services as a guide for the following day. His wife was a friend of the Sheikha.

This tall young refugee from the opposite side of Arabia had a history as confused and traumatic as any of his countrymen. Relegated to a refugee

camp as a young child, miserably poor and constantly hungry, he amused himself by haunting the dig of an archaeologist. He became a runner, doing errands which earned him enough money for food and a little over. With sheer dogged persistence, a lively intelligence and an insatiable curiosity the child was eventually rewarded with an education in how to 'dig', what to look for, and that most important asset in life - a knowledge of 'the way to go'. Eventually he became a skilled stratigraphic excavator and accompanied British Museum archaeologist Katherine Kenyon on her expeditions in Jordan. He began to climb the ladder of success. Then, sniffing the Arabian pot of gold, he left the security he had found with the Jordanian Department of Antiquities and made his way toward the Gulf.

From public relations man to antique collector, from museum guide to Sheikh's assistant, Abed was the classic Jack-of-all-trades. What was needed, he would find. Whatever the job, he knew the way. He had a fund of miscellaneous knowledge and a smattering of languages with a special facility for English. He escorted, arranged, informed and served. Scorned and admired, used and needed, he was neither tribe member nor servant and though an Arab himself, he was then as foreign to the natives of Abu Dhabi and Al Ain as I was.

When I first knew him he lived with his wife in a two-roomed corrugated zinc shed, but he had already started on the collection of Arab antiques that would gain him a villa and an antique shop, the first such shop in the area. Eventually he would acquire the habit of wearing Arab dress, a sign of his final absorption into the life of the place and the life of his patron Sheikhs. Now it was shirt and trousers.

'Welcome. Welcome,' said Abed. 'I will collect you tomorrow early and show you the area. It will be a day or two before you see the Sheikha. They need to settle in.'

He seemed to know more than I knew about my plans, which was puzzling until I learned that his wife was not only a friend, but a sort of go-between for the Sheikha, going between the market, the school, other homes and other hareems.

'Thank you,' I answered, 'I'd enjoy it.'

Early the following morning Abed arrived in a sort of jeep-cum-pick-up.

'It is best for crossing the sand,' he explained. One had the feeling that the Abed guided tour was part of his progress plan for moving up in life. Who could blame him?

We set off, the truck reeling across sand and shale on its way towards the Jebel Hafeet. Through aroyas, over hummocks of sand, shifting from gear to gear, Abed managed to avoid the worst of the dangers. He finally

stopped at the foot of a sharp rocky incline. Leaving the truck, we began to climb·that cut-out mountain. The air was dry and hot. A wind blew in soft gusts. We paced the climb slowly.

On the way to the summit we came upon a group of young archaeologists from France who were excavating a site. A grave had been carefully opened and re-constructed. Centuries ago robbers had removed any worthwhile artefacts or valuables and even now the tomb in its rediscovery seemed no less raped. The young French showed us their finds. Some beads, part of a hair ornament.

'There is nothing spectacular as yet, you understand, but we are trying.'

They were earnest, involved. We shared tea with them there in the blazing sun before walking along the razor back of the mountain.

You can see the whole oasis from there. What a prize, what a jewel of green. No wonder tribes had fought over it, fought bitterly, for here were water and soil and trees, all more precious than gold as they meant life. Directly below us was Al Ain. In the distance were the look-out towers where men once waited and watched for the dust of marauders. To the south were the jagged mountains of Oman. West, north and east were desert and more desert. It was all a barren nothingness except for this great green jewel large enough to be registered in a British atlas as the Buraimi Oasis.

There was evidence of a bronze-age civilisation in that great oasis. There was evidence of trading over two thousand years before Christ. The green carpet lying beneath me had sheltered and succoured man since the days of Tutankhamen, since Alexander, since Marco Polo and up through the steps of history. Down there, under those trees they had lived and died and fought and farmed for thousand upon thousand of years.

As I stood on the summit of the Jebel Hafeet, I could see the black road worming its way across the desert towards Abu Dhabi. I could see another inching toward the mountains of Oman. I could see the lorries and cars. It was the beginning. The next invasion was beginning. The carpetbaggers were coming. The pampered, dependent, petrol-absorbing darlings of the industrial world were already busy plotting, planning, scheming as to how to get a private chunk out of the pot of gold at the end of the Arabian rainbow. The West and the East were building them schools and hospitals. They were bringing boutiques, decor shops and supermarkets; television, video and radio; Mercedes, Cadillacs and Range Rovers; jets and the jet set; bankers, diamond merchants and oil merchants; constructors and demolishers. Air conditioning and mind conditioning had arrived in about equal proportions.

The people of Al Ain had survived the sun's torments, the sand's storms, invasion by desert, by Arab, by Greek, Portuguese and English. They had survived small wars and large wars. Now they were being given the greatest test of all. The invasion of money. Yards of it, acres of it moving steadily down that road. I felt a sudden coldness, as though a cat walked over my grave. Abed touched my arm.

'You are shivering. Are you cold? It is very hot. Perhaps the wind. We will go down. You will have lunch, a rest and then I will take you over there to Oman.'

He pointed to the far distant side of the oasis, then turned and began to lead the way down. I was glad to move, glad to shake off the sudden chill which had risen inside me. I began to pick my way carefully down the path.

As with all things, the way down was far easier than the way up, but effort and concentration were needed. It was enough to paper over the nervous shivering I'd felt on the summit. By the time we reached the truck, the sun's heat had reached my bones again.

Half-way back to the streets of Al Ain, Abed stopped at a mound of pebbled sand. 'You like fossils and these old things?' he asked. 'Maybe we'll find one.'

Once in some prehistoric age the sea had covered this sand. Fish had foraged through the hotel gardens. They had left their calling cards for me to collect a million years later. I found a shell, old, hard, thick, petrified. Abed found three which he gave me. I still have them and several others which he continued to give me over the years.

After my lunch and my rest we drove round the edge of Al Ain and crossed into Oman. There were no borders, no guards, no lines, no-one to say no. The Oman section of the oasis was at that time still on a par with Al Ain in development. It was all one. People moved as they had always moved from one area to another oblivious of the machinations of politics.

We stopped beside an ancient, crumbling fort, its thick sand-coloured walls rising ominously, exuding an inexplicable odour of fear. Beyond the fort tall date palms stood with a contrasting benevolence, hiding beneath their massive fronds a network of lanes and walks and narrow, shallow canals called *falaj*. Precious water had poured through them for centuries, water from the underground rivers and lakes of the Oman mountains.

We walked into the shade. The lanes were as yet free of modern litter, the tins of Pepsi, plastic detergent bottles and silver paper sweet wrappers which were soon to come. It was cool, welcoming, restful. You could hear the movement of the water, a sound which soothed the mind.

'These canals are old,' said Abed. 'Hundreds, maybe thousands of years.'

What an extraordinary people, I thought. We dismiss them historically as bedouin herders, traders or fishermen, but they were engineers, builders, navigators, farmers, soldiers and sailors and ... My thoughts drifted at the broad expanse of learning in front of me.

As we walked along the shadowed lanes I looked over a wall into the slowly moving canal water. On a ledge a woman squatted, she had been washing a sheepskin which she was now spreading out to dry. Further on two small boys padded about, learning to swim. Then beyond one of the intermittent bridges which led to the inner fields I looked over a particularly high wall and, lo and behold, there was an old man having a bath. Rebuked by his eyes, I jumped back as embarrassed as if I'd caught my uncle in his tub.

'How was I to know he'd be there?' I muttered to myself, retreating rapidly to the opposite wall.

Abed was convulsed with laughter when I told him and went back to make my apologies. I could hear the old man railing at both him and me.

Still laughing, he came back and said we'd better go.

'Did you see the old market by the fort? I'll take you there,' he said.

It was a quiet market. The one long alley was roofed with strips of wood overlayered with dried palm fronds. Crickets whirred and sang. Flies were present but unobtrusive. Market boys stretched out on sacks, dozing, waiting for a prod from a customer.

There were sacks of beans and lentils, of spices and seeds, of dried herbs and coffee, bundles of cloth, small china coffee cups and heavy brass coffee pots, hand woven donkey bags, long rifles and swordsticks, leather saddles for camels and tin pans for cooking. The smell of the spice, coffee and herbs rising in the warm air was delicious.

It was there, in that market, that day with Abed, that I met a slave. We were walking slowly, looking into each market shop, talking with the shop keepers. We had reached the shop with the swordsticks when Abed suddenly turned and gave a shout.

'It's Nubi. *Marhaba*, Nubi. *Ahalan*. Welcome,' and he hugged an old man. A small old man. Small and brown as a nut. He had a neat grey beard covering a toothless mouth. The white of his Arab dress framed his face, a face which smiled everywhere even though the eyes were being invaded by cataracts.

'He was a slave.' said Abed. 'Truly a slave. This is Nubi.'

They called him Nubi because he came from Nubia, that land south of Egypt, which was once a favourite hunting ground for slave traders. When Nubi was a small boy, small enough to be tossed into a sack, a slave trader

had done precisely that. After a tormented trip, he had eventually arrived at this oasis village. Here he had been ever since. A slave who now belonged to no-one, a very single old man, and yet an old man of such warmth and affection that I longed to pop morsels of solace into his mouth and watch them melt into his soul.

He reached into the pocket of his gown and pulled out the smallest pipe imaginable. The bowl was less than thumbnail size and rimmed with a small band of silver, as was the stem. He had tied a piece of coloured cloth to it perhaps to protect or clean it. It was my first sight of these miniature pipes which I was to see again and again. The tobacco used in them is so violently strong that one puff is more than enough. And one puff is all they hold. Nubi tried to explain where the tobacco came from but Abed said his Arabic was rough. No-one had taught him properly and the ancient Nubian language was his only inheritance. So he remembered it, talked it, kept it polished. Year after year, speaking to himself, remembering, he kept this one Nubian thing.

Years later I went to a film with the Youngest Son. It was called 'Ashanti' and was the story of a young wife being kidnapped by modern slave traders in North Africa. It horrified me. Most of the Arab characters in it were despicable. I asked the boy whether this trade was still true. He turned to me with wide, honest eyes.

'Yes, it is true. It happens still. It happens in Afghanistan as well.'

'But why?' My dismay was palpable.

'Because they want workers,' he answered.

'They?'

'The people of the Gulf, of Arabia. The people. Arab people.'

'But such a thing is dreadful.'

'Yes. It is dreadful, but there are dreadful people everywhere. You have dreadful films about these Mafia. Or about criminals. Are they true? Yes, they are true. There are good and bad everywhere. This is one bad thing about Arab.'

There are many Nubis in Arabia. Many, many. The hangovers of slave trading are everywhere. You've only to go there to see it.

Illegal by law and by decree through the British influence in the area, slave trading continued nevertheless with only a thinly veiled cover. It was only when oil wealth brought an influx of foreign business people and when the infrastructure began to expand under Zayed bin Sultan, the present ruler, that slave trading began to disappear and the lives of slave families changed. Free education was the prime factor coupled with passports. The former ruler, Zayed's brother, had a penchant for keeping his people close

to him. Neither Sheikh nor slave was allowed a passport. Only temporary documents of travel were issued for limited periods.

Limitations of education, travel and money breed a slave mentality even if in law there is freedom. If a man or a woman were traded as a slave, then told, some twenty years later, that they were free, where were they to go and how were they to manage? Most would have married and settled within the broad life of the family that owned them. They were psychologically bound even though the extraordinary growth of the area might have made them economically free. Many took jobs in the new trades and industries but all remained attached to their former masters who in turn felt responsible for them.

Once, a young black Arab talked with me about his future. He wanted a 'real job', not just to be in service to a Sheikh.

'I want to be free,' said the boy. 'My friend is free. He works in the petrol company. I want to be free.'

Though he was, in the legal sense, as free as any man, financially and psychologically he felt bound. Unquestionably, he had the sort of life many youngsters from the Liverpool docks would long for. At least on the surface. He ate with the Sheikh, sat with him, travelled all over the world with him; his family was cared for by him.

Once they became part of an Arab household or tribe, slaves were both servants and companions, often becoming trusted keepers of the purse, bailiffs or navigators of desert and sea. Slaves ate from the same plate as their masters, wore the same clothes and though their hours were long and the work hard, they were no longer or harder than those put in by their masters or mistresses who had the same elements to battle. Of course there were bad masters and mistresses, but normally the attitudes to slaves were wholly different from that of the West in the days when human beings were traded there.

The unusual roles filled by slaves or descendants of slaves have led to strange complications in modern life. The Sheikhs need trusted 'captains' in their civil service and industry. They always allocated such work to men who were wholly dependent. How then to find such men today in their developing world where slavery as historically known is unacceptable? Before, their 'captains' were brought up in the tribe, developed, so to speak, for the work.

Was this where the Abeds came in? And the educated Palestinians, Egyptians, Syrians, Armenians and Lebanese to be found everywhere on the Gulf, hoping for their 'chance'? They certainly were given every chance in those early days of oil. Many have become wealthy, but all held an

allegiance to a Sheikh and must continue to hold it if they are to continue working or trading in the area. Life is changing, but this is still generally true.

I was never to see Nubi again but I have heard that he is still alive, growing older and drier with each passing year. His face is as vivid in my memory as the day I saw him. Other faces, other places are wiped out as cleanly as chalk from a blackboard. Was it because it was a first visit? Does the memory hold something new and lose the repeat? Or was there truly something rare and special about that old man and that ancient place?

When Abed drove me back to the hotel I was foot-weary and mind-stuffed. There was a message from the Second Son that they had come but I was not there. 'We come tomorrow 10.30,' the message said.

I went to my room with the message paper in my hand. I scattered my dust-layered clothes, showered and lay down on the bed to digest the sights I had seen. The sounds. The smells. The light began to fade and the call for prayers echoed over the town. I drifted off to sleep with one final vision. The Sheikha smiling behind her mask.

5

At Home in Al Ain

THERE IS ALWAYS a first time, a first moment to dip your foot in a new place. Never easy, it is a hiccup that has to be got over. The first time in the desert the simplicity of the camp had quickly smoothed over the rough places of newness. Now there was the fear that the constriction of walls, the aroma of urbanity, the layering of a new world on to an old would unravel those too recently woven cords of understanding.

Promptly at 10.30 the next morning there was a sharp knock on the door. I opened it to see the two smiling faces of the sons.

'Are you ready?'

'Yes, ready,' I answered and walked out of the door, closing it firmly behind me.

We were all a bit nervous. In the desert they had had complete authority. There was no possibility of an invidious comparison between our worlds. Houses were another matter. Especially the houses which were being built on the Gulf in a building boom the like of which the world may never see again. The old Al Ain homes with their thick walls, castellated or balustraded roofs, wrought iron screens across the windows, finely carved doors and high ceilinged rooms were being abandoned and destroyed. They were replaced by new, often jerry-built cement bungalows. The vast palaces with bowing servants were dreams yet to be realised.

I don't know quite what I expected to see on that first visit to their home, but I do know I wasn't prepared for its homeliness, nor for the extent of it. The boys had tried to describe it when they were in London, but I couldn't

envisage the place. The meals for fifty. Why fifty? The different gates for men and for women. Why two gates? The houses, the guest houses, their grandmother's house, the kitchen house. They'd tried to explain but I just couldn't understand.

The first thing I saw that day was the wall. Long, high and studded with round globe lights, it surrounded an area of about twenty acres. Date palms, mango trees and lemon trees pushed their heads over the top of the wall in a jumble of cool green that cast clean-cut shadows over the flat roofs of several houses just visible inside.

We entered through the 'women's gate', the family gate. The men's gate was on another side. That was the 'main gate' but it was only used by male guests, especially those who were not part of the family.

The women's gate or family gate was high and imposing, rather like a Middle Eastern version of an enormous lych-gate. A sleepy gate-keeper dozed quietly in the sun, tilting his old wooden chair against the wall. The gates were always left open for cars, trucks or bicycles going in and out laden with family or friends or food stores. I would never see them shut.

The 'home' was a village of small houses which stretched around a square court studded with date palms and weeping kenna trees, each growing out of its own pitted circle of earth, pitted for the quantities of water that needed to be poured around them. There was a fountain in the centre of the court but no water played from its mouth and no water tipped into the blue pool surrounding it. Perhaps it had been set there in a flight of fancy forgetful of the constant flow of children of assorted sizes who might have taken a header into the pool; or perhaps water was too precious to be used for such a frivolous purpose.

Baluchistan pedlars with packs of cloth and boxes of perfume sat patiently waiting on the paths hoping for the attentions of a mistress or servant. Drivers polished their cars on the court drive and women servants walked from one house to another with trays or bundles on their heads, or coffee thermoses in their hands.

On one side of the court was a row of bungalows, each with its own porch and broad flight of steps.

'That's our house,' said the Second Son pointing to the largest. 'I told you it is all different from your house.'

'Over there is my father's majlis and guest rooms for his friends,' said the Youngest Son, pointing to a long, low building on the opposite side of the square. Beside it was a group of smaller box-like structures which proved to be the kitchens and store rooms. The same cooks whom I had seen in the desert with their white crocheted skull caps presided here.

'And what's that one?' I asked pointing to an amazingly ornate house on a third side of the square. It was twice as large as the largest bungalow and had been built to impress. Heavy cement arches crouched over fretted tile screens which bound another wide porch. Carefully constructed cement boxes hung from the porch like outsized window boxes waiting for plants which had never been planted, and never would be planted.

'Ah, that,' they answered, the words jumbling over each other in their eagerness to explain. 'That is for our brother. The first one. We told you of him. The oldest. The one in Jordan studying. He will come home very soon. Then he will marry and bring his wife there.'

'He is the number one son,' said the Youngest Son smiling.

'He is the eldest,' said the Second Son with a shrug of his shoulders.

On the fourth side of the square were a few small cubes of houses screened by a large shade tree. These were the senior servants' homes, servants who had families. Tucked up against them was a pigeon house from which flights of white tumbling pigeons rose periodically and performed their strange sky dance before returning to roost.

'They are my pigeons,' said the Second Son. 'I told you about them. And I have a camel and a horse.'

'And my mother has cows and sheep and goats. Many things. Over there,' said the Youngest Son, taking my hand and turning me about to point out a farm of some ten to twelve acres which stretched to the far corners of the wall behind the bungalows.

They led me toward their house, the Sheikha's house, the family house, and I had my almost constant prayer in mind, 'Oh Lord, don't let me put my foot wrong and especially not in my mouth.'

I remember mounting the steps to the front door and being amazed that they were carpeted. Carpets on the outside steps. They would have been a soggy mess in no time in front of my own home, but here they were comforting for bare feet, far better than searing marble or burning cement.

I remember there was no bell to ring. There were front doors, massive, panelled, wooden double doors which were wide open. They were apparently opened in the morning and left open all day. No bell was needed as there was always someone around to announce the arrival of guests. Selma, my Pakistani companion of the desert, was waiting for us now. We kicked off our sandals which joined a pile by the front door, and she led the way into a modest, comfortable room with simple yellow couches lining the walls, beautiful carpets and a built-in unit, a 'library' which had all manner of television and hi-fi equipment fitted into it.

They were all there. All the women I had met in the desert. I was entirely

surrounded by women with masks and veils and silks and soft voices all eager to show me everything or anything, to explain, to urge me to talk, to laugh. No-one spoke English except the sons and daughter, but it is extraordinary how eloquent the hands and the eyes can be. Furthermore, I was beginning to understand more and more phrases.

'Welcome,' said the Sheikha. 'Welcome. Welcome. Come. Sit with me.'

We sat, some of us on the couches, some on the floor. Little girls in their best dresses ran in and out among us and the sons stayed beside me, constantly translating, constantly teasing both me and their mother.

Coffee was served. Arabian coffee. It still seems to me to be the ultimate coffee sophistication. To them it is the symbol of hospitality and is made and drunk with care and respect. During that visit I heard for the first time the ringing sound of brass pestle on brass mortar as cardamom seeds were pounded with the freshly roasted coffee beans. The sound announced to all and sundry that a guest was in the house. How many times over the coming years would I hear that sound? How many times would I walk into the coffee house to see the big square brass brazier with its charcoal fire warming the enormous fire-blackened, brass Arabian coffee pots? How many times would I watch Selma make the yeast-risen, spicy breakfast pancakes, squatting on her haunches over a gas ring? The smell of coffee, fresh pancakes and ripe fruit would draw me like a magnet to that special little box of a house standing next to the Sheikha's, where sacks of coffee beans and crates of fresh fruit waited to be prepared and served.

Selma sat in front of me now, pouring from a long-spouted pot with an expert hand. It's not easy. I've tried it. You need a strong left wrist and a good eye, for the coffee is poured with the left hand from a height into the miniature handleless cups, a stack of which are held in the right hand. About two good swallows are poured and then the cup is brought smartly up under the guest's right hand.

Everyone was served in strict protocol. The Sheikha first as though she were about to taste the wine, but she never accepted a cup until all were served, unlike our wine-tasting hosts. Protocol demanded that the eldest was served next, the eldest being the most respected. In every facet of life youth serves age. It is a rule of their society. The youngest wife, the youngest daughter, the youngest sister, all serve those older than themselves. Young brothers hop to the commands of their older brothers. Young sisters run the errands of older sisters.

In this hareem the eldest was the Sheikh's mother. That morning she sat in quiet dignity on the carpet. I recognised her not by her age but by her bearing. They all had straight strong backs but Sheikha Grandmother's

back seemed to extend into her swan-like neck. She had the back and bearing of a queen. And her eyes. I recognised her by her eyes. They were exceptionally beautiful even in age. Slightly slanted, not upward but downward. The falcon eyes of the Second Son. Yes. He was like his grandmother. I could see it now.

A cup was placed in my hand. I was served next as the chief guest and finally all were included in the welcome ritual.

Coffee was offered again, and then again. Round and round it went until someone gave the short, sharp shake of their cup that meant enough. I tried to imitate the almost insignificant tremble that the Sheikha gave when she had finished.

'That's good. Good, Um Yusef.'

It was the first time I heard the name which would become as familiar to me as my own. Um Yusef. There, in that place, you are known as the mother of your eldest son. I had only one son, Joseph. The Sheikha used the Arabic pronunciation of his name, Yusef. Um Yusef I would be from that day on.

I became so involved in watching the customs of the visit that I forgot to be nervous, forgot for a moment that tentative wariness which plagues me in every new situation even today.

Coffee was only the overture. Next came the incense pots, those sparsely decorated little pots made of coarse, brick-coloured clay which stand about five inches high. A few chunks of charcoal were taken from the coffee brazier and put in the top. Then the incense. It was sandalwood. I watched as the Sheikha selected slivers of the wood from a large screw-top jam jar which held a perfumed oil of her own recipe. She told me that everyone had their own mixes of oils and perfumes; recipes that were carefully handed down from mother to daughter and shared much as we share a special recipe for a souffle or a cake.

I was beginning to understand that their social mores and traditions were far more complex than I'd envisaged and that the Sheikha beside me was ruled by them and ruled too, by her own innate desire to do everything well. She was a perfectionist in manners, a perfectionist in morals but much more, a perfectionist of the spirit, worrying continually over everyone's happiness and comfort, over whether sufficient prayers were said, sufficient welcome given, sufficient attention paid to the commandments of Islam and the commandments of Arabian hospitality. In time I would discover that she was just as afraid of putting a foot wrong as I am. In time I would know when she was worried by the way she quickly turned her head, like a young deer when it hears a discordant sound.

Now she said, 'This is the way, Um Yusef,' as she placed a few small chunks of the perfumed wood on the coals and poked at it delicately with the tip of her forefinger. As she gently blew on the coals a thick perfumed smoke began to rise. She passed the pot to me and told me to pass it to my right: just as port must be passed to the left, so incense should be passed to the right. The ladies lifted their veils first on one side and then on the other, their heads and hands arching to allow the sweet-smelling fog to permeate their veils and hair.

Next their skirts were lifted and the pot placed underneath. This terrified me then as it does now for when skirts and veils are dropped back in place the pot smoulders away until curls of smoke issue from the fabric. I am always afraid that they will catch themselves alight. The object of this frightening act is to permeate all their clothes with the scent of the incense, so they smell sweet everywhere.

Conversation was kept up all the time in an unintelligible stream. They spoke to me as though I understood. I didn't. But they didn't begin to speak louder as we do when someone doesn't understand us. I don't know why we do it. Do we think that the louder we talk the more some pre-Babel cell will react in our brains? God knows, but the ladies of Al Ain kept talking to me in Arabic as though I understood and I kept smiling and nodding like one of those wobble-headed dogs sometimes seen in the back windows of cars.

As we sat steeping ourselves in smoke, me struggling to be understood, they laughing at my efforts, the fruit arrived. It arrived on a large round aluminium tray carried by Selma and another young Pakistani servant whom I'd never seen. There were many more servants in Al Ain than in the desert. They seemed to have multiplied by two or three.

Selma and her helper carefully placed the tray in the centre of the room and the Sheikha took my hand to bring me near to it. We all sat around this great tray with its fruit piled high. Apples, oranges, bananas, grapes, tangerines and melons were pyramided in the centre while enamel dishes of Arabic sweets sat on the edge, solid masses of a light nougat and a spiced glutinous candy decorated with almonds and cashews.

The women gathered around and the boys disappeared. It would not be seemly for them to be where women were eating. Little boys, yes. Not big boys.

The Sheikha reached for a large plate of dates, those sweet, sticky Al Ain dates oozing sugar which are the only kind I've ever liked. She picked one up and with a quick twist of thumb and forefinger, de-pipped it and handed it to me.

'Are these your dates? Did you grow them?' I asked.

She threw back her head and laughed. 'Yes. Yes.'

For the life of me I can't remember who did the translating, for when the sons were gone, I was often in a vacuum. Perhaps it was the Sheikha's daughter whose smattering of Egyptian-taught English had been such a help to me in the desert. She was about eleven at this time and painfully thin, but her sweet open face with its large brown eyes was always a welcome sight. She spoke her strangely accented English carefully and distinctly.

Then again, perhaps Abed's wife had arrived with her halting words newly learned. I don't know. I don't remember, but somehow we communicated. I know that I discovered that the dates were from their own trees and that dates were at one time all they were able to serve on the tray unless the mango trees were in season. I learned that women had sometimes climbed the date trees themselves to harvest the dates if the men were away at war or hunting; that for many years they existed on a little dried fish, some rice and their dates. Camels' milk and a hard yoghurt cheese varied the diet.

'One dress was all I had to wear. Sometimes one in the box for good,' said the Sheikha.

All the while she spoke, she peeled and sliced the fruit urging me to 'Eat. Eat.' She peeled and sliced apples, peeled and segmented oranges, sliced the heart out of melons and pipped plums, passing the prepared fruit to her guests. Just as we preside over the tea pot, she presided over the fruit knife.

I was urged to eat more and more as though every mouthful was a compliment to my hostess. Finally, after swallowing yet another mouthful of nougat, I lifted my hands and made grand gestures showing that I was becoming explosively fat. With smiles and nods of understanding the tray was finally removed, its carefully pyramided fruit a jumble of peel and pips. Selma brought a silver wash bowl and matching kettle. Warm, scented water was poured over each of our hands in turn. Then instead of passing a towel they handed around boxes of paper tissues, that universal commodity which crosses every international border.

Coffee was served again, the incense pots passed once more and then came the *pièce de résistance*, the final courtesy. At a command, a treasure box of perfumes was brought in, a velvet box studded with jewel-like stones. Nestling inside in silken slots were gold-trimmed bottles containing a collection of rich and rare perfumes. Attar of roses, attar of jasmine, essence of sandalwood, attar of henna, attar of musk - strange, heady scents so strong that they are used only as a base for modern Western perfume.

Long, gold dipsticks were placed in the bottles which were then passed around. A little perfume was placed on the side of the thumbs, or on the sides of the face or on the veils or just beneath the nostrils - 'to make the breath sweet'. This heavy scent was added to the already incense permeated clothes so that these ladies moved in a cloud of musky Eastern odours strange to the Western nose, but totally identifiable. As identifiable as their masks and veils.

Perfume was an imperative and it is just as important for a man to smell sweet as a woman. The Arab male sprays himself liberally with cologne. He is not alone. The custom is slowly wafting its way across Europe like some aromatic cloud.

For women, however, it was a mark of identity. Babies and toddlers hung on to an old piece of veil like a security blanket. And I'm just as guilty. I have an old veil of the Sheikha's which she gave me years ago to protect my head from the sun. It's in a drawer in London and whenever I come across it, her perfumes still lie in it and the sights, sounds and smells of Al Ain roll into my mind magically and nostalgically.

'Come. Try a little. Here, on the thumb. Now like this.' The Sheikha dotted my thumbs and hers with attar of jasmine, then rubbed her neck and chin while I copied her. She dabbed her dress and handed me the dipstick to do the same.

'Good. Good. She does well,' she said to her sons when they returned. The youngest settled himself soberly in front of me.

'Ask your mother for me please whether she has ever ridden a camel and how long did it take from Al Ain to Abu Dhabi in the old days?'

'Ask your mother.' That phrase would be used tens of thousands of times over the years to come.

When the boy translated, she immediately sat up and began to pretend to ride a camel.

'*Aywa*. Yes, yes, many times. We rode in the spring and in the autumn. When the weather became hot, we moved from Abu Dhabi to Al Ain. It is hotter in Al Ain but more dry. Then when the weather cools we go back to Abu Dhabi where the boats go out for fish and for pearls. Big pearls we call the danna, small ones the lulu. There are many names for all sizes and colours. We dry the fish and sell the pearls.'

'How long was the trip?'

'Maybe five days, six nights. Sometimes we move at night. Too hot in the day. I am small then. Once I fall in the water going over to Abu Dhabi. There is a tower there. I fall.' She tossed her head back and I could see her broad smile. 'My back still hurts from this fall.' She began to laugh. She

had that ultimate grace, the ability to laugh at herself.

The boys teased her for her bad riding. The women joined in the laughing. I remembered seeing that watch tower when we crossed the bridge from Abu Dhabi island to the mainland. It is still there today, one of the few bits of history that have been visibly preserved. I never pass it without thinking of the Sheikha.

'Tell me,' I said. 'No-one is truly poor any more. Everyone has wealth from the oil. Tell me. Are you more happy now?'

The Sheikha straightened her mask and veils. Then using her hands to explain she patted the pockets at the sides of her dress. Turning her face toward me so that I could see her eyes, she said, 'Happiness is not a matter of the pocket.' She moved her hands to her heart. 'Happiness is a matter of the heart.' It was a moment I have never forgotten. A moment of truth. Everything was said.

I have rarely known a woman with such innate good manners. Not imposed, ritual manners, but manners which rose out of some spiritual orderliness. Her hospitality contained qualities of respect for the needs of both the body and the spirit. She had opened new vistas for me, vistas with tempting horizons.

I packed for London the following day and the sons drove with me back down the long highway to the airport. I had been on the Gulf barely three weeks but as the plane lifted off the runway I knew as well as I knew my own name that my life had taken another imperceptible turn.

They say that once you have placed your hand near the heart of Arabia you are drawn closer and closer until you are hopelessly bound, as in a tormented love affair. I had come dangerously close to the heart of Arabia. Was I caught? Would I ever be able to leave them now?

6

At Home in Park Lane

'IT IS YOU WHO likes the desert. Not us. It is a hard place. Nothing is there. Nothing. Nothing. Nothing. Here there is green everywhere. No people were so blessed by God as you. You have water. You have rain. You have kind weather. You have green everywhere,' said the little Sheikha whom I had visited in the desert.

Hyde Park stretched before us. Its trees flattered each other. The grass was that rich green which only England can produce. It was indeed green everywhere.

'Paradise has green everywhere and water in abundance. Do you not know that this is like Paradise? To walk on the green, in the cool, away from dust, from sun. For children to run in rain - is that not like Paradise?'

We sat on the hotel balcony high above the traffic of Park Lane. We sat cross-legged passing the incense pot among us, watching the London scene as though we were observers on some magic carpet suspended in space. Beside us was a plate of dates and a bird cage with its captive canary. The clear, cool, English air had been invaded by the heady odours of the Gulf.

They had arrived the week before. Like a flock of black birds, Shamza and her mother and her mother's friends, all the women I had breakfasted with in the desert had descended on a London hotel to roost.

In London but not a part of London, they brought their own culture shell with them. They sat aloof - above the rushing of the city. They watched, walked and luxuriated in the cool, damp weather, soaking up the

46

rain as we soak up the sun.

Shamza had called me a few days earlier, her immaculate schoolgirl English coming down the telephone line.

'Madame? Madame? How are you? Are you well? Are all your family well? How is your health? How is the health of your family?' The words of courtesy came floating down the telephone wires.

'Shamza? Is that you?'

'Yes, Madame. You remember us?'

'How could I forget you?'

'We are here in London. Will you visit us?'

'It is my pleasure,' I answered and tried to remember all the words of courtesy that I should now reply. 'How is your mother? How is your father, your sister? And your brothers? All in your house? God bless your home. And what is your news? God willing all is well.'

Shamza told me where they were staying and said to please come at any time. I suggested six that evening and she said they would wait for me.

Shamza's mother was like a sister to the Sheikha. Their home compounds bordered each other and their husbands were cousins. Their families were so intertwined that in the early days they all lived together in one compound. Now Shamza and her mother and their group were here. I decided that the most polite thing to do was to wear my long skirt again, so I put it on with a feeling of reminiscence and drove to their hotel.

Not many Gulf families had English homes in those days, but they had the wealth to escape from the blinding heat of the summer months. So they arrived at London's great hotels, taking suites of rooms and sometimes whole wings.

The rooms were quickly transformed into Arabian oases in the desert of European hotel life. Couches were pushed back to make more room for sitting or eating 'bedu fashion'. Boxes of fruit were bought and stacked in the bedrooms or corners of the sitting rooms. The smoke of the incense pots seeped through the doors of the suites and out into the corridors. When the lift door opened on the tenth floor of their hotel, I lifted my head like a hound and headed for the scent.

A Pakistani maid answered my knock. I knew I was in the right place when I saw her long skirts and black veil and I knew instinctively that I had been right in wearing mine. Little courtesies meant a lot to them. Once I was inside, the doors shut behind me and Shamza appeared from her hiding place in the bedroom. She could never have risked the possibility that some strange man might have been at the door, some Arab from her place, though I soon saw her speak unveiled to floor waiters or foreigners

with an extraordinary dignity in one so young. Foreigners were from beyond the pale. They didn't count.

She greeted me warmly and led me to the balcony where her mother and the others were sitting. The little Sheikha whom I now knew as Um Hamed rose and kissed me English fashion on the cheeks. She was a head shorter than her daughters and indeed myself. She was young. I reckoned that she couldn't have been much more than thirty. Delicately boned, graceful, shy, deeply religious, she exuded through masks and veils a rare femininity and attractiveness. Um Hamed was a beauty. Nothing could hide it.

'Welcome, welcome, my house is yours. How are you? Your husband? Your children?' Her voice was as gentle and alluring as a child's, and she seemed as glad to see me as I was to see her. The servant brought coffee and we sat in our eyrie observing the evening and exchanging news while Shamza translated back and forth.

They were there for the summer. Al Ain was very hot and her husband needed treatment. They would keep him company.

'I hope it is not serious?' I asked.

'He is well and in God's care,' was the answer. I felt rather than knew that the illness was probably chronic and not acute.

'My friends. The boys. Their mother, the Sheikha. Are they well?' I asked.

'Very well and send you greetings. Perhaps they will be here later in the summer. The Sheikh and his sons will be here. We are not sure about the Sheikha.'

I absorbed this news, wondered when I would hear more of their plans, realized that it would not be until the last moment, and held my cup out for more coffee as it was passed.

'It is delicious. How can you find this coffee here?' I asked.

'We make it, of course.'

'Make it? How?'

I was shown an electric kettle with a plugless lead, the bare wires poking into a hotel socket.

'But this is very dangerous,' I said with considerable alarm, adding that they might have a bad accident. Shamza smiled and said that she knew but what was her mother to do? They must have coffee. Other women did the same everywhere in all the hotels, she said, explaining patiently that when hareems visited each other they needed coffee for hospitality. I promised to bring a plug and fit it on and turned my eyes away from the potential disaster area. Then swallowing the few swallows in my cup, I held it out for

more.

They had brought their own coffee, cardamom and cloves with them, all packed carefully into their suitcases along with incense, incense pots, perfumes, perfume dipsticks, prayer mats, coffee thermos, Arab medicines, kohl for their eyelashes and, of course, the henna and oil to make the patterns on their hands and feet. They travelled as my grandmother or great-grandmother might have travelled, taking the whole of their personal lives with them, distrusting hotels, public transport, European food.

In the first years that the Sheikhas and their hareems began to travel to the West, the hotels despaired at their strange customs and tried to make them fit into Western conventions. A useless exercise. After hundreds of thousands of pounds, perhaps millions, had been passed into hotel coffers, these same hoteliers began to take considerable pride in their ability to cater for their masked guests. Large baskets of fruit slowly began to replace the boxes of oranges, peaches or apples. Maids were alerted and room-service waiters were ordered to provide tablecloths, plates, cutlery and glasses when demanded for the meals brought in from one of the specialist restaurants which soon began to spring up.

Before these Armenian and Lebanese restaurants began to sprout in Kensington, Knightsbridge and Earl's Court the Sheikhas struggled with room service, not knowing quite what would arrive.

'Madame?' Shamza asked - she was too young to call me Um Yusef, 'Madame, is there no fish in England?'

I assured her that there was, and recommended Dover sole.

'Dover sole?' She repeated the name and her mother tried it amid quiet laughter.

'But how can it be fresh? How far is the sea?'

I tried to convince them that it was perfectly fresh and quite delicious, but they were doubtful and I don't believe they ordered fish in London for a year or two.

'Come. We will move inside,' said Um Hamed. 'It is cool. You will stay with us for supper? Yes, of course you will stay.'

I said that I must call my husband and they laughed with delight at the thought that I must consult him.

'Call. Call,' said Um Hamed and we rose to move inside.

Shamza picked up the bath towel her mother had been sitting on and we followed her into the sitting room where the same towel was placed on a chair. When she saw my surprise Um Hamed said softly, settling herself on the towel, 'But who can tell what has been here before, Um Yusef? There might have been a dog and I would have to change all my clothes every

time I wish to pray.'

Dogs are forbidden as unclean. They find our dogs very hard indeed to take, especially our having them in the house. When I said that I had a lovely dog but he was certainly not allowed to sit on the couch they exclaimed almost in unison, 'A dog!' It became one of the curious announcements which one masked lady made to another when they spoke of me. 'She has a dog,' they said, much as we might say, 'She has a lion.'

'How can you stop them watering the carpets?' said a friend of Um Hamed that evening in the hotel suite. 'Would you have a horse in the house? Imagine.' And they laughed aloud at the joke.

Shamza lifted the phone to order supper. Chicken soup, 'baby' chicken, kebab, salad and of course the universal chips plus tomato ketchup were the summer menu. As the months wore on two desserts were added. Black Forest gateau and crème caramel. These plus orange juice - 'fresh squeeze' - Pepsi and later English tea with hot milk completed the diet. The number of 'baby' chickens slaughtered in any one of those London summers must have been phenomenal, for the Gulf Sheikhas began to come to England in droves.

When, after a lengthy wait, supper arrived we all ate bedu style, the hotel's pink damask tablecloths having been spread on the floor. The well-trained waiter didn't blink as he placed the platters on the covered carpet. It all seemed quite natural.

'Can you eat this thing, Um Yusef?' asked Shamza, delicately holding up a mushroom. I urged her to try it but she wrinkled her nose after one nibble. The platter of vegetables was pronounced delicious by one member of the household and shoved far away by another.

The following day Shamza called to ask me to go shopping with them. It was the first of many shopping expeditions I would make. The long 'stretched' limousines pulled up at our London home, a driver rang the bell and, much to the amazement of my neighbours, I joined the group of masked and veiled women. Off we all drove like some incongruous Arabian fairy tale.

They shopped. Oh, how they shopped. It was a delight which they denied themselves at home in those days, for it was neither seemly nor correct for a Sheikha to be seen in the markets or shops of their own new towns which were growing so rapidly out of their old villages. Here, among the strangers of the north whose customs and attitudes were so odd, so immodest, so bold, they could walk, shop, select and reject with the canniness of a Scot.

That summer, whenever I was busy and unable to go with them, an

Egyptian, Syrian or Lebanese woman, whose English varied from good to dreadful, went along as guide. Provided by the Embassies, they conducted the Gulf ladies up and down Oxford Street and Regent Street or to the 'Sunday market'. Shamza's English improved so quickly, however, that Um Hamed's hareem was soon able to manage the 'markets' for itself and markets they were, whether it was Bond Street, Knightsbridge or Shepherds Bush.

I myself am the world's most impatient shopper and have been known to pay over the odds in order to escape from a store. Anathema to my new friends. Um Hamed would pick and put aside, examine and re-examine, while the shop assistants watched and waited, knowing that the rewards in the end would be great. I would find a chair in some corner of a fabric department and try to relax while the bolts of cloth were unreeled. A sales girl who didn't know her silks from mixed cloth was soon replaced by the buyers or heads of department, for the hareem could tell pure silk or wool almost by the smell. It was quite useless to try to fool them. Many did. The store was discarded like an old boot.

'Ignorant, Um Yusef, or cheating. Both bad.' And we would waft out to the waiting limousines and move on to another store.

At first they were embarrassed by the stares of shoppers but they very soon learned to stand their ground.

'Shall I tell you what happened today?' asked Um Hamed as we sipped coffee on the hotel balcony one morning some weeks later that summer.

'God willing,' I answered.

'We were in the big store. Upstairs. Where they have things for children - for boys and girls. All of us were there.' Her hand with its henna circle in the palm and carefully drawn henna finger-lines swept out to include her friends and Shamza. The 'big store' had apparently been Selfridges.

'We were waiting for the lift. Standing. Waiting. Some boys came up. Big boys. They point at us and look at us in a bad way. Then one says to me, "Hello, Batman."'

Her eyes behind the mask were bland and unreadable. I felt the wave of helplessness which comes when I'm caught in a mind vacuum somewhere between their world and mine. I wanted to laugh. I wanted to cry.

Um Hamed sat stone still. No one spoke. Then she lifted her hand again, palm forward, in the stylish way they all have when telling a story. Her eyes began to sparkle.

'I turn to these boys. I look at them. I say very loud in English, "Thank you." And that minute the lift arrives, thanks be to God and we get in. The door shut but I see their face. They did not know I understand their words.

Thanks be to God. They look very funny.'

They all laughed with her, each one adding a detail or nodding agreement, but I saw once again the chasm between our two worlds. Two cultures examining each other. Each calling the other backward.

Oh, yes. The West is backward. Not in technology, not in mechanics, not in sciences. But in the eyes of these women our immodesty, loud voices, atheism, careless treatment of our elders, orphans and widows are signs of barbaric behaviour from which their daughters must be protected.

Thinking to change the subject, I asked Shamza whether she and her mother would like to see one of the museums. I knew that so far the limits of their adventure into English life were the 'markets', the occasional walk in Hyde Park, or visits to the doctors of Harley Street.

'Would you like me to show you the Tower of London where the Queen's crown is kept? Or the British Museum where there are many things from Egypt?' I asked.

'Thank you, Um Yusef. Shall we go today?' As always I was surprised. I had thought I would have to persuade them to move out of their cocoon. I had forgotten that they carry their cocoon with them.

Our first visit was to the Science Museum and progress was slow. Unlike Western tourists who 'do' a museum in under an hour, my flock of black-veiled butterflies stopped at each exhibit, taxing my imagination to the limit as I tried to describe the age of certain time mechanisms, the workings of the first motor cars or antique equipment for mining.

The following day we progressed at a snail's pace through a room of Egyptian artefacts in the British Museum.

'Did the English steal these?' asked Shamza blandly. I found the courage to answer the truth, saying, 'Yes, probably,' but then in deference to the British archaeologists added, 'But I believe some were taken by agreement with the authorities in Egypt.' What more could I say?

When we eventually returned to the hotel, footsore and weary, they pulled all their veils and coats around them for the short walk from limousine to lift. To them it was a sort of gauntlet to be run. The shops and museums were impersonal. The hotel was their 'place'. Anyone could be there. Sheikhs, sons of Sheikhs, men from their country, women from the West whose disdainful stares would sting, men from the West whose amused eyes tried to unveil them. Beneath their layers of black they could look out, and no-one could look in. They were safe. So they covered themselves doubly and proceeded with haste. That does not mean running. These ladies never run. Haste is walking steadily without detour from one point to the next. Walking together looking neither to left nor to right.

At the lifts we stood and waited for an empty one. Occasionally they would ride up and down with Westerners but they preferred their own lift and numerically it was sometimes a necessity. When we arrived back in the suite, Shamza shut the door firmly and soundly. She was not only shutting the door, she was shutting out the stares.

She kicked off her sandals and I kicked off my shoes. Her mother ordered coffee for us all and went off to change and pray. Shamza took the coffee thermos from the maid and dropped to the floor in front of me. She poured cup after cup for me but would drink nothing herself until I was quite finished.

As she thanked me for this day out I watched her. Her beauty, her serenity and dignity. She was a woman of thirteen, not a child. Her life and that of my daughters were as opposite in experience and habit as it would be possible to conceive. What parts of our way of life would eventually be absorbed by her? Or by her children? What would they gain or lose?

Like a typical mother, I longed both to keep the status quo and to see growth. Impossible. Completely impossible.

The Second Son telephoned in the first weeks of August.

'We are coming. My mother, my sister, Selma, the little ones. Hussa. You know Hussa, her friend. All of them. Not my grandmother of course. She never leaves. But all of them. You will be there?'

'Yes, I will be here,' I said, pushing away tempting thoughts of a week in Cornwall. 'I will be here. Shall I meet you?'

'No, never mind. We come by private plane and this is difficult for you. I will call you when we are settled.'

'Good,' I answered and after giving him the news of Um Hamed for his mother, I relaxed.

Not for long. Within two days I received a frantic telephone call from Claridges. It was the Second Son.

'Urgent, urgent, my English mother. Come now. Please. Come now. Urgent.'

I didn't wait to put on my long skirt but flew out of the house, convinced that something awful had happened. Arriving at the hotel, I found the hareem all sitting in an expensive suite with their cases still shut. After the usual greetings I was taken into a bedroom and quietly shown the beds by the Sheikha.

'These things have been used by other people, Um Yusef?'

'Yes, but everything has been washed for you.'

'How can you be sure, Um Yusef?'

53

'It must be so,' I answered helplessly.

'Please, we must have new.' I was offered a large sum of money to purchase new linen for all the beds. Finally, with the help of the hotel management and housekeeper, I was able to satisfy them that all was indeed clean. But without turning a hair, and with calm and smiling courtesy, Claridges changed every bed and provided new blankets before a single case was unpacked.

The Second Son, who was escorting the hareem, had thrown up his hands in despair when I arrived and made off for his own room. He stayed well out of the way until this 'woman's business' was sorted out, eventually phoning to see if 'the birds had settled'.

Then the visiting began in earnest. Um Hamed visited the Sheikha, the Sheikha visited Um Hamed and I visited them both. We shopped, or rather they shopped and I watched. I took the Sheikha to visit the dentist and for 'check up', and then escorted Um Hamed and Shamza around Syon House, an historic, once royal mansion.

The Sheikh never arrived, but the Youngest Son joined his mother's party, bringing his charm and sense of humour to an already good-tempered scene. More appointments were arranged by the Embassy medical section for all the members of the hareem.

There was an awful innocence about these visits to Harley Street. They still had a faith in all things British and especially the British medical profession. Doctors were at the top of the totem pole of knowledge and the more paraphernalia involved in the tests, the better. The number of pills, potions and lotions prescribed was phenomenal. Having received the advice of one man, appointments were made for a second opinion. Then a third. All the tests were repeated each time. As they had made the long trip to London, they felt compelled to devour as much medical advice as possible. Their own new clinics and hospitals were largely staffed by Arabs or Indians whom they rarely trusted.

In London, the way to Harley Street was already richly paved. Once Arabian gold had been spotted, fees grew like the green bay tree. Commissions and cuts from Embassy big apples were already common practice. Private clinics began to pop up all over the West End, clinics with gourmet kitchens and luxury suites. The clean edge of the medical profession started to crumble here and there, softened by the constant flow of Arabian dirhams, riyals or dinars. As you entered a waiting room you could assess almost at once how much erosion had set in.

During the day, I would take my little Sheikhas to their appointments, try to translate the medical jargon into understandable language and do

my best to steer them away from medical clip joints towards men of principle.

During the evening, at dinner parties or receptions, I would suffer the derisive stories of the 'in' Harley Street groups. The lack of understanding of the culture and customs of their patients was total.

It was that summer, a summer of Harley Street visits, sight-seeing expeditions and trips to the fabric departments of every major store, that the Second Son made an important decision not only for him but for us. He decided to go to university in England.

'Now, please. This September. Or October.' He had consulted his father and his father thought it was a fine idea. The Sheikh sent a message to my husband which in substance said please get the boy into an English university near you. Now.

It took long conversations with the Second Son, long telephone calls to Abu Dhabi and days of work for both my husband and myself to persuade both the boy and his father that nothing was simple about entering a British university.

We eventually found that certain red-brick universities would accept fee-paying foreign students provided the standard of their secondary school certificate was sufficiently high and that they passed the Oxbridge English paper for foreign students. A particular West Country university was establishing a Middle East department and was prepared to take well-based Arab students. We entered him there. The boy returned home and set to work with a will. Senior tutors were found in Abu Dhabi with the help of the British Council. His school certificates were sent to us by courier. Telephone calls became longer.

In the autumn I travelled to Abu Dhabi for a brief visit with my husband; I longed wistfully to visit the hareem in Al Ain but there was no time. Instead, plans were made for the boy's accommodation at university, his finances and of course his companion. He wouldn't, he couldn't live alone, said his father.

'Hassan will go with him to university,' said the Sheikh.

It was another of those moments that stagger you. A mental body blow.

'But. . .' My voice trailed off and I looked helplessly at my husband. He, being far cooler than I, simply stared back at the Sheikh who was calmly staring at him. At a given moment, as if on cue, both men smiled and my husband said, 'I will arrange something, of course.'

The Sheikh laughed and held out his hand. They understood each other. What neither of them understood was that it was I who would do the searching for some way to accommodate Hassan. My Cornishman was as

much of a Sheikh as the Sheikh. He had a sublime confidence that whatever was necessary to be done, could be done. Neither of them was interested in the amount of beavering that lay ahead.

In the end, Hassan was entered in an English language school near the university. He would work for entrance to a polytechnic. When we finally met, I realised how well the Sheikh had chosen. He was a tall, handsome black, intelligent and well-spoken. His English was better than that of the Second Son. Here was an ally, I thought, for I knew that ahead of me lay three years of responsibility. I would be responsible for the Second Son's peace of mind in England. I would be his English mother in earnest, providing the haven which his own mother and her hareem provided in Al Ain.

My hareem consisted of my two daughters, my daily and myself. Not much of a comparison, I thought, with laughter welling up from somewhere inside.

Part Two

7

Changes in the Desert

A YEAR CAME AND a year went and another began to tick its way into the clock of time. It was a year in which the emphasis of my life changed. Imperceptibly, slowly but definitely the eyes of my mind focussed more and more on that eye in the desert, Al Ain.

The Second Son had sweated through an orgy of study and entered the university of our choice. In term time he spent nearly every weekend with us in London, sleeping in a small room which overlooked the garden, a room which we'd previously used as a dressing room. Occasionally he brought Hassan or a new found friend with him but usually he was on his own, relishing being 'at home'.

He made friends easily though he occasionally collected the odd hanger-on who I felt sure was only waiting for a Sheikhly hand-out. Outside of their own milieu, Arabs seem to have a penchant for choosing the hustler as confidant, or the shyster as business companion. In those early oil years they were easy marks and millions, perhaps billions, were lost in the pockets of the sleazy where the pounds and dollars grew in a muddy climate.

I disdained the half-baked friends he chose, encouraged the good ones, pushed him into buying the right shoes and jackets, T-shirts and jeans, explained endlessly the use of 'could I' and 'may I' instead of 'give me' and 'I want', the right way to make tea, the right way to use a fork and knife. He was a medieval prince. I was an American-born British mother. It was a weird combination.

Intelligent, quick, his studies were never a problem. Once he'd mastered

sufficient English to use it without thinking, he surged forward, but his handwriting never improved.

There were awkward times as well as good times, and subjects on which we could never agree. I hated it when he bribed rather than tipped, left without saying goodbye or arrived without saying hello, all perfectly acceptable in his world, but not in mine.

'It is my home here?'

'Yes.'

'Then I come and go as home.'

'No.'

'Why not?'

'It is not our way.'

'Oh.'

We learned. I learned. He learned. God knows who learned the most. But the learning wound cords around us both and a strange half son and mother, half friend and friend relationship was made.

We had long talks together, usually over breakfasts of pancakes with maple syrup. I must have made thousands over those university years, much to the annoyance of my own family, as I'd rarely made the effort for them. I suppose I'd wanted to lure the boy into an acceptance of our ways and if pancakes were the bait, I'd use it. I desperately wanted him to see the right 'way to go'.

Spice cake, too, was made more frequently in my kitchen than ever before. It ran a close second to pancakes on the list of his favourite foods. Like all boys of his age, including my own son, he never seemed to get enough to eat, and yet in spite of the bread, pancakes and cake he remained thin and hard with muscle. Perhaps this was due to his near passion for exercise. It was as though he thought keeping fit would compensate for the image of the decadent Arab which was reflected in most of the press. The stories startled him and stung him. No matter how I tried to explain, he couldn't see how the odd fifty pound note or bottle of whisky he spread around contributed to that image.

'They're just presents,' he'd say. 'They're nothing.' And I'd try all over again to explain the Western way of life.

Sometimes I'd stamp my foot and cry in a completely feminine burst of frustration and he'd stand bewildered, pleading ignorance and apologising. Sometimes he'd throw up his hands and storm out of the front door, returning to my apologies and his apologies and yet another spice cake. Rough or smooth, it didn't matter for the bond that grew between us was strong.

It was made even stronger by my visits to his home and my increasing understanding of his own way of life.

Every holiday he'd fly back to the Gulf to be with his family, to put his feet on the familiar sandy soil of his own land, and every holiday he'd want me to go with him. It wasn't always possible, but when the long winter vacations of his university came, it was hard, if not impossible to resist.

'Come. Come soon. It's a good time. We go to the desert.'

His calls were repeated at increasingly frequent intervals.

'Come. Come. You know it is possible. Everything is good here. My mother invites you.' His voice strained like a young stallion on a halter. He knew his mark. He knew me well. He knew the temptation he was offering me.

The winter of his second year of university he began to do some special research on the Gulf for a project he'd been assigned. His time in Abu Dhabi would be longer than usual.

'Come. Everyone is waiting for you.'

Eventually I gave in, just as both of us knew I would. Besides, I argued with myself, the trip would work out well. My husband was going out to Qatar, that pear drop of moonscape pitted with rich oases and edged with ancient trading posts, the Emirate that had refused at the last moment to join Sheikh Zayed's dream of unity. Canny and careful, the Qataris had watched Abu Dhabi grow like a hot-house flower, but decided themselves to follow the path of the tortoise. My husband had many friends there and they sometimes called on him for his help and advice. We could travel together as far as Doha and I would go on alone to Abu Dhabi.

'You will meet me?' I asked the Second Son.

'What do you think, Mrs Tea Cup? Of course I will meet you.'

So I packed once more, stuffing my cases with presents which taxed the imagination. Presents from returning travellers or presents for your hostess are as much a sign of manners to the hareem as they are to us. The seemingly endless lengths of costly fabric which the masked ladies bought when they were in London were almost entirely presents for family and friends. I couldn't possibly compete in those stakes, so I racked my brain to think of small things which they might like. Sewing baskets, manicure sets, perfume bottles, all sorts of ornaments, soaps, shampoos and creams were packed into my cases with the skill of a Chinese puzzle maker. It was a battle of weight versus cost, a battle which, to my husband's dismay, I usually lost and we would have to pay over the odds to have my cases stowed in the hold of the Jumbo.

The flight that winter was a quiet one, a good one. The plane slipped

easily down out of the night sky on to the Doha runway. I watched as my dear man made his way across the tarmac to the small Doha airport. There was an hour of cleaning and a change of crew before we finally lifted off for the short leg down to Abu Dhabi. The final landing after the long journey was welcome. There's always that sense of relief when the wheels touch down evenly and the plane taxies to its last stop.

From my window I saw a tan Mercedes sports car pull up to the moving steps which were being fitted into place. Three young Arabs got out and stood quietly talking together. I recognised the Second Son. Through the years that I'd known him, I'd watched him grow in mind and body and now felt a twinge of pride that he had grown so well. Gathering my things, I moved out of the plane and on to the stairs. As I stepped down the steep treads I heard the too loud click of shoe leather on metal. I was already in that other world where unnecessary noise is taboo and loud voices are undignified.

We greeted each other with the warmth that people have when they enjoy each other, and my passport and luggage tickets were taken by one of his friends who moved off toward the airport building. Hassan, who was usually with him in Abu Dhabi as well as England, manoeuvred into the rear seat of the Mercedes and I took my place beside the young son who had long since graduated into a licensed driver.

We drove off into a gentle January night. The air was like a child's kiss, cool and sweet.

'How is your mother?' I asked.

'Well, thanks be to God.'

'And your grandmother and father and brothers and sisters?'

'Well, all well, thanks be to God.'

'And where are they now?'

'Waiting for you, Mrs Tea Cup. We will go tomorrow.'

His face turned briefly to me, smiling broadly. It was a handsome face, thin to the point of gaunt, quiet and still, but with the stillness of a parked Maserati. He now had the neatly trimmed beard which his father expected his sons to adopt as they grew to manhood. His hair was closely cropped, giving no concessions to the fashionable long-haired male coiffures which he had once enjoyed. It was covered with the white crocheted cap demanded of his tradition. This was topped by the long white scarf and plain black, double twist crown. The simplicity and white purity of this costume were gradually being adopted by all Arab men working on the peninsula whether they were Egyptian, Palestinian or Lebanese. It seemed that by donning the white kandora, they were declaring allegiance to the country

of their patron Sheikhs. It was a loose patronage and a loose allegiance, but it was there, nevertheless.

We drove on toward the city. It had continued to expand and change. Everything was taller; the trees, the bushes, the flowers and the buildings.

'You will find change,' said my young driver.

'Yes, there are many new buildings.'

'Of course, but not Abu Dhabi. You will find changes in the desert.'

My heart missed a beat. Some things needed to change, but some needed to remain the same and I usually found myself in this place pulling at the forces of change as a child might pull at the reins of a runaway horse. Uselessly.

'What changes?'

'You will see,' he smiled again.

The following day he arrived to collect me from the hotel where I had spent the night. He was early as usual. Arabs always seem to be either in a great hurry or without any sense of time at all. He had a new Range Rover. It was dark green with the inevitable thin layer of dust. The seats, I thanked God, were now wonderfully comfortable, a great improvement over the hard utility of previous models. Hassan and two other young men were in the back, with some boxes of food and a pile of neatly laundered men's wezaar. My suitcase was stowed and I climbed in, drawing my long skirts around me.

We drove out of the city on the now four-laned highway, passing the airport and driving over the bridge where I silently saluted the ancient tower standing in the tide-water below, the place where the Sheikha had fallen from her camel. Beyond the bridge were more signs of building. The new refinery was expanding. I remembered the black tents I had seen on this same spot on my first visit. Where were they now? Stored and forgotten, or out in the deep desert beyond?

A few miles further on we turned abruptly off the highway and the Range Rover sped into the desert leaving landmarks behind. This was a new way. A 'short cut'. Hassan seemed a bit wary and doubtful.

'Are you sure you know the way?' he asked.

'Of course,' answered the Second Son. 'Anyway, we have the radio if we get lost,' he added, laughing.

The boy was driving like the wind when suddenly we hit something. It might have been a rock, a rill of sand, who knows, but the car took off. Head-dresses flew in all directions. There were shrieks of laughter and I felt a thousand bruises rising. The laundered clothes had fallen every which way and my cases were in a jumbled heap in the back, but we didn't stop.

The car went racing on while the friends tried to tidy up the mess.

Later we were forced to stop. Quite suddenly we had driven into soft, damp sand, grey and treacherous. Sinking sands are everywhere in this area. Sucked into their vortexes are camels, sheep, goats and too many men, women and children to remember. They are the nightmares never forgotten, the reminder that the earth will have all our bones one day. We were on the edge of such a pit.

The boys eased themselves carefully out of the back of the car and pulled out some of the stores with care. I was told to stay where I was while slowly, slowly with delicate patience, the young son tried to inch the two embedded wheels out of the stuff. Hassan and the Omanis put their shoulders against the tail-board, Hassan cursing as he moved too close to the edge of the pit. They shouted commands to each other, the Second Son speaking to the engine as he might to his horse, commanding, urging, praising. I felt the sinking whir of the back wheel as it dug its own grave. Hassan's curses grew louder, ringing out over the sounds of the engine. The Second Son shouted to him to pray instead of cursing and we might get somewhere. He moved the gears down once again and once again and spoke to the engine, 'Come my beauty, come, come. Take us home, my love.'

Imperceptibly we moved. Slowly, slowly, at the pace of a snail, both front wheels gained traction and in a matter of minutes, of seconds, the recalcitrant back wheel gave up its suicidal spinning and followed the others on to firm ground, if sand can ever be called firm. We carried on in a more sober mood, each repeating his own prayers. At such a moment God is never to be forgotten.

The whole incident made the short cut longer than the long cut but in time we reached the approach to the camp, much to the relief of Hassan who seemed to have less and less faith in the Second Son's navigation. There at last was the fire burning hot, high and welcoming. There at last were the now familiar figures moving back and forth across the sand. And there were changes.

Yes, there were changes. Many changes. Though I'd visited the family in Al Ain and Abu Dhabi, it had been two years since I'd been to their camp on the Gulf. A new water tower stood sentinel and only two or three tents were scattered outside the perimeter of a newly erected wire fence. Inside the fence were six palm-frond houses identical to those which were once used in the old Abu Dhabi. I saw these invitingly cool and comfortable, old-fashioned homes for the first time.

The children were the first to greet me, their brown eyes looking up, asking silently and then audibly for presents, knowing that my cases must

hold something for each of them, if only a ribbon or a sweet. They were shooed away by the Sheikha, who rebuked them for being naughty and greeted me almost in the same breath.

'*Marhaba*, *Marhaba*, Um Yusef, welcome.'

The Second Son threw his arms about her, disturbing both her veils and mask. He winked at me with a slight shake of his head. I caught the message which in effect meant, 'Please, no word to my mother about our adventure.'

She rebuked him for being so long. He said it wasn't long and that she worried for nothing and I changed the subject.

'The houses!' I exclaimed.

She smiled and took the bait. 'You see them now? You have never seen before? Yes, my husband wanted them exactly as the old ones. Everything is the same except they have electricity and water. Come, I will show you.'

We walked to a house at the far end of the fenced area. Half shyly, half proudly she opened a pair of narrow, carved wood double doors and I went inside. It was cool and dark, a beautifully built long-house with decoratively carved wooden uprights, carved cross beams and a dormer roof.

The walls were made of stripped palm fronds, closely woven and tied with hemp to the wooden uprights. The roof was split palm lath, tied and pinned as thatch, then covered with a finely woven matting which made it quite weather-proof. The walls were lined with another fine matting woven in a large diamond design of red and green. The floor was the beaten and smoothed sand of the desert covered in layers of mats and overlaid with fine carpets. Cushions, the large hard Arabian cushions, stood neatly along the back wall.

At one end of the house, a separate small room was sectioned off. It had traditionally been used for stores and dressing. Now this little room was subdivided into a dressing area and a cement-floored shower.

A palliasse had been laid for me and in a corner were the rolled palliasses of others.

'Who?' I asked the Sheikha.

She named the same two hand-maids who had been with me on my first visit. Selma and her friend Nadia. I had known them now for some time and smiled at the thought of their good company.

'Rest,' she said and made her way to the door. 'I must pray and will see you at lunch.' She stood a moment in the sun, pulling her veils around her in one swift movement. 'This is your home. Welcome. God keep your life,' she said and moved serenely toward her own house.

Closing the doors against the brilliant light, I padded about, exploring

each nook, forgetting the drive, forgetting the pit, the danger, the desert traps. Running my hands over the matting, fascinated by the craftsmanship, I searched vainly for nails. There must have been some, but I couldn't find any. Every wooden join was tongue and groove reinforced with knotted rope. It was a house made as they once made their ships and I wondered how many would now learn either craft. The big ocean-going booms with their kite sails were becoming as rare as square-rigged schooners or clipper ships. There were small motor-powered *jalboots* which hugged the coast, fishing or cargo hopping, but they rarely lifted sail, plying in and out of the Emirates using the region's cheap petrol. Freighters, tankers and a modern fishing fleet trafficked the old sea lanes.

As for the old houses, there were none in the immediate area that I knew of, other than these which had been built as a nostalgic memento, as a reminder, as a gift both to himself and his family from a man who must have known innately that in discarding the past his people were in danger of losing their touchstone. How long would these *areesh*, these palm-frond houses be wanted, I wondered. Were they just another novelty? How long were they meant to withstand the pressures of wind and weather, and the galloping growth of all things bright and buyable?

I heard a light knock on the door. My cases were brought in and stacked against the wall. They were closely followed by the children who settled down to wait for their treasure trove. Is there a child in the world who doesn't hope for presents from a returning traveller?

A returning traveller. That was a startling thought. Was I now so enmeshed in this world that the role of visitor had changed? How many times had I heard, 'This is your home,' 'These are your sons,' 'You are my sister,' 'They are your daughters'? At first out of courtesy, but then, almost imperceptibly, as a declaration, a statement which carried with it inevitable responsibilities, inevitable pain, inevitable joy.

I laughed silently as I sat against a hard cushion in the palm-frond house looking at the brown eyes around me. What strange quirk of the heart made me feel so much a part of the life of this place? God only knew. I wondered for a moment at the intricate patterns of life. Then a familiar feeling of peace and warmth surrounded me. I felt comfortable and at home and began to search my cases for chocolates and ribbons and toys.

8

Walking to the Island

THE FOLLOWING DAY dawned clear and cold. Half awake, I lay listening to the silence. During the night the wind had risen, skating sand over sand to build drifts against the windward side of the house. It died as suddenly as it had risen. Nadia and Selma lay sleeping quietly, their black hair tumbling out of their braids. Selma snored gently in the weight of her sleep. Her round, hospitable face was totally relaxed, the face of a child. Nadia slept as she worked. Neatly.

A sharp, heavy knock sent Nadia scrambling out into the cold half-light of the early morning. It was our shovelful of hot coals for the brazier. Grumbling in Urdu while the bearer joked, she soon had him out of the door, motioned me to sleep on, and leapt into her own blankets for another half hour of rest. I buried myself deeper in the warmth of my own blanket and slept again. The clink of cup against saucer woke me. Selma was pouring my morning tea. 'Good morning - you are sleeping well, eh? It is good. Breakfast soon, Bibi.'

We drank tea together. It was hot and thickly sweet from a new tin of condensed milk. After a short, complicated conversation in our melange of languages, she left me to battle with my clothes and the shower, returning only to tell me to come to the house of Sheikha Grandmother. The women's meals were always served in the home of Sheikha Grandmother whether that home was a tent, an *areesh*, a bungalow, or, as it eventually proved, a palace. She was the titular head of our hareem. The men ate in a large tent outside the perimeter of the fence.

The fire beside the storage tent and cook-house was still burning and trays were being carried to tents and houses when I made my way across the sand wrapped in shawls against the cold. It would be another two hours before the sun rode high and hot.

'Peace be with you,' I said, kicking off my shoes as I crossed the threshold of Sheikha Grandmother's house.

'And with you, peace,' the women replied softly.

I went first to Sheikha Grandmother to make my good morning, then greeted all the others in turn. The Eldest Son's young wife was there. They had married the previous summer. At long last the large new house in the Al Ain compound would be occupied. A shy, thin, very beautiful young girl, she was already pregnant. The Eldest Son had his own areesh, his own palm-frond house where his bride sat buried in her shyness while the Sheikha's daughter did her best to make her smile. Her smile was that of a half-child, half-woman. It was wholly lovely.

I sat beside her and we waited for those who had not yet arrived. The tray with its conical basket 'hat' covering the food was in the centre of our circle but no-one would consider starting until we were all together.

I had grown used to these meal gatherings, to the formal greetings. Whatever the time of day, entering a room or joining a group demanded a blessing. 'God's peace be with you all.' As for the children, 'Hi, Mom' would be as startling as a bikini. Every morning and every afternoon after siestas, the children and young people were expected to greet their mothers, grandmothers and aunts with a kiss in the centre of the forehead. For fathers, grandfathers and uncles there was the nose kiss.

This strange greeting is used in this particular part of Arabia and parts of Oman, not the northern Gulf nor the inland deserts of Saudi Arabia. Hands at the sides, nose quickly touches nose one to three times. Men greet their friends this way, women greet their women friends.

'Where did this come from? Why?' I had asked.

'Perhaps it is because the nose is the first part of you to come forward. And you can be dignified still. An embrace is more intimate,' was the answer. Who knows? One thing is sure. It is an ancient form of recognition that civilisation drowns. Here in the Abu Dhabi/Al Ain area it was both a statement and a signature used only by those whose lives were rooted in the place.

As we sat waiting, each wrapped in her own morning thoughts, a small three-year-old girl came quietly through the door, dragging a piece of black veiling behind her. It was Amina, one of the Sheikha's foster daughters. Intensely shy but always wanting to be good, she went round the 'table',

kissing each one of us and hoping for a hug in return. The veil was her security blanket. She was never without it.

The second foster daughter soon followed, coming in with a bound. Miriam was five and about as different from Amina as possible. Extroverted, quick and full of enthusiasm, she hopped about the carpet without a word of greeting to anyone. No-one scolded her. Scoldings were reserved for more serious offences.

Although many children were fostered, especially girls, few were adopted. True adoption is rare. Adoptive children should nurse at the breast of one of the immediate family in order to have the freedom of the family when they are adult. They are then accepted as true brothers or sisters. Marriage between a blood son and an adopted daughter who had nursed at the same breast would be incestuous - *haram* - forbidden.

Miriam had been an orphaned refugee child brought from the Lebanon at the Sheikha's request. Amina had been orphaned in the Emirates. Both were kissed and cuddled and bandied about like special toys.

In most of the hareems there were usually two or more of these little girls. Sheikhas were always looking for homeless orphans to take under their wing. There was one wonderful story of a little Pakistani girl of some four to five years who accidentally wandered on to the edge of the Abu Dhabi-Dubai road. A Sheikha passing in her stretched Mercedes saw the child and picked her up. The little girl seemed to have been abandoned, so the Sheikha took her home, cared for her and made all the necessary preparations to keep her. Only when the police and parents advertised the child's disappearance was the mistake discovered and the child returned to her family.

In any event, that is the story.

Miriam and Amina were not foundlings. A careful search had been made for two orphaned children whom the Sheikha could foster and love as her own. These two lucky little girls were chosen. They were being brought up with the same affection the Sheikha gave her own daughter.

All these little girls ate their meals in the Sheikha's majlis with their nurses - in the nursery, so to speak. They wouldn't join the grown-ups for a good many years, though the Sheikha's daughter had been my meal companion before I myself had been accepted by the 'grown-ups'.

Once the little ones had left the room, I shifted my position on the floor and sat cross-legged, trying to cover the soles of my feet with my skirt. It is as rude as spitting to turn the soles of your feet toward anyone, so stretching your legs in front of you becomes nearly impossible. Leg cramp, therefore, is always imminent. This, plus the fact that sitting *tahat* - down on the

carpet - is no excuse to lounge, makes it a problem for me. You are supposed to sit up with a straight back. In fact the back should be straight at all times. My back with its two slipped discs sometimes ached unmercifully. Indeed one of my more embarrassing moments was when a child was told not to sit like Um Yusef. In Arabic, of course, thinking I didn't understand. Shame. Shame on me.

When the Sheikha finally arrived we all rose to greet her. We always rose to greet each other. They did it easily. I was always getting my feet caught on my hems.

Breakfast was my favourite meal as it was the easiest for me to eat. I had become quite skilled with harees, that glutinous porridge of lamb and cracked wheat which I had met at my first meal bedu style. Bilaleet was less enjoyable for me as I couldn't get used to sweet vermicelli, but then I never liked rice pudding either. My real favourite became *mahala*, a very thin pancake about twelve to eighteen inches across which is torn into pieces with the fingers and dipped into a mixture of honey and butter. Delicious. Then there were the hot, spiced, yeast buns with their shine of sugar on top. Oh yes. Breakfast was always a pleasure.

After nibbling away at piece after piece of mahala and making a large hole in the harees dish, I said my *Alhamdulillah* - Thanks be to God.

'No, no. This is not enough. You must eat more.'

I shook my head and was saved from further entreaties by the arrival once again of the children who all wanted choice titbits from the grown-ups' 'table', kisses and praise. The washing bowl with its kettle was passed. Coffee was served and we sat sipping cup after cup.

'Will you walk today, Um Yusef?' The Sheikha turned to me as she spoke. She knew that I loved to walk along the inlet with the children, looking for shells or pebbles or a wild flower.

I hesitated, for I already had a plan but wasn't sure whether it would be acceptable.

'I would like to walk across the inlet to the island,' I said.

'Walk? Through the water?'

There was consternation on the one hand.

'It is surely too cold.'

'It is too deep.'

'You will get wet.'

There was laughter on the other hand.

'I'd like to see Maha walk.' Shrieks of alarm from Maha, a divorcee from Qatar who often visited in those days.

'She'd never make it.'

70

'Never.'

'The fish would eat her.' This last from Hussa, the Sheikha's great friend and lady-in-waiting.

Hussa was a large, enveloping woman with a large, enveloping sense of humour; she walked with the rolling gait of a shore-bound sailor and her veils had such a haphazard permanence, you felt they were an outgrowth of her personality rather than a covering. When camping, she generally wore an old-fashioned dress with little or no decoration. Her jewellery consisted of a sound gold watch and a fine turquoise ring. Nothing else. Her hands were strong, her body was strong. She knew everyone and was always in the know, always had some news. She was a catalyst.

The daughter of an ocean-going boom's captain, Hussa understood and loved all things relating to the sea. When we walked along the shore with the children trailing us, she would name the shells, the fish and the scrub grass. She marked the paths of birds and insects, pointed to the homes of lizards and carried a fishing line which she would occasionally cast, watching for the rough bobbin to lurch, winding in a small, flat saafi fish which danced on the hook until she released it and tossed it back.

Yes, Hussa would walk with me.

'We'll put the children in the boat and pull them across,' I said. 'We can pull Maha too if she is afraid to walk.'

Maha was a lushly beautiful woman who had left the husband who had been arranged for her. She cut her masks daringly until there was little left of them. She had dancing eyes and a full figure. There was little doubt that she would marry again and hopefully it would prove a more comfortable arrangement.

'She will walk,' said Hussa.

'I will go in the boat,' said Maha.

'She will walk,' said Hussa.

So it was decided.

'Will you come?' I asked the Sheikha.

'No. Another time. I have much work.' Her eyes smiled, and I knew it was true. I knew, too, that she felt such an excursion would be just a little too unconventional for one of her position.

We set out for the inlet, pulling a shrieking Maha, surrounded by the usual bevy of children and urged on by the boys, maids and especially the Youngest Son, who was always ready to tease and laugh. It was only a few yards to the water. The sun shone somewhere between warm and hot.

At the water's edge a rowing boat was beached. The tide was ebbing. We gathered round the boat with all the sense of adventure of Drake

71

rounding the Horn. The children began to jump in and out of the boat, arranging and re-arranging themselves. Maha tried to join them but was cast out and good-humouredly began to push the loaded craft into the water.

'I'll pull the children in the boat. You pull Maha,' said Hussa.

'Pick up your dress so it won't get wet,' I said to Maha.

She gingerly lifted her skirt to reveal perhaps twelve inches of heavily embroidered, ankle-tight white pantaloons. Hussa didn't bother. She plunged forward, skirts dragging, heaving on the tow rope.

At its deepest I reckoned the water might be waist high. The whole inlet couldn't have been more than fifty yards across, but to Maha it was at least a mile wide, as deep as the ocean, wet and cold. To add to her worries the sandy bottom was thickly covered by myriads of minute creatures in their delicate shells.

I took her by the hand and stepped into the water. She was game so step by step, her eyes growing bigger, her shrieks louder, we inched our way across. Lifting our skirts higher and higher to avoid the water we carefully dropped them as it became shallow again.

As we reached the shore of the island Maha threw her hands in the air, clasping them in a boxer's sign of victory. With her veils damp, her mask awry and her skirts bedraggled, she danced a little jig.

'Thanks be to God. I crossed,' she shouted.

Hussa had beached the boat and the children made off in every direction to explore. Maha followed them but Hussa and I threw ourselves face down on the warm, white sand, both of us smiling at the success of the project.

This was the same island we had visited on my first trip. On its Gulf side, the collection of flotsam and jetsam could still be found. To reach it other than by boat or wading in low tide would have taken an hour's drive, so it was not often visited by the women. They rarely ventured more than ankle deep into the inlet. Hussa was the exception. She could swim, read the signs of the sea, forecast the weather. She was a fund of knowledge in a thousand unexpected ways.

After resting and lazing for nearly an hour, after the children had slid down enough dunes, chased enough birds, fallen in the water enough times, we returned in much the same way as we started out, except this time Maha leapt into the boat and would not move. With gunnels close to the water, much shouting and sharp warnings to sit still, Hussa and I dragged the boat back home. It had been an adventure.

9

The Djinn and the
Slave of the Devil

THE MORNING CLOUDS had withered and disappeared. The distant
winter sun still held enough heat to dry the sky of every shred of
moisture. It was siesta time, that full-stop in the day which divides the long
morning from the long evening.

I never could sleep in the middle of the day, so as usual I took a sketch
pad and sat sketching and making notes with my back against the wall of
my house. It was calm and still, that rare sort of peace that feeds the soul.
But it didn't last long.

The children were up first. They always found me no matter where I hid.
As they demanded sketches of themselves, I drew first one and then
another. Any sort of likeness would bring choruses of 'Good, good' - 'Again,
Mrs Tea Cup, again.' I'm a poor artist and only draw to make notes, but in
this company everything was flatteringly good.

Around four o'clock I packed up my books and went into my house to
wash and change. A little mirror had been hung on the wall of the dressing
area. It looked rather like a closed tryptic. Two doors shut the glass away
when it was not in use, as if to remind me that too much self-admiration
was unacceptable. I could just see my face in it. Mirrors were still very
dubious household items. It was not seemly to look at oneself and although
every lady had her hand mirror tucked into her personal box, mirrors on
the wall were still not quite nice, still slightly risqué.

Turning on the shower, I let the water run over me. The cement floor
was cold underfoot and the water colder, so I washed quickly and jumped

73

out on to the carpet, gratefully rubbing myself with a towel which the Sheikha had given me. I was sure the tryptic mirror was one of her own treasures and I opened it carefully to see myself as I brushed my hair and applied a quick dab of lipstick, the red paint which marked me as a Westerner as surely as my blue eyes and blondish hair. They never used lipstick. It was not only unnecessary but slightly scandalous.

Pulling on a sweater and wrapping my long kilt around me, I made my way towards Sheikha Grandmother's house. We greeted each other for the afternoon, but before I could sit down she took hold of the fabric of my kilt and gently fingered it.

'Wool?' she asked. Her eyes were keen and direct. A wool skirt was a strange thing to one whose life had been spent battling the sun.

'Yes, wool,' I answered and tried to explain the idea of tartan, the 'tribes' of Scotland with their foreign names.

'And they play the pipes, just as the Arab plays them with a bag holding air,' I added.

That fact didn't surprise her. We all expect others to be like ourselves. But wool skirts - that was strange.

'It is good,' she said, as she held the cloth and told me to sit. Ordering coffee she then pointed to my pullover and shook her finger. I knew she didn't like my roll-neck pullover. Polyester cardigans were sometimes worn over their silks on a cold night, but pullovers were rather rough and for children, not for ladies.

It suddenly occurred to me that just as I wanted the boys to dress according to Western ideas when they were in London, so the Sheikha and Sheikha Grandmother would like me to dress according to their ideas of fashion when I was with them. I never wore the roll-neck out there again and as the years passed I was gradually given a large wardrobe of beautiful traditional dresses, which I wore with comfort and delight, each dress reminding me of the giver.

Having drunk my first afternoon coffee with Sheikha Grandmother I went to greet the Sheikha. She had settled on a carpet which had been unrolled on the sand in front of her house and the family had gathered around her. She liked to be outside, liked to watch the day waxing or waning, liked to be where she could see her household moving about.

It was quiet. Relaxed. Coffee was poured again. Smoke rose in a thick spiral from the oil-perfumed sandalwood smouldering in an incense pot. A second thermos was passed with hot camels' milk, yellow with saffron and heavily sweet.

The men of the family began to join us. The Sheikh with his now tall

sons wore their long grey and brown winter kandoras. On their heads were checked winter head scarves twisted into turbans that showed by the particular shape the area from which they came. Al Ain. The tassels of the head scarves spilt down the sides of their faces. It is a handsome style, now sadly relegated to holidays in the desert or hunting excursions.

The Eldest Son joined the family. He was on holiday from his university in Jordan; he had yet to finish his studies even though he was now married. Heavier than the others, excitable, he reacted to any given situation with sudden outbursts of what he then felt was a Sheikhly authoritarianism. Underneath the prickly exterior, however, was an inherently sweet character with a deep interest in history and the machinations of international politics. We would have long, complicated discussions whenever the days allowed a stretch of time between us. He, too, was blessed with that sense of humour which seemed indigenous to them all.

As we sat together in front of the Sheikha's areesh the conversation began to move back and forth, gathering speed and laughter. Tales were told of trips abroad and their social pitfalls. The hopeless English or French of one or another was mimicked while stories of European or Asian drivers, hotel waiters or doctors were traded. They mocked each other mercilessly, made a comedy of the simplest incident and drew the world into their pantomime.

'And so they don't know which button to push in the lift,' laughed the Youngest Son. 'First up, then down. Then up and up and down and down. Hussa got out the *della* and began to pour coffee. Up, down, up, down.'

Once the sense of the ridiculous had begun it was like waves gathering into a crescendo. Animals, birds, insects, people were all pulled into the joke of life. The laughter rolled up until we were weak and weeping, and the sky turned pink, and the air began to cool.

Suddenly the tempo changed. Two spirals of dust had appeared on the distant horizon.

'Who?' asked the Sheikh and rose to get a better look. His eyes had long been trained to see deep into the flat light of the desert.

'The trucks with the stores,' said the Second Son.

'Yes, but three are coming.'

I could still see nothing but the spirals of desert dust.

'Your sister?' asked the Sheikha.

'No, not that car.'

'Who comes to the desert then?' asked the Eldest Son.

'It is a holiday. Anyone might come,' said the Second Son.

Anyone might, anyone could, anyone would be welcome for a time or

half a time.

The trucks eventually swung into the camp's orbit and moved off to unload stores. A car pulled up to the fence. Two women shook themselves out.

'It is Halema bint Mohammed. She said she might come,' said the Sheikha softly and went to greet her.

A bundle of black walked toward her, round, bobbing, and bubbling with good cheer. She was accompanied by a dark, well-dressed woman. As she had no mask, she was no doubt a hand-maid-cum-companion to the cheerful bundle. Only women who are indigenous to the area wear masks, so she was a foreign Arab - probably a Sudanese or Somali. The women exchanged their multiple greetings, quickly and quietly, rattling off the familiar courtesy phrases, nodding and gesturing with their hands - small gestures.

'God's peace be on you and all with you,' said the black bundle.

'And God's peace on you and all with you,' we all answered.

'How are you all?'

'Well, praise be to God.'

'How are you, sir, *tawil omrak*' asked the bundle of the Sheikh, 'and your mother and sisters and aunts?' Here a long list of everyone by name.

'Well, praise be to God,' answered the Sheikh.

Interspersed throughout the conversation the Sheikha added, 'Welcome, welcome.'

We had all risen to greet them. The men, after more formal greetings, moved off to their majlis tent. The circle of women had grown beyond the immediate family. If the men didn't move off, the woman visitor would have had to remain completely veiled as well as masked. For friends such as Hussa and Maha who had spent a lifetime with the family such formalities scarcely mattered any more. But for real visitors it was a must.

Once the men had left, the hareem settled down on the carpet once again. Now the welcome greetings continued.

These greetings are always positive, for with these women all life is of God: whatever trials or disasters are endured, they must be God-sent so all is well. Not for them our Western confidences: 'How are you?' 'Awful, I've got a lousy headache' or 'My uncle just died' or 'Suzie's got a cold.' All news on greeting is good. Even if a daughter or son or husband were seriously ill, the answer to 'How are you all?' would be 'Well, praise be to God', thus giving all into God's hands, and relying on his wisdom and mercy. Like the Biblical Shunamite woman, whose faith in God was such that when her only son died she answered the prophet Elisha's question 'Is all well with

the child?' with 'It is well', so these women answer 'All is well' when humanly all is a disaster.

Halema, however, had no sad news to share. The coffee thermos and cups were fetched, the incense came again but this time it was passed more slowly, so that everyone could enjoy the sweet-smelling smoke to a greater extent. Halema moved the pot down her dress, then folded it inside her cloak, waiting for the smoke to rise. Her companion did the same, but the Sheikha in her usual way lifted her veil and with a graceful inward movement of her wrist held the pot under her arm, first one side then the other, her neck arching above the rising smoke. The pot went again to Halema, who pulled up her skirt, revealing blue pantaloons trimmed with four or five inches of the requisite silver and gold thread at the ankle. She placed the pot between her legs, knees drawn up, then pulled her skirts down carefully and her cloak on top of it all.

I watched and waited. Soon the smoke began to leak through her clothes until the ensuing fog convinced me as always that she would set herself alight. She looked like a little black chattering chimney pot, for as the smoke rose up through her veils she kept up a constant conversation. Periodically she turned to me and spoke to me like a teacher to a beloved but dull-witted child. '*Shoo hadha?*' she'd say pointing to her nose or chin or mouth or leg or wrist. 'What's this?' When the Arabic word would come roughly out of my mouth she'd correct and correct - '*La, la*' - 'No, no' - and would carefully mouth the right pronunciation. Right at least according to this area.

She sat steaming away, telling her news. It was a holiday. She wanted to see Sheikha Grandmother. She wanted to see the palm houses which she had heard the Sheikh had built. The news of this or that Abu Dhabi family was given. Some I knew, some I didn't.

The talk began to waft over me, Halema's guttural Arabic being too quick and too difficult for me to catch. I covered myself in myself and became the observer, an easy role to assume after years of struggling with their throaty language and its local eccentricities, its dialects and apposite linguistic twists and turns. Years of the language battle seemed to have given me an inner eye. If you are lost in language you must find other roads to understanding. So I put my own invisible veils over me and began to watch.

Halema was a black-covered dumpling, delicious and rich, perhaps not in money, but certainly in the joy of life. She was a traditionalist - her jewellery gave no concessions to modern fashion. Not for her the shops of the Boulevard or Bond Street. She was content in her own city. She was

either divorced or widowed. One sensed the aloneness, and would she be roaming the desert if there were a husband to worry about? She was a member of this or an allied tribe. Sheikha Grandmother, whom she wanted to visit, was a renowned figure, but such a trip would not be made for one outside the tribe circle.

She was filled with an inner energy. Her small hands flew like gold-ringed birds as she told the news, rocking back and forth with laughter at one of her own jokes. Red hair escaped from under her veil. Red with henna. White hair is sign of great age, a sign that one no longer really cares about appearance. When her veils eventually parted a waft of smoke engulfed her and she laughed again, a deep-throated, jolly laugh. You could see her whole body shaking and I remembered Clement Moore's *The Night Before Christmas*: 'a right jolly old elf ... with a little round belly that shook when he laughed like a bowlful of jelly.'

As I watched, the sun dropped toward the horizon gathering momentum as it fell. Almost at a signal, though none was given, the women rose. '*Sulleh*, Um Yusef. I go to pray.'

Halema handed the incense pot to one of the maids, and the women moved off in a wave of black veiling. The Sheikha gave me a questioning look and I answered, 'I will stay here.'

The twilight began to move in around me, that strange half-light which sometimes gives way to an afterglow. All the beauty that ought to be but rarely is, all the promises of perfection are caught in a few moments of that iridescent light. An exquisite unreality catches the earth, or perhaps it is the ultimate reality.

They say - the records say - that twilight is a moment equal only to pre-dawn in its tenuous hold on life. More lives begin and end in those pre-dawn or pre-night moments than at any other period in our twenty-four hour cycle.

Islam covers these arcs of time in a blanket of prayer. Certainly in the desert at dawn and dusk it is impossible to ignore the need to relate to an intelligence, to a protective power beyond oneself. In the shimmering half-light, even the earth seems to breathe. Inevitably, consciously, I added my own prayers to their paeons of praise.

That evening, long after the dark had finally driven even me inside, I mentioned the beauty of the twilight.

'Ah,' said Halema, with her eyes laughing, 'she does not know how she is protected by our prayers from Boudariah.'

Boudariah, the slave of the Devil, the evil spirit of the sea. I had heard of this spirit creature. 'They say that he is very tall and very thin, but no-one

is really sure,' I said. 'Is that right? Do you know?'

She looked at me and laughed. 'Who knows? Who knows? But do you believe?'

'I only know that there is more that I do not know than that I know,' I answered.

Halema seemed satisfied with my answer and the talk turned to the lives of such spirits and then to the djinn.

It is said that these underground beings, djinn, rise in the half light of pre-dawn and in the twilight. Are they mind creatures, hallucinations or semi-realities? Is it belief that gives them reality? If we disbelieve do they cease to exist? Or is the carefully structured Arabian djinn world a remnant of some extension of communication which we once knew how to use and control but have now lost?

All of us have our underworld and nether world creatures with whom we carry on some inner conversation. On black nights in Cornwall the piskies fairly leap out of the twisted holly trees and granite stones and I rush inside, grateful for the light, the fire, the warmth of a human voice.

Cornwall. Our family's heart home where the sea smashes against cliffs in winter, and the sun pulls life out of its rich earth in summer. The piskies could be anywhere. In the hedges, under milk churns, by the stone stiles. Anywhere.

And what of hobgoblins, gnomes and the little people of Ireland? What of fairies? What of Zeus himself and Medusa, the Cyrenes and Orpheus?

Halema settled herself more comfortably, adjusted her veils and began to question me.

'You know of the djinn? What do you know?'

I explained that before I came to Arabia the only djinn or genie that I knew was Aladdin's genie of the lamp.

'You know of Ah-lah-deen? How do you know?'

'She reads of him,' said Hussa. 'And of Sindebahd.'

These characters have become so much a part of our own childhood that we almost forget their origin.

'Tell me, Halema, is Boudariah a djinn or a devil? What is the difference between djinn and devil?' I asked.

She looked surprised at my ignorance.

'Devils are not djinn. Djinn are not devils. One is one. Other is other.'

'You mean djinn or we say genie as in our story of Aladdin?'

'Whose story of Ahlahdeen?' A slight lift of the eyes and no doubt eyebrows which were hidden under the mask. Then a quiet laugh. I was chastened.

'Forgive me,' I said. 'Your story. But it is such a famous story that we all mistake it for our own.'

'It belongs to the world,' said the Sheikha, not wishing to see me embarrassed.

'You mistake the story for the realities,' said Halema. 'Djinn are real.' She saw the moment of disbelief in my eyes. 'Come, Um Yusef, you believe in God? Yes, of course you do. Then you must believe in djinn for they are written in the Qur'an.'

The finer points of the differences between being a Christian and a Muslim were rarely discussed between us. For them it was enough that I, a Westerner from a God-forgotten, immoral country, believed and made some attempt to practise. On my part I would not presume to disturb their faith.

'Tell me,' I said. Halema began to describe the life of the desert djinn who people the underworld. They have a complete society, I was told. A family life. Homes. They marry, have children and die. Some go to Paradise, some to Hell. There are black djinn and white djinn. They have been known both to help and to hurt the desert people. They can guide you or confuse you. When they rise at dawn and in the twilight people should not be abroad, but at their prayers indoors. Four elements protect you from them. Fire, steel, salt and the Qur'an, but the Qur'an, of course, is considered the most important.

'And they hate electricity,' Hussa added. I suspected this was the reason compounds and camps always had rings of protective lights.

Djinn are of another dimension but can take possession of all living things. Sometimes they are in trees, sometimes in animals and sometimes they take control of a human. When this happens the human is capable of extraordinary acts. They will do things that ordinarily would injure them, and yet they are not injured; superhuman acts, from lifting enormous weights to self-wounding.

At twilight it is most important to be kind to animals, to refrain from throwing anything on the ground, from riding either horse or camel over the desert, for you might injure a rising djinn and they are vengeful spirits.

'Now you know of the djinn.' said Halema. 'Yes, you know. But you do not believe. Come, I will tell you of Aisha. She knew Aisha?' Halema turned to the Sheikha who said that I had known her well.

Aisha had been both a tribal companion to the Sheikha and a 'nanny' to her children. She had been a wet-nurse for the Sheikha's youngest child, her daughter. A kind woman, she had had three children of her own and a heart as large as her ample body. I had visited her often in the London

hospital where vain efforts were made to stop the spread of cancer. She had been stone deaf, as well.

'Can't anything be done for her deafness, at least?' I had asked, 'Surely some hearing aid or something?'

'No, nothing,' was the answer. 'She has seen the best specialists in Europe.'

As the wind began to rise outside the palm house, Halema told the story of Aisha's deafness.

It had happened when Aisha was first married. She had been cooking rice for supper. Not realising that the afternoon hours had passed, she had gone out and thrown the boiling rice water on the ground. It was just twilight. The following morning she was struck with a heavy fever and by the end of the day she was stone deaf. There was no damage to her eardrums, no apparent cause other than the fever.

'She threw the rice water on the djinn,' said Halema. 'It was a strong curse. The djinn will always pay you back. They will always take revenge. You must always be careful.'

As she spoke, the women listened carefully, interjecting a soft prayer or injunction to praise God. They watched me even more carefully, their eyes expressionless, waiting. They waited for my comments, waited to see whether I would condemn their beliefs or laugh. They waited for the moment when I might put myself beyond their pale.

'Aisha was a good woman,' I said. 'A kind woman.'

'Thanks be to God,' they answered.

'She died as she lived, with patience and courage,' I went on, for I knew more was expected of me. 'I believe that only God could have saved her, but for some reason - perhaps her fear or our fear for her - we could not realise His mercy.'

'Thanks be to God, this is true.'

'Praise God who has created all things.'

'Praise Him. Thank Him.'

All was in God's hands. All of my life, all of theirs. We were breathing together again and there were no barriers of disbelief between us.

The Sheikha called for coffee and some sweet to be brought. An enamel pot arrived and we dipped our fingers in the sweet, gelatinous stuff. Then I turned again to Halema.

'But what of Boudariah?'

'Ah,' she said, handing back her coffee cup with a shake to Selma, who was never far away. Adding a quiet 'Thanks be to God', she turned to Shama. 'You tell her of Boudariah, Shama, for of this you know much.'

Shama was the mother of Hussa. She was an ageless woman, this widow of a sea-captain. She sat with a lame leg tucked under her. It was the result of a fall from a camel on her way to Mecca. In the days to come she would tell me the story, she would teach me many things. How to watch the stars, how to number the days for the planting of dates and how to forecast the weather. I never knew her young, but she has never grown older in the years since I began to sit with this hareem.

'Boudariah,' she began, slowly repeating his name as she settled herself more comfortably and tugged at her long, old-fashioned mask. Her voice was deep and low. A contralto. 'He comes out of the darkness. He is not a djinn. His spirit is black. He is the slave of darkness, of the evil one, of the Devil himself. The Devil is not a djinn, Um Yusef, but is as with you. The whole of the bad. The one who takes you and makes you do the wicked thing. Boudariah is his slave.'

As she spoke, the wind rose again and the brazier burned hot. We warmed our hands as though a sudden chill had come upon us at the mention of his name.

Shama continued.

'Off the coast of Ras Al Khaimah and off the coast of Muscat, too, the Slave of the Devil has been known to catch a boat by the middle, break it - break its back and pull it down and down until all is gone. Nothing seen and no-one found. Never and never. This is true, for we know some travellers who were on such a ship. A great ship. They were going from Ras Al Khaimah to India. There was no wind. No storm. It was calm. Boudariah caught the boat and sank it. This time, thanks be to God, some were saved to tell the news.

'I tell you, if anyone went near the beach in those days before everything became new - if anyone went near the beach at night, the Slave would come from the deep sea and make a light. The light would pull you. You go toward the light, always toward the light. Then Boudariah takes you, kills you and throws your body on the beach.'

The Sheikha caught my eye and shook her head as if to say, 'This is all very old and not for today.' She often seemed to worry that they would appear strange to me and out of key with the age. It saddened me. I answered her look with as much affection in my own expression as I could muster and added, 'But I want to hear, my lady, *tawil omrich*. I want to hear, my friend.'

Halema began to speak again. 'Here is a strange story for you, Um Yusef. A story of Boudariah which is not so very old. I will tell you, but I think you will not believe.'

'Tell me, God willing,' I said.

'I will tell you now that the Slave can take the shape of a human. Some djinn are like this. It makes difficulties. But when the Slave takes a human form it is always a bad thing.' Her voice was strong and clear, that of a true storyteller. Nothing disturbed its cadences as she spoke, except the low accompaniment of the Sheikha's schoolgirl daughter, who translated gently and continually for me. Only this and the hissing of the wind.

'There was a man. He lived in Abu Dhabi,' began Halema. 'A good man. A straight man and a good fisherman. Fish come up from the deep sea in the early morning and the early evening. You know this?' I nodded. 'You know this,' she repeated and then went on. 'This man - Ali - had a cousin named Ahmed. They like to walk together and to fish together. Ali and Ahmed made a time to meet on the beach to fish. But they were careless. Careless of the sunset. They like fishing more than their prayers perhaps.'

She leaned back and waggled her forefinger to show her disapproval. Then she continued.

'That evening Ali made careful arrangements with Ahmed. He said he does not want to be late returning home. Perhaps his wife was ready to deliver a child, perhaps his mother was ill. Who knows? But we know the arrangements were exact. The meeting should be at a place far down the beach. Far from houses. Fish come in quiet places. You know this?'

Again I nodded and she said, 'Ah. You know this.' Then the story went on.

'Ali came, but he sees Ahmed there before him. Then he sees Ahmed start to walk away from him. Not come to him. Away from him. This is strange, you understand. Strange. Why does he do this? Ali called, "Ahmed. Ahmed. Stop. We fish here. It is good here." But Ahmed only walks faster. "Ahmed. Ahmed. Stop. Don't go running like this. It is good here. Not up there," Ali shouts. Then he runs to catch his cousin. Ahmed turns and smiles and runs faster. Now both run on the beach.

'"Stop. Stop joking. Ahmed. Stop this joke." shouts Ali. He sucks air for breath. But Ahmed laughs and runs straight into the sea. Far, far he goes until he goes under the sea.

'Ali follows. He follows in the water until the sea is all around him. He calls and calls his cousin but nothing. He cries. Tears come down. Salt tears. Salt as the sea. But he can go no more. Ali cannot swim. Cannot. So he cries and he goes back to the beach. He falls down on the sand. He lies looking at the waves touch the land, crying for his cousin.

'Then he hears a voice. It says, "Ali. What are you doing there? You told me to meet you further back." It is his cousin Ahmed coming. He comes

late. He had slept all through the sunset prayer. Through the time of meeting. Now the sun had gone leaving only this dangerous light. What you call it?'

Halema looked at me. I answered, 'Afterglow.' She tried it in English, then returned to her story.

'I ask you then, who had been on the beach? I tell you it was Boudariah, the Slave of the Devil. He had taken the shape of Ahmed. Ali was saved by someone's prayers. Now, how many have died from fright? How many pulled into the sea? No-one knows. But this story is true.'

Murmurs of 'Praise God' went around the circle.

Halema looked at me. The Sheikha again said that it was a story from the days past but Halema did not say another word. Only her eyes spoke and her words stayed, 'But this story is true.' Had Ali and Ahmed been her cousins? I could not ask.

That night in my areesh, wrapped warmly in my blankets, the wind rose again and began to make odd wind sounds as it pushed through the fencing. The water in the inlet beat roughly against the shore. I shivered, looked at Selma and Nadia sleeping quietly and felt grateful for their company.

10

The Mercy Plane
with Gold Taps

HALEMA STAYED FOR three days, just long enough for her round figure bobbing up and down the beach to become familiar, long enough for the affection she exuded to be returned tenfold.

When she left, we all stood around her car to wave her off. Setting out into the desert was still regarded as important. It was not a casual departure which warranted little attention. Water bottles and coffee dellas were stowed on the back seat. She got in the car with as much ceremony as if she were mounting a camel. Settling herself, settling her skirts, her veils and her abaya, she motioned to her companion to get in, gave a nod to her black driver and with a quick firm 'Ma'salaama' (goodbye) and an even quicker 'Bismallah' (in the name of God), the doors were resoundingly shut and she was off. No waving. No looking back. They never look back. I have not seen her from that day to this.

Our own days in the palm-frond houses seemed to dwindle as quickly as sand through a sieve. I knew the hareem would soon return to Al Ain. The caravan of cars and trucks would move up the highway, the women driven by sons, all of whom were now old enough to take the wheel, the Sheikh driving his mother and wife. The cars would pass and re-pass each other in a game of motorway weaving, the sons manoeuvring their powerful Mercedes around each other until the women eventually objected or they themselves tired of the sport.

I would not be a part of the caravan that year. Word had come that my husband had arrived in Abu Dhabi.

'He is there,' said the Sheikh one morning. 'Now you will leave us.' He held out his hand to me, palm up. I slapped mine into his and we both laughed. His hand was dry, fine-boned and strong.

The Sheikha joined us and we sat together while arrangements were made for me to leave.

'She will come to Al Ain when her husband goes? This is for sure,' asked the Sheikha.

'She must,' said Sheikha Grandmother who was walking towards us, leaning on her granddaughter.

'She will,' said the Sheikh, rising to greet his mother and kissing her on the forehead, the kiss of respect, of the younger for the elder.

That afternoon I left for Abu Dhabi with the promise that I would indeed see them in Al Ain in a week's time. I knew that on this trip my husband would go on to Oman and Cairo before returning home. I would stay on in Al Ain, making my own way to London in time for his return.

We met at the Hilton. He looked tanned and well and our room was comfortable and quiet. It was extraordinary moving from one environment to another, from the desert to that very modern hotel. That very morning I'd wakened in my khama. I'd sat on my palliasse writing notes, watching Selma plait her hair, trying to decide when to get up and walk down the inlet far enough to be out of sight in order to go to the loo. I'd dressed in my long dress, eaten breakfast bedu fashion, discussed the children's health with the Sheikha over coffee - the Youngest Son had had far too many headaches and his usual teasing and joking hadn't been seen for days. She thought she might try a purge. I thought a cup of sweet English tea or warm camels' milk and clove and a sleep, and certainly not to take the wheel of one of the cars on their way to Al Ain.

Now, in the afternoon of the same day, I was resting in a perfectly made bed after a hot bath in a perfectly designed bathroom. I was discussing business contracts with my husband and waiting for a call from my own children who would rock with laughter if I prescribed a dose of warm camels' milk and clove for a poor stomach and headache.

Like a chameleon, I absorbed and reflected the place where I was. My clothes and conversation changed according to environment and companion. It was almost automatic. Almost, but not quite.

My mind, my inner eye needed more time. It needed time for reflection before reflecting was possible. I found myself wanting longer and longer times of quiet, longer arcs of contemplation. I had begun to rise earlier and earlier, sometimes watching the sun lift itself off the horizon, first red, then yellow, then white. Then I'd remember the hareem at their dawn prayers,

standing, bowing, kneeling, bowing down their heads to the flat surface of their prayer mats. Up and down and over and over, again and again and I'd marvel at the bulk of prayer they made in any one day.

For me peace and prayer melt into one attitude and as my life grew ever more complex, I needed, in direct ratio, ever more peace. Whether in London, Abu Dhabi or Al Ain, in a hotel or in the desert I searched for times of quiet as a starving man searches for food. I found them in those dawn hours.

That week in Abu Dhabi my days were spent beside the pool under a shade umbrella, with my books and notes at my side. Around the pool the hotel guests sunbathed religiously, oiling their sleek bodies in order to achieve deeper and deeper tones of tan. I had already learned to relish shade and arranged my umbrella continually in order to be under its protection. Sand-coloured bastion walls rose around the pool, hiding us from the desert world outside.

In the mornings my husband walked the endless corridors of oil power, hoping for patience to overcome impatience. By one o'clock he'd be staggered by the reels of shiny new bureaucratic red tape and return to the hotel fort where we would lunch by the pool, talk, plan, watch, and he would slowly recuperate. The evenings were filled with dinners given for us or by us and then the night would become day again and the same pattern repeat itself.

The week passed quickly. Far too quickly and when he left for Oman, I felt that aching void which, after decades of marriage, never lessened when he and I separated to travel alone.

After he had gone, I packed my own cases, checked the drawers and cupboards of our room and called for a porter. In the lobby, I braved the stares of the milling guests, for I was in long skirts again and long skirts on a Western woman at ten in the morning were a bit peculiar, even in that centre for strangers in a strange land.

I waited, sitting as quietly and unobtrusively as possible on the low backless benches in front of the ground-floor lobby windows. It was a short wait. The tan Mercedes sports slipped up to the main door. The Second Son had come for me. My bags were stowed and we set off.

'How is everything? How is your mother?'

'She is well.' He said nothing more. His face was still.

'And your father and your brothers? They are well?'

'Thanks be to God.'

'What is the plan? Who goes with us today?'

'My mother is here. In my father's house. She asks will you go there.

Maybe we stay a few days. You can sleep in my room. They make it for you,' he said with the same lack of expression.

I knew his father had a small villa in Abu Dhabi. We had stopped there once or twice, but as yet I had never been inside.

'I hope it is not a problem. I could stay in the hotel,' I said.

'No, no,' he said quickly. Now a slow smile. 'You are one of us now. My mother would not like this.'

'I hope all is well with her,' I said, longing for a little break in the atmosphere, a little news.

'She is perfectly well,' he said. Then a pause. 'But my brother is a little sick.'

Ah. Now the news.

'A little sick? How sick? Your young brother? What's the matter?'

I knew it must be something more than flu. They usually ignored colds and flu, dragging themselves around with fevers and allied aches.

'It must be something difficult for your mother to stay in Abu Dhabi,' I said. 'Have the children gone back?'

'Yes, they went with my grandmother and Hussa, and the others.'

'And your young brother?'

'He is not so good,' he answered.

'He wasn't very well in the desert last week,' I said, remembering his headaches.

'He sicks up blood,' said the Second Son. 'It is nothing. The doctor thinks maybe malaria.'

'Malaria!' I knew this plague of the tropics had found its way to Abu Dhabi. The fast expansion of the place had brought its inevitable curses.

'Don't worry, Mrs Tea Cup. We go there. He will be all right. There are many doctors here. One came. My father looks for another. We go there.' For my liking we couldn't 'go there' fast enough. The car swung off the Corniche and within minutes we arrived.

A dusty sentinel's box held a bedouin guard who saluted us as we drove into the parking area. Opening the car door, the boy took my hand to lead me towards one side of a three-sided, bungalow-styled villa. We went up a few steps and into a small majlis which was nearly choked by deep couches pushed against its walls. What space there had been was taken up by two glass-topped tables. The Sheikha rose from one of the couches to greet me. From another the Youngest Son began to struggle to his feet.

'Lie down, my son. Lie down,' I said and he eased himself back on to the couch. His forehead was tightly wound round with a torn piece of an old checked head-scarf in an effort to ease his headache. His face was the colour

of *café au lait* left standing overnight. There were pain lines around his mouth. I sat beside him and took his hand. It was too dry, too hot.

'I am sick, my English mother. Can you believe it? I am sick.' His eyes closed as much in anger as in pain. He hated illness, hated it with an inner anger as though sickness were a devil attacking his life, his plans for his future, his energy.

'Hush,' I said. 'We all have these problems at some time. Anger is not the weapon to use when battling with them. Rest.'

I turned to his mother, whose lips were continually moving in silent prayer. Through the Second Son I asked as many questions as I thought sensible and it didn't sound like any malaria I had ever heard of. The boy was bleeding inside somewhere. He had no cough. It wasn't his lungs. He was passing blood and sicking it up.

The door opened and the Sheikh stood there with two of his men. The Sheikha covered her mask with her veils. I rose, as did the Second Son. The Sheikh motioned us to sit down, left his men outside, and picked up the phone on the table. He was strained with worry. He had been trying to reach the doctor they used but the man was out. Infuriated, he looked at me with a hard, steady stare. His eyes were totally unyielding, the eyes of the Arab ready to do battle with me, with any man, with the wind or the devil.

'What you think?' he said in English. Each word was distinctly, carefully and sharply spoken.

I sat forward and stared back at him with all the strength of my pioneering ancestors.

'You want to know what I think?' I asked. 'Send to the hospital and bring the head doctor here. The top one. Bring him.'

He picked up the phone and started to dial again. Perhaps ten, perhaps fifteen, perhaps twenty minutes passed. I don't remember. I only remember the interminable dialling and re-dialling, and the short sharp commands given by the Sheikh. I remember the boy rose once to go to the bathroom, his thin, adolescent frame weaving in pain. I remember his brother catching him and helping him.

At last the Sheikh put down the phone, looked at me and said, 'He comes.' Then he rose and stalked to the door. Turning to give his wife a look of gentleness and a few words of encouragement, he opened the door, his men fell in behind him and they left.

It was perhaps half an hour to an hour later that the Sheikh's Mercedes drew into the parking lot and a man got out. He was short, stocky and had short-cropped, almost Afro hair which was greying slightly. He wore glasses

and a Western suit and moved with the authority of a man of his profession. This was *the* doctor, the top medical man of the area. He was already used to being called out by the Sheikhs for the slightest problem. His expression was a mixture of resignation and annoyance.

The Second Son opened the majlis door, greeted the doctor and called a servant to send for his father. When the doctor saw me sitting beside the boy a puzzled look crossed his face. He greeted the Sheikha formally; she apologised for troubling him and explained the problem. Then he turned to me. Before he could speak I introduced myself as a friend of the family. He spoke perfect English, which was a relief. He was a Syrian and there is no question that he knew what he was about.

After a cursory examination, he turned to me and said that we must get the boy to hospital quickly. I felt a surge of shock rise in my throat and mentally commanded it to recede. The Sheikha was completely veiled but I knew her eyes would have turned black with distress. They would have been the only outward sign of strain as her voice continued to keep its same even tenor, its same quiet courtesy.

The Sheikh arrived while the doctor was on the telephone to the hospital. Cars were called, engines revved, the Sheikha ordered coffee and water for the cars. Then the Sheikh went over to his Youngest Son, spoke a word of blessing and lifted that tall boy in his arms as though he were a small child. He carried him easily, placing him gently on the front seat of his car. The Sheikha and I got in the back while the Sheikh took the wheel. The Second Son drove the doctor. The Sheikh's men followed in yet another car. But the vivid memory, the unforgettable picture, is of the tall son carried in his father's arms, carried so easily, so gently.

A perforated ulcer was diagnosed. A perforated ulcer in a boy of not yet sixteen. What volcano of emotion must have been boiling inside that youngster under his teasing and laughing, under his occasionally expressionless face?

Now he lay exhausted, angry and restless in a vast bed, jogging his arm and pulling at the drip which a nurse kept watching and adjusting. The bed was far too low for ease of nursing and so large that its cotton sheets didn't fit. They slithered about on a plastic mattress cover, bunching up under the boy every time he moved.

The bed was in a large room, in a large suite, in a large bungalow. The whole hospital was made up of various bungalows which surrounded one newly built principal building.

The Sheikha settled herself in the dressing room, determined not to be

too far away from her son at any time. Hussa and the boy's sister soon arrived from Al Ain and installed themselves in the adjoining bedrooms. I continued to stay in the Second Son's bedroom in the villa.

Within hours, the paraphernalia of their lives began to appear. Coffee thermoses, incense pots, boxes of fruit, trays to serve it on, suitcases, prayer mats. Selma arrived escorting two braziers, one to keep the coffee pots hot and another for hot coals for the incense pots. A young prince was ill. He would be surrounded by his family and court just as Henry VIII might have been. The only difference was the ambience of a twentieth-century Arabian hospital.

The Sheikh sat on one of the large couches in a bay window opposite the bed and watched and waited, his pearl prayer beads going round and round through his fingers. The Second Son walked in and out with various friends. They stood in groups around the bed smiling and talking, joking gently as though their words were necessary medicine. The Sheikha, her veils over her mask, went from room to room injecting order into confusion. The braziers were placed in adjoining bedrooms and promptly lit. Nurses and doctors, oblivious to the scene around them, came and went with pills and potions, drips and plasma.

Two days later the boy's condition slowly began to stabilise, but the activity around him had increased measurably. Shama had joined us along with the Sheikha's mother, a tall, fine-boned woman with compassionate, intelligent eyes. They added their prayers to those of the other women.

Hareem prayer mats were spread next to the braziers and the women began petitioning God for the health of the boy. They set about their prayers with a will, always, of course, adding the final coda that His will be done. Sometimes after their formal prayers, which were said a minimum of five times a day, they continued to sit with their feet in front of them while they carried on long conversations with God. Informal though respectful chats. 'Thy will be done of course but meantime . . .' The soles of their feet were near black with henna. Their nails were painted with henna and the palms of their hands striped with it.

At night the Sheikha slept in that great plot of a bed with her son in her arms, trying to keep him quiet, allaying his fears and anger. I wondered briefly what a British nursing sister would have said, but the act of motherly comfort may well have made up for the lack of quiet during the day.

Four days on, I sat with the Sheikha's brother, the boy's uncle, on the bay-window couch. I did not know the uncle well, but he knew my husband.

'He is in London now?' asked the uncle.

'Yes,' I answered. 'He arrives there today.'

'That is good.'

He, too, was tall, taller than my husband, which put him over six feet. He had a neat beard and moved almost laconically. But there was nothing laconic about his mind, which was known to tick over like a well-oiled clock.

We sat together, watching the Youngest Son drift in and out of a drug-induced sleep. A large group of his young friends had just left.

'He needs peace,' I said, despairingly.

'Yes, but the road from Al Ain is filled with more visitors. It is our way.' He looked at me kindly. 'Surely you know this.'

'God willing, I am learning,' I answered with some sadness.

'Don't worry,' he said. 'His father is arranging for him to go to London. Then it will be better.' He saw my relief. 'You will go with them?' Again the statement made in the tone of a query. No grammatical change. No concession to the question. In this case both uncle and I knew that the answer would be 'yes'.

'Sheikh Zayed is loaning them his private plane. They will leave tomorrow, I believe,' said the uncle. 'You will be ready?'

'I will be ready,' I answered. When they move, they move.

I had heard of the many mercy missions of the ruler's private planes. They were often used for one or another of the Sheikh families, or for some accident victim who could not get to a specialist hospital in any other way.

That night I packed, ordered the cook to prepare some chicken soup for the journey and to find some cows' milk. The following morning I rose early, dressed and asked for a driver to take me and my suitcase to the hospital. The Second Son had gone to Al Ain the previous night on errands for his mother. When we reached the hospital, four cars and a Land Rover were drawn up at the bungalow. Cases were being loaded and mine was unceremoniously tossed in with the rest. There was no ambulance. The boy had refused this show of illness and the Sheikh had agreed.

An Omani doctor had been assigned to accompany us to London. He couldn't speak Arabic, as he'd been brought up in Zanzibar. Instead he gave orders to everyone in Swahili. His English was reserved for me and he kept shouting at me and pleading with me to check that 'all equipment' and 'my suitcase - the brown one, you know' were all safely stowed. I think he thought I was a nurse or hospital official. We never got it straight but he was a good MD.

At final count there were eleven black-veiled ladies in the hospital suite and three gentlemen. All relatives, all there to wave us off. Smoke from

smouldering sandalwood permeated everything.

With sudden inspiration and at the last moment, I stripped the big bed of its blanket and pillows and stuffed them on top of the suitcases. Needless to say, things were forgotten. Both the milk and the chicken soup were left behind. A pity, as both would have been a godsend.

When the Second Son drove up with a whoosh, I ran over to him and after kissing him both hello and goodbye, told him to call my husband in London.

'Call him. Don't forget. There must be an ambulance to meet us. Don't forget. No-one has ordered the ambulance. Tell him to check the hospital. Don't forget, my son. Remember your brother.'

The Youngest Son walked to his father's Mercedes with the Sheikh on one side and the uncle on the other. I got in the back seat with the doctor. The Sheikh drove. In the following car were the Sheikha, her daughter, Hussa and Selma who were to accompany us to London. Behind them came two of the Sheikh's men and a Pakistani male nurse. We drove in cavalcade to the airport, through the runway gates and up to a Grummond II Gulf Stream, one of the larger of the executive jets of that time.

We were met with cool efficiency by the English crew and I shall never forget my relief at the sight of them. They had been on stand-by since 10.00 a.m. and it was now after one o'clock, but they were as crisp and well-tailored as if they'd just stepped on to the plane. A handsome lot. A pilot, co-pilot, engineer cum navigator and stewardess.

Eleven of us boarded. The Youngest Son, pale and drawn, but smiling and trying to tease, walked up the steps with a drip of sodium, sucrose and potassium attached to his left arm. The doctor had fixed it in place in the car, as we waited for the luggage to be stowed. We lay the boy on a couch in a sort of majlis area toward the rear of the plane. I wrapped him in the big blanket we'd brought as he was already shivering. The doctor fixed the drip to the bulkhead with adhesive tape.

The male nurse was totally overwhelmed by his job and by his new trousers which, being a couple of sizes too large, kept threatening to drop to half-mast. Poor fellow. Throughout the trip my feelings toward him varied from fury at his incompetence to humour and pity.

The plane was elegant. Simple but elegant. It was the first and last time I was to fly on one of its mercy missions. It had pale green upholstery with matching carpets and teak tables. The only signs of opulence were the gold kleenex boxes and the gold fittings in the loos.

The jet was small compared to commercial aircraft and to the new, private 747s sported by the oil Sheikhs today, but it was large enough to

have three separate compartments. The Sheikh, the doctor and his men adopted the forward section. They drank coffee and played cards throughout the long haul to London, only interrupting their concentration for the Sheikh's frequent visits aft to watch over his son.

The Sheikha, her daughter, Hussa and Selma occupied the second section. Coffee was on the go there as well but I noticed that the Sheikha never drank a drop. Her prayer beads were constantly moving and a steady stream of soft petitions to Allah were just audible.

The third section was the majlis. Two long couches faced each other. The boy was stretched out on one and the male nurse took the other. For half the trip I sat on the floor of the plane, holding the boy's hand, watching the drip. The other half I sat in the Sheikha's section trying to be as inconspicuous as possible.

It was a strange trip. All of our attention was focussed on the boy. When we weren't actually nursing him, we were upholding him with prayers - either Muslim or Christian. Another haemorrhage at 25,000 feet would have been disastrous.

After about five hours we dropped down on Athens in a soft rain. The plane was too small to make London in one jump. The Sheikha got up and stood in the door, thanking God and declaring it a fine day. The boy turned toward her and smiled.

'Will it be fine for me?' he asked.

'God willing, my heart,' she answered.

The Sheikh and his men stretched their legs while we refuelled. The only sign he ever gave that anything was amiss in his family was the number of times he got out his thumbnail-sized pipe for the comfort of the single puff it gave him. He, too, was addicted to the powerful Oman tobacco. His eyes revealed nothing. His straight back and determined walk were commanding. He paced back and forth on the tarmac, occasionally stopping to talk to his men.

Eventually we took off again, this time into the cloud-spattered European sky and finally arrived at Heathrow well past dark.

Suddenly it was like living out a Grade B TV movie. There were the spotlights, the ambulance, the cars, the officials. There were the sirens, the waiting clinic, the waiting surgeon, the green-gowned theatre nurses and all the alarming accoutrements of modern medicine.

To the boy's worried parents the whole scene which ended in the exclusivity of an intensive care unit must have been a Faustian nightmare. Where was he? Why couldn't they be with him? Why wasn't he in a suite? Who could stay with him?

His exhausted mother was finally persuaded to rest in a hotel. His father, once satisfied that the intensive care nurses were doing their best, left his own men to watch over them as they watched over the boy while he, too, was persuaded to rest.

Remarkably, by the time the boy reached London, contrary to the general prognosis, the ulcer had healed sufficiently to avoid any major surgery. With the aid of one of those minute cameras with which specialists investigate physical disorders internally, they discovered that he was healing, and healing well. Though it would be some time before he was released from hospital, he was already better and we were all able to relax with relief.

Throughout the long days of his recovery, the Youngest Son was never left alone. His mother or his father or one of the group was always with him. I took my turns as well. The Second Son, on his return to London and to his university, spent his week-ends beside his brother. Every night someone slept in a chair-cum-bed provided by the hospital. There was a night nurse and a day nurse but these were not the same as either 'family' or 'friend'.

The hospital was the Wellington, built to cater for an ever-growing Arab clientele and its special needs. So nothing was said. All was understood. On the British part, the staff regarded Arab customs as weird and slightly annoying. On the Arab part, they regarded the British as unfeeling, as cold as the weather but clever and efficient. As usual I watched and wondered and defended one side to the other.

Each day the boy improved. Each day he gained strength and with strength came impatience. He groaned with impatience, broke out in a rash and longed to toss himself in the sea.

'I must go home,' he shouted. 'My lessons. My work. I must go home.'

It would be several years before he was truly fit. The massive amount of blood that had been dripped into his veins brought its legacy of jaundice, followed by a seemingly endless skin irritation, something akin to prickly heat. It was largely his own determination to be rid of the tag of illness that brought eventual healing.

When the London doctors finally granted him his freedom, he bolted like a child let out of school. They left within two days of his release, leaving me tired, dazed, relieved and waiting for the Second Son to come 'home' for yet another week-end.

Part Three

11

Words and Music

WITHIN WEEKS OF the family returning to Abu Dhabi, the spring 'vac' had begun and the Second Son was off again with the ever-faithful Hassan. As usual I drove them to Heathrow and as usual we parked in the Terminal 3 car park. We then made our way to the Gulf Air desk for first class passengers. This time they were overburdened with luggage which was far too heavy for even the lenient Gulf Air to overlook.

'They will let me through,' he said as he watched the cases and boxes being weighed. 'I'm not going to pay for all this. It's not mine.'

He was acting as courier for some of his family's purchases earlier in the year.

'How will you do it?' I asked suspiciously.

'Never mind.'

'A bribe?'

'Maybe a present.'

'It's all the same, my son, all the same and it does you no good in the end.'

I never saw him pay anyone. Perhaps I missed it. Perhaps it was his manners and his words. Authoritative, expecting obedience, quick and then the slow smile.

'After all, it's our airline. Not theirs,' he said nodding in the direction of the British staff who then managed Gulf Air, and we walked toward the departure gate.

Hassan followed silently. I looked toward him for some answer to my

curiosity but his eyes were expressionless.

'You will come next week, then?' the Second Son asked.

'No,' I answered. 'It is Easter. I will be at least ten days.'

'They wait for you,' he answered. 'I will wait for you. I will meet you.'

'God willing,' I answered and kissed the boy goodbye. Hassan now smiled his wide smile of understanding and genuine friendship, and they walked through the gate.

I spent Easter in Cornwall with all our family. It was a late Easter and the daffodils, or 'lilies' as the Cornish call them, were in full bloom. The hedgerows had begun to burgeon with violets, primroses, wild garlic and early pink campion. Our elder daughter, a budding journalist, had her birthday a few days after Easter Day, so we seemed to be stuffed with Simnel cake and birthday cake and chocolate eggs. Long walks by the sea were needed to shake it all down and shake off the pounds that could so easily accumulate.

We are a family that enjoys each other, relishing each day we're able to spend together. That particular spring our son brought home a dark-haired, dark-eyed, lively lady who would become a third daughter, moulding into the family clan as though born part of it.

It was a holiday of celebrations, but all celebrations must end. We all had our separate ways to go. My husband to Tunis, our son to Saudi Arabia, the girls to London and I turned my face toward Abu Dhabi and the pains of collecting money that was owed to our business.

The Second Son did indeed meet me as always, but this time I stayed once again in his bedroom in his father's Abu Dhabi villa, and this time I ate my meals with the Sheikh, his men and his two eldest sons. It was a strange experience and I felt out of place, like the old duck out of water. They were all kind, all courteous and the Sheikh seemed delighted, ordering special fish and salads and making his sons translate for him. His English was scanty and his Arabic hard for me to catch. He spoke very quickly.

Mercifully, I was able to complete all I had to do within a very few days and I wondered whether the Sheikh had put a few words in the right ears. Hassan escorted and drove me wherever I needed to go and acted as general red-tape cutter by referring to me as the English Sheikha, friend of this or that Sheikh. It's wonderful what a little name dropping will do. Money was quickly traced. Each evening the Second Son would lift his head from his books to ask how it was going, adding a 'hurry up' to Hassan as his mother was waiting in Al Ain.

When the last telex was sent and the last cheque banked, we almost

threw our things into suitcases, loaded them into the sports car, said our goodbyes to Hassan who was off to see his own family, and set out.

The drive to Al Ain was a pantomime. There were four of us. The two Omani brothers had joined us, their head scarves twisted into the flat turbans of their own country. We slipped along the now four-lane Al Ain highway, winding in and out of the sections which were still in the process of being built. I watched the Second Son as he drove. His thin face had recently assumed a look of severity and responsibility. When this imperceptible metamorphosis took place, it would not be long before another marriage was arranged. It was like the change of seasons. Inevitable. Now he was still single and there was time for a little madness.

He had a passionate love of music and in another world at another time might have made a fine musician, but there, held in that place at that moment, there were other plans, other duties, other paths. Now he held the wheel in his long-fingered brown hands, tossed a tambourine in my lap and marked a beat: 'Wahida, wahida, wahida' - 'One, one, one.'

From the narrow seat behind there was a sudden thunder of sound as the two Omanis began playing drums. One was of beaten metal, a sort of aluminium alloy with a modern fitted skin. The other was brown-painted pottery, its skin held down by strings. It gave a sharp, light tone to the modern drum's bass.

The fingers of the Omanis were quick and their hands firm. As they played, their dark eyes flashed with all the hidden mystery of their own mountain country.

Admonished and instructed by turns, I occasionally had the tambourine snatched away from me by the Second Son, who would rap it sharply against the wheel. We sang and drummed our way to Al Ain in an explosion of sound which riveted cars as we passed them. Now and then friends were sighted and passed. They would hail us, waving their arms to the beat, as we thumped and bumped our way along the highway.

When we neared Al Ain I saw once again the Hazhal Bush, those massive waves of red sand hundreds of feet high which had once protected the oasis from marauders. The Sheikh had crossed them by camel as a boy; then as a young man with a wife and small children, including the boy at my side, he had camped overnight on one side of the range waiting for the engines of his jeeps to cool before grinding inch by inch, around and over. We were through in minutes.

Al Ain seemed to be moving to meet us. Houses were being built ever further down the road which now completely bypassed the old fort. 'Main Street' had a plethora of new shops. Indian and Pakistani shopkeepers stood

in doorways, waiting to sell bolts of cloth, household pots and pans, fridges and cookers, videos and TVs. We passed a new supermarket, a miniature imitation of the American drive-in, and then some large furniture shops whose massive suites of heavy, over-stuffed couches and chairs filled the windows like obese pashas waiting for ladies to settle in their laps.

The old general store had gone but the shade thorn tree was still there, bewildered by its surround of concrete pavement. Trees and bushes had been planted everywhere. We veered to the right.

'My God,' I breathed. A Wimpy Bar stared at me. Armageddon. 'Al humberger' had joined 'les chips', 'Coke' and '7-Up' as powerful contenders in the international stakes for one world. Since the arms merchants were busy separating us, the odds seemed a bit uneven, but who knows?

After one more roundabout and one more tune, we drove through the compound gates, drawing up to the house with ringing ears and a mild sense of both exhaustion and satisfaction. The Youngest Son waited to greet us, and what a contrast from the last time I saw him. When he'd left London his face had had the pinched, strained look, the hollow eyes that long illness seem to give. Now his eyes were bright and he stood straight and strong, the whole incident having been relegated in his mind to the unimportant, the not-to-be-remembered.

'Mrs Tea Cup,' he said. 'Welcome. Welcome back to Al Ain.' He greeted his brother nose to nose, welcomed the Omanis and took my hand to lead me up the steps of the family bungalow. On the porch outside the front door, I kicked off my sandals and pushed them to one side where they joined an already substantial pile of varying styles and sizes. You could generally tell who was at home by glancing at the sandals.

Inside all was cool, calm and welcoming. The Sheikha rose to greet us. Her sons kissed her on the forehead. I kissed her on the cheek. Her gentle 'welcomes' and those of the women around her were like balm on my thudding head.

I began to abandon my Western habits and within minutes crossed the bridge into the Sheikha's world, self-contained, unhurried, conscious of movement, aware of sound, small sips of fragrant coffee as against gulps of hot tea. The boys, the drums, the tambourines, the highway disappeared. I was enfolded in the women's world.

We talked, exchanging our news. When the Sheikha heard that her son had kept me beating the tambourine all the way to Al Ain she was horrified and no amount of pleading on my part helped. Such antics were taboo to the women, especially the Sheikhas. Playing any instrument was taboo, but playing it along a public highway - shocking.

It was not my tambourine-playing that worried her, however. With her generosity of spirit, she always forgave my sliding back and forth across the East-West or male-female barriers. She was upset because I had not been allowed to rest on the drive. She knew too well that my afternoon times of quiet were often cut short by a 'jam session'. Her sons would often invite me to some remote corner where we hoped against hope that we would not disturb the siesta of the compound, though we were rarely successful. The drums made a thundering noise. What's more, the boys sang at the top of their lungs - old songs, new songs, songs in the tradition of the place.

That afternoon was to be no exception. After a large lunch in the women's majlis, I had just settled myself to do a little reading when there was a knock at my door.

'You coming, Mrs Tea Cup?' asked the Second Son.

'*Na'am* - yes.' I couldn't resist.

We found a space in a hopefully distant room. One by one the Youngest Son, and the Omani friends arrived, drawn by the urgent invitation of the drums. I was placed in a good watching position and given instructions on how to clap my hands.

'Like this. Together. Hard. Make the hollow places come together. Not clapping. Not just clapping.' The Second Son showed me how to make the hollow of one palm meet the other. There was suddenly another sound. Sharp. Loud. Different.

'Good, good,' he said. So I graduated from watcher to player and clapped as the sons and the Omani drummers played and sang.

When I first heard Arabic music I was fascinated, then tormented. Now, hopefully, I have reached the beginning of appreciation. Penetrating, complex and totally different in structure, it pulls the single line of melody up and down and spins it out to leave you dangling in some sort of musical nirvana. While our music has become thick with harmony, theirs twists and weaves the solo voice or instrument into intricate patterns searching for some impossible horizon of sound.

It was the sons who tried to train my ear. In our afternoon sessions they would explain the differences between folk music from the Gulf or from the Levant, between the good and the mediocre, the great and the awful.

'Listen, Mrs Tea Cup, listen,' the Second Son would say as he slotted yet another tape into the nearest stereo or tape machine, whether in the car or the family room or the garden.

'Watch him, watch him,' the Youngest Son would say, pulling me around to see a TV video of a lute player, or a religious song celebration with long lines of men chanting Islamic verses in a sort of mouth music

with hand-clapping accompaniment.

The music that we beat out in the afternoons was their music, the music of the place, sea shanties and sand-sea shanties. But poems set to music were the ultimate challenge; love poems or poems of great events; deeds of valour, victories, tragedies. Epic poems.

When I first knew them in those early London days, I'd often find the Second Son picking out some phrase on the piano in our living room. His younger brother would say a verse and then they'd put it together. Over and over the one phrase would go. Never two notes together. Just single notes. They would never get more than a phrase completed before an argument would break out as to the merit of either the words or the music.

The younger boy's passion for the poetry of his own place was as real as the older one's passion for music. His fascination for words would often keep him awake at night as the poetry of the place is a kind of Rubik's cube which can become obsessive. Though the Youngest Son had an essentially scientific mind and was impatient with the finer points of literature, his pleasure in puzzling over poetry was never ending. Getting him out of bed in the mornings in time for school became a real problem for his family when he'd been up most of the night with pencil and note book.

As for our music sessions and lessons, they went on intermittently for several years until eventually the drums were abandoned, put away for the sake of both higher education and marriage. But if the day is fine and still and I am alone, I can hear somewhere in myself the sound of the hollow-ended drums, the clapping, the tambourine, the young voices singing, laughing. I can see them in my mind's eye rising and dancing slowly around the room, their bodies undulating in a controlled exuberance as if lifted out of the world of motor cars, rockets and computerised mentalities into some universal heartbeat, some rhythm of the day, of the night, of the sea, of life.

12

The Woman from Oman

THERE WAS A knock on my bedroom door and it opened. A new maid from Sri Lanka came in with my English morning tea which the Sheikha always sent. The Sri Lankan's bare feet moved silently across the carpet.

'Good morning,' she said in her schoolgirl English.

'Good morning and thank you,' I answered, mouthing the words carefully.

We talked for a while in English, grateful for the ease of communication. At that moment her Arabic was even poorer than mine, for she was new to the household, but on my next visit she would be rattling away in this throaty language and I would be struggling as usual. Why is it that Eastern peoples acquire languages so easily while we in the West make such heavy weather of it? Padding out as silently as she came, she left me to the early morning quiet.

Stretching my feet to the end of my bed I felt the tightening of the sheets. They were flowered sheets, brightly flowered sheets which sometimes slipped about on the plastic mattress cover which had never been removed. The bed was tucked modestly into a corner of the room. In fact all the furniture hugged the walls as if frightened to put its feet on the carpet.

A long, rather stark couch held neat piles of clean kandoras and white head scarves which were laid there daily. These would disappear by evening, the boys having collected them, for this was the 'boys' house'. It had been built ostensibly as a future home for a son and his future wife, but

105

tastes and pocket books had changed. The house had become a kind of bolt hole for a clutch of growing and maturing sons.

There were three rooms in the bungalow. One held a pool table, another seemed a jumble of drums, school books, volley balls and footballs. The pool table was the only piece of furniture in those two rooms. The third room was my bedroom. I looked around it, recording my impressions. There was the stark, pale yellow couch. There was my bed with a wooden chair beside it and there was a small chest of drawers on top of which were a pile of Arabian newspapers, a few snapshots and two or three bottles of cologne.

My suitcases were stacked against the wall along with those of the boys which contained the rest of their clothes. They never seemed to use the drawers of the chest, so sometimes I confiscated them. In those days they had very few clothes. They needed very few. A pile of white kandoras, a pile of head scarves, a pile of wezaar, an extra black braided circlet, a few underpants and an extra pair of sandals. When they began to travel abroad they invested in a couple of suits and a jacket which they passed around each other. The Second Son had his university uniform of jeans and T-shirts, but these were always left in England.

These days whenever I visited, the sons vacated this house, rolling up their palliasses and sleeping in the family majlis. I don't believe the little bed was ever used by anyone but me. It was undoubtedly bought for me. How easily we accept everything, expect everything. That first visit when I stayed at the Al Ain Hilton seemed in the dim past. Now it would be unthinkable for me to stay anywhere but with the family.

I stretched again, feeling content and at peace, and watched the curtains lift in a light breeze. I had opened my window in the night. I liked the night air but the night watchman didn't like the open window. He'd come around and poke his hand through the outside wrought-iron grill, trying to close it. Eventually he'd give up and walk away, his grey beard moving up and down as he mumbled to himself, the words spilling out of his almost toothless mouth.

Kicking back the covers, I let my feet touch the carpet, put on the white and blue striped kaftan which my journalist daughter had made for me and walked to the window overlooking the central court. A Baluchistan gardener was working there, his voluminous turban perched like a cushion on top of his head, his baggy cotton 'jodhpurs' tan with dust. He was trailing a long, thick, green hose. Water belched out as he drenched each tree, pouring the costly stuff into the deep trench which circled their trunks.

Beyond the court, beyond the wall with its globes of protecting lights, I could see the bulbous tower of the family mosque. Once upon a time

muezzins had had to climb such towers to call the people to prayer, the little round room at the top giving resonance, enlarging the human voice. Now they used a microphone and loudspeaker system and the mechanically multiplied sound echoed off walls.

The bedroom door pushed quietly open. Amina and Miriam crept in, clutching each other's hands. Their long, black hair, still damp from washing, was tightly braided and tied with pieces of torn white cloth.

'Hello, Mrs Tea Cup,' said Miriam in her singsong little girl's voice.

'Good morning,' said Amina, rolling the 'r' around with her tongue.

Then, falling into each other's arms, they tumbled about laughing at their own precocious English. The big red and white polka-dots of their identical dresses made a tangle of colour on the floor. I'd seen a lot of that splashy material. It must have been bought by the bolt, for it kept showing up all year in pantaloons and children's dresses, or on servants.

Amina and Miriam were continually wandering from house to house in the compound, searching for something new to amuse themselves. Sometimes they were to be found in a corner, solemnly talking to a rather battered doll whose arms and legs were always popping off, waiting to be clipped on by a passing 'brother' who was inevitably obliging.

Now they untangled themselves to watch as I layered face cream on to my face and hands in the endless battle to save my skin from drying up altogether. The jars of Cornish hand cream, with their pictures of St Michael's Mount, looked incongruous somehow. The children opened each jar and sampled them all. Cologne was sprayed about and lipsticks swished up and down.

'Me, me,' they cried, pointing to their lips. I dabbed a little on each puckered mouth to further shouts of laughter and much dancing about the room.

The door opened again, this time with a gentle touch, and the young Sri Lankan maid came in. She caught sight of the children and, in a sudden paroxysm of words, tried to admonish them in her own language interspersed with Arabic, while announcing breakfast to me in English. Grabbing the children by their arms, the three of them left in a welter of confused sounds and I began to dress. There was no time to linger. It was Friday - the Muslim holy day, the equivalent of our Sunday - and visitors would be expected. A quick shower in the bright pink bathroom with its already peeling tiles, more cream, a fast selection of long skirt and blouse, a final comb through my hair, and I walked out into the sun.

The young wife of the Eldest Son emerged slowly from her own home. She was heavily veiled and masked to walk the few yards to the women's

dining majlis, which was, of course, in the house of Sheikha Grandmother. As slim as a reed and as shy as a bird with the eyes of a gazelle, were all the aspects of beauty once described to me by the Youngest Son as most desirable in a woman. This young girl usually had all these qualities, though now, in the last months of her pregnancy, she was hardly as slim as a reed.

'*Sabah el khair* - Morning of dawn,' she called softly.

'*Sabah el nur* - Morning of light,' I replied.

The words echoed in the court. We walked carefully together, clicking our sandals on the cement drive. I wore my dark glasses even for these few moments, as my blue eyes were always straining in the brilliant light. Known as 'Um Yusef's *burgah*' (Um Yusef's mask), they were always getting lost and being found by some kind soul who returned them to me.

We reached the bungalow of Sheikha Grandmother, crossed the porch and pushed open the carved wooden doors of the dining room. Kicking off our sandals we walked barefoot into the air-conditioned cool of the big room. The thick carpet felt comfortable.

There was no furniture in the room other than a cupboard in the far corner in which were kept special foods such as plates of dates selected from the great storehouse or the enamel pots poured full of the sweet of the area. Sometimes the *ghee* (clarified butter) which was offered to pour over the plain rice was kept there along with big spoons for dishing up.

The windows were curtained in heavy velvet. In the hottest months these curtains would be tightly shut in one more effort to get away from the heat and glare. Above us hung new crystal chandeliers announcing the growing wealth of the place.

Breakfast was laid on the floor at the near end of the room. The tray this morning was about three feet in diameter, an average family size, and would have been carried across the court from the cook house on the head of one of the maids. Its size indicated that no extra visitors were expected.

We sat cross-legged on the floor, our skirts splaying out around us. We waited for the Sheikha. We could see her as she proceeded from her house. First she stopped at the coffee house to see if all was ready, then she stopped to speak to one of the servants. She stopped to catch a child by the hand and whisper some word which was rewarded with a kiss, then caught the corner of her veil to cover her already masked face as the chief driver came towards her for a quick answer to a query, always given and received after the words of greeting and queries as to health had been exchanged.

She moved nearer, her silks and veils rustling about her, and we all watched with the same affection that she invoked from family and friends alike. As she came into the room we rose to greet her. She greeted me.

'*Marhaba*, Um Yusef, my English - no English,' she apologised as always.
'And I have no Arabic,' I answered as always.

She motioned to me to sit beside her and we settled into our limited
verbal exchanges. Our friendship is a triumph of overcoming every known
barrier. The things we have in common have outweighed the problems of
communication, culture and education. Love of family, of children, of life
itself; love of God, though she is a devout Muslim and I am a Christian;
shared curiosity, and genuine pleasure in each other's company. All these
links have bridged quite unbelievable distances.

As it was the Muslim holy day, the tray seemed more loaded than usual.
I knew I would eat too much and mentally planned to restrict myself at
lunch, which would be equally difficult. Being Friday, we would have
something delicious. There was a new cook and he was determined to
impress. Perhaps it would be one of the Sheikh's favourite dishes.

Men speak very little when they eat. They down the food quickly and
fairly unceremoniously. Women take more time, talk easily and still adhere
to the strict rules of manners.

The most vital rule, the rule never to be broken, the rule which marks
the true Arab and lifts him above the morass of intrigue and materiality
which now dominates his world and indeed ours, is the rule of hospitality.
'In the hospitality of the Arabs is kinship and assurance in their insecure
countries,' wrote Charles Doughty in the nineteenth century. Hospitality,
he said, was 'the piety of the Arab life ... the sanctity of the Arabian
religion'. I was certainly a subject of the generous hospitality of this family,
but I was not alone. There were others. Many others. That Friday morning
as we sat enjoying each other's company and the fresh bread and pancakes,
I was to see the rule practised once again. We felt, rather than saw, someone
arrive. I looked up, a mouthful of harees waiting on my fingers. A figure
stood in the door, silhouetted against the light. She had no sandals and
walked barefoot.

'Peace be with you.'

'And peace be with you - welcome, welcome,' said the Sheikha.

The figure moved into the room, closing the doors behind her. She
slipped a small bag off her shoulder and, leaving it by the wall, sat a little
way off. The heat of the sun seemed absorbed into her black veil which was
ragged and dusty. Underneath she wore a traditional dress, high-necked
with small hand-made buttons but without decoration. Heavy silver bracelets were on her wrists and two similar ones on her ankles.

But it was her burqah, her mask, which was startling. It covered her face
from the top of her forehead to the bottom of her chin. It was made of a

dark blue, rough, woven cloth and left only two small oval slits for the eyes. Those eyes were bright and lively and her voice was young and eager.

I had seen the women of this tribe only once before. They came from the edge of the desert, between Muscat and Salalah in Oman, hundreds of miles to the south. She was a Wahiba, a true bedu.

The Eldest Son's wife had gone quickly to fetch her a glass of tepid water, which she drank carefully, tipping her mask back fractionally to accommodate the glass.

'Welcome, welcome,' repeated Sheikha Grandmother, and motioned the guest to come to the tray, arranging bread and pancakes for her, bringing the honey butter and harees nearer and urging her to eat. Her simple, dusty clothes made a sharp contrast with the rich fabrics around her.

The wash basin was brought, with its tea-pot-like jug. Again the Eldest Son's wife served her, pouring water over her hands as she lathered the soap, the dirty water dropping through the perforated lid of the basin. Then, thanking God, she began to tuck in hungrily with the rest of us and was plied with questions.

'What's the news, Sayeeda?'

They addressed her as if she was the equivalent of a Sheikha. Her extended family group was camping in the Buraimi, in that part of the oasis which belonged to Oman.

Had they walked from the South? Yes, they had walked and sometimes ridden as well. They were here to buy and sell. They would stay for a few months and go back. All the while she talked, she gesticulated with one small, thin hand and with the other tore off bits of bread, dipping them in the honey butter and tilting them under her mask into her mouth. Her eyes were continually smiling. Her poverty could not detract from her enormous dignity and presence. She completely fascinated me.

No-one moved until she had quite satisfied herself. The straw 'hat' was put on the tray once again, a maid was called and the tray lifted on to her head. The wash basin was passed again for us to wash, the soap and warm water carrying away the grease from our hands. Kleenex was handed round so that we could dry our hands and we settled together for coffee. The Eldest Son's wife took the della and poured. After several rounds, Sheikha Grandmother rose to leave, the other women rising with her. Knowing that I wanted to speak to the bedu woman to learn more of her life, the Sheikha signalled me to stay while they moved out of the dining room, pulling their veils over their masks.

There were now just the two of us left in the dining room. We sat and

stared at each other, Sayeeda and I. I could see she was smiling and I marvelled once again at how much the eyes can say. Then she apologised for her mask, which was indeed extraordinary, and said it was the custom of her people. I said I understood this, but did not add that I had been told of the beauty of these women and their attention to make-up, of their fine skin and care for the traditional in their clothes and way of life.

We began to 'talk', though my 'kitchen Arabic' was only good enough to ply her with questions and to catch perhaps half of the answers. How I wished that one of the English-speaking sons or the Sheikha's daughter was with us. She told me of her children, of how life had changed in Oman once the old Sultan had gone and the new Sultan began to rule, of the Sultan's mother who was 'covered in gold from her neck to her waist' and who lived in a palace in the city of Salalah.

'I have seen her,' she said. 'I have been there.'

She chatted away, her hands illustrating her words. They had come up to the Buraimi for the men to look for better opportunities. They would work and trade a little and then go back, but after the summer, as it would soon be too hot to go far.

'But it's too cold in here,' she said, nodding to the already whirring air conditioner. 'Not good for the bedu but it's good for a rest.'

She told me about the Sheikhas of Al Ain, which were good and which were not truly hospitable or kind. 'This Sheikha is one of the very truest, so very good,' she said and I agreed wholeheartedly.

An hour quickly passed in this nodding and talking. Then she rose to leave, picking up her bag. She adjusted her veils and put the little bag over her shoulder. It was hand woven of sheep's wool and dyed the same deep indigo colour as her mask. Mysterious indigo with its connotations of protection was a substance and colour full of symbolism in the distant places of Arabia. It carried a quality bordering on the magical. Even the modern masks of the Gulf hareems had their indigo linings which left little tell-tale purplish marks on the noses of the women who wore them. Sayeeda's indigo-dyed satchel with its colourful, patterned shoulder strap looked like a carry-all. Out of it she drew a little distaff, much as we would draw out a pair of knitting needles. It was threaded in such a way as to twirl and twist hand-spun wool into a twisted string which would then be used for the saddle bags she made. She adjusted the loose threads in one hand and held the distaff in the other.

As she bade me goodbye and began to walk down the drive, she used her left leg while walking to set the distaff twirling. Every third pace the left knee bent, the leg rose and she slapped the distaff against it in a kind

of walking dance. The distaff whirled, twisting the threads. Her bare feet were silent on the drive. The rhythm of her walk never faltered. She never wasted a gesture or a movement. She never looked back.

It was Sayeeda who gave me an insatiable desire to open the doors of Oman, doors which were locked to most foreigners and needed a special key. In time, I found that key and discovered another world, a world full of mystery, beauty and the rare wealth of a dozen cultures bound together in an ancient empire.

13

One Morning and
The Man in the Moon

FRIDAY PASSED AND Saturday arrived with its Monday feeling. It would be another week before the men returned for their 'week-end'. The Youngest Son would stay with us in Al Ain, catching up on his studies in order to graduate with his class from secondary school, but it would be a week before the Sheikh and his elder sons drew up in their big Mercedes and brought that filling of the house that always comes when men are at home, the heavy laughter, the smell of pipe smoke, screeches of excitement from the children as they are tossed high in the air. On Friday afternoons the road to Abu Dhabi moaned with the traffic of returning Sheikhs, would-be Sheikhs, expatriates and the new merchants. They returned for their week of work in Abu Dhabi, a few with their families, but most without, for the women preferred Al Ain. The air was dry, the atmosphere pure, the scenes more familiar. Al Ain was an island of stability in their oil-overturned life.

The Second Son had returned to the coast with his father in order to fly to Doha to see a friend who went to the same university in England. A Qatari son of a Qatari Sheikh who had many falcons. No other temptation was needed.

For the hareem it was another Saturday. Another *sabat* or seventh day. As with the Hebrews, Sunday is the first day of the week. This would be a quiet day. No special holidays were on the calendar. No marriages. No babies expected. Yes. It would be a quiet day.

I walked over to the Sheikha's house. As it was unusually cool for the

time of year, two great carpets had been unrolled on the porch and a smattering of cushions rested invitingly against the wall. The coffee della and a stack of cups waited for someone - anyone.

The women began to congregate and we rose to greet each other, even though we'd met at breakfast less than an hour ago. Hussa arrived with her mother and while Shama eased herself on to the carpet and settled against a cushion, Hussa picked up one of the newspapers which a driver brought from the village each morning. She carefully digested the headlines and then read only the news that interested her. News of the Sheikhs, where they were going and where they had been. She was always sceptical about international news and found it difficult to trust the reports. Who could blame her?

Shama meanwhile had begun to sift through a small sheaf of numbered pages. She was always busy with these pages, working out the correct day for planting date trees, for pollinating or foretelling the week when the pods would burst and the golden maidenhair would tumble out into the sun, each hair holding the promise of a cluster of dates. Shama's systems seemed enormously complex to me. They involved the cycles of the moon, the positioning of certain stars and a numerology which may have had its roots in Zoroaster. But she was relied on to be correct, so no-one disturbed her as she worked, her arthritic hands holding a stubby pencil, her long, old-fashioned mask covering her mouth as she murmured to herself.

The little children moved up and down the court playing their own private games. It always surprised me how few toys were actually used, even though there were cupboards full of them; toys which indulgent fathers or uncles or stepfathers brought home from trips abroad or from some new shop in Abu Dhabi. Sometimes a toy car would have its moment of glory, but it would soon be forgotten.

Other games went on and on. 'Five stones' was a favourite and a collection of good smooth pebbles of the right size and weight was a treasure, something like a really champion conker. The children hid little caches of five stones in the most unlikely places, like reserves of nuts a squirrel would hide. The game was played like 'jacks' without a ball.

I sat watching the children, sipping coffee and trying to pick out words from one of Hussa's newspapers. When I deciphered one I would announce it to all and sundry. The women would look up and congratulate me and encourage me to 'go on, go on, you can, you can'.

Looking up from the paper, I saw Sheikha Grandmother moving slowly toward us, on Selma's arm. Thin and tiny in stature, her back was as straight as an arrow, but her legs often pained her in the cooler winter and spring

114

weather. Thus she used a stout stick which was nearly twice her height to walk across the court, or she leaned on the arm of the nearest grandchild or servant.

We rose to greet her and then settled back into place like so many fluttering pigeons. Cups were rinsed and coffee handed round again. She turned to me and asked if I had spoken to my husband today, was he well, and the children.

'All well, thanks be to God,' I answered. 'My children wait for me in London, I will have to leave soon.'

'But not yet, not yet. You must stay a while. It is too small, this visit.'

She looked at me with an elegance of expression that is difficult to describe. Authority and humility? Her extraordinarily beautiful and intelligent eyes were always carefully lined with kohl. She was the true head of our hareem and her word was law.

She would never travel abroad other than to Mecca or Medina, the holy cities of Islam. The world beyond seemed to her to be filled with treachery; treachery to the spirit, abandonment of principle. She would not take up the cudgels of such a battle. Not now. So she remained in her place and someone always had to remain with her. The Sheikha herself usually chose this role, thus limiting her own travel.

Sheikha Grandmother's mind was now almost wholly concentrated upon the Qur'an, its words and their inner meanings. Day after day she could be seen sitting cross-legged on the carpet in front of her house, a pair of silver-rimmed spectacles perched across her mask, a copy of the Qur'an or a book of the Hadith on her lap, oblivious to the movements of the household. Then she would close the book, rise with difficulty and take a slow, often painful walk to join her daughter-in-law, the Sheikha. Settling again, she would observe the scene, rarely entering into the conversation, still held in her own thoughts. After perhaps a quarter of an hour she would rise again and return to her books, as though satisfied that all was in its place.

It was she and her friends who kept this small area as an oasis of tradition. The other Emirates up and down the coast, even Abu Dhabi itself, were crumbling, slipping. Men, trapped by their own wealth, were caught in the economics of billions, lost in some bankers' monopoly game. Women were hungry for a new life away from the heat, from the cloister, hungry for education, hungry for travel. But they had no-one to explain the uses of what they learned and knowledge of itself could easily overbalance a carefully structured society.

The weight of the new wealth drew maggots that frightened Sheikha

115

Grandmother. They were everywhere, slowly inching their way across the desert. She spent her time building the only defences she knew. Traditionalism, manners, morality, a conservatism coupled with massive bricks of prayer. The bastions would stand during her lifetime, but she would soon be a great-grandmother.

Such a tiny little woman, I thought as I watched her, imagining her building and repairing her mental walls, her endless labour. Such a tiny woman.

A rustle behind us broke the silence. The Sheikha had come to join us, her veils and silks carrying their aromas of attar of roses and jasmine and musk. She greeted us all in her various roles of mother, friend, daughter-in-law, mother-in-law and mistress of the house, bringing with her an air of reality and practicality. She was followed by the Sri Lankan who held a pile of cloth. She settled herself on the carpet and the fine cotton was stacked beside her. She ordered the coffee della to be passed yet again and began to work.

She was making serwal - pantaloons, the jodhpur-like underpants worn by the women and children which tie at the waist, fasten at the ankle and are loose, cool and comfortable. Laying a piece of liberally flowered cotton in front of her she hand-spanned it, her long fingers measuring the size needed. Then she took up the cloth, worked at the edge a moment and tore it neatly along the weave. Neither measuring tape nor scissors were needed here. She knew the hand span necessary for each member of the hareem and piles of measured cloth began to rise beside her. Needle and thread were brought and they were rapidly basted into shape. Pair after pair of serwal were made ready for the tailor's sewing machine. Eventually they would return, plainly finished at the ankle for the children and young girls, heavily embroidered for the ladies. At one time the ladies of the area did all the embroidery themselves. Now it was left to Indian and Pakistani seamstresses.

As the Sheikha worked, her smiling eyes caught mine and she said, 'Come, Um Yusef, you must learn,' and she tore a bit of cloth into a four-inch square. 'You must learn to make buttons for my mother.'

Sheikha Grandmother would have nothing but hand-made buttons for her traditional dresses. The Sheikha usually made them for her. Now I sat beside her and watched as the cloth was folded and refolded until it became a nubin. Then the Sheikha took her needle and drove it up through the middle of the quarter-inch nub, anchoring the fabric.

She showed me how to cover the cloth with an embroidery stitch which finally created a small, neat, round button. The trick was to get them all

the same size. Mine varied from too large to too small but I was encouraged by the laughter of the women around me and their urging me on with 'good, good' or 'work, work'.

I sat absorbed in my button-making, warmed by the winter sun and content to let the quiet conversation move around me. Then, like a break in the rhythm of a fugue, I heard the Sheikha say 'Um Hamed', and looking up saw Um Hamed and two of the women of her hareem walking through the court toward us.

It was a special moment, a rare occasion to see them walking. These days the ladies will ride if only for a few hundred yards. Um Hamed came through the court, covered in her black veils which brushed against climbing bougainvillaea blossoms, sending down showers of petals. We rose to greet her and her companions with delighted cries of welcome, mingled with congratulations for her walk.

'But it is such an easy walk on such a cool day,' laughed Um Hamed, lifting her veil off her face and adjusting her mask so that it settled properly on her nose. We agreed that it was indeed a fine day - a perfect day. The wind had changed, bringing strangely cool, fresh air to the oases. It was a day like those searched for by Northerners in the south of France or the Greek islands. Hot enough to embrace you - not hot enough to bake you.

Another carpet was called for and our circle expanded. Fresh coffee and fruit were ordered and soon the sound of the big brass pestle pounding the cardamom and coffee beans in the brass mortar rang around the court, announcing that we had visitors, come and make them welcome.

I had not seen Um Hamed since those frightening days when the Youngest Son was in hospital. We greeted each other with affection. She was always the same. Always welcoming, always beautiful, always that charming voice. I asked about her daughter and her son and husband. Was he better? Would she come to London this summer? She in turn asked why I hadn't been to visit her. Would I come that very evening or soon? The Youngest Son would bring me.

'God willing,' I answered.

The chatter and gossip began to run among us. The serwal were admired and my own efforts at button-making were applauded. I felt like an eight-year-old showing her work in class. The tray of fruit arrived. There were dates and a delicious bowl of freshly made cottage cheese. We talked and ate, exchanging news and views. Someone had gone to Germany, someone had returned from London, someone was in hospital, someone was to be married.

Then the talk turned to the West and I found myself at the centre of

questions.

· 'But why do they wear so few clothes? Why do they kiss on television?'

'And more.'

'Yes and more. It is very rude. I have to close it off.'

'And why do they speak so roughly to their husbands and why do they have so few manners? You are not like this to Abu Yusef? Surely not.'

'No, surely not, surely not,' all agreed while I sat silent.

'They do not visit and do not know their neighbours. They do not know who lives beside them. How can they live like that?'

'Once, when shopping in London with my friends and daughters, one young man comes and stares at me. It is very rude to stare. And they look and look all the time. It is very uncomfortable.'

'In London I go from the room to the car quickly.'

'I only go to small shops now. Not the big ones.'

'Ha. Let them stare. It is they who are rude. Not you.'

'What I do not understand is where is the water? There is nowhere to get water if you are thirsty. I always take a bottle of water in the car for the children.'

I tried to answer and explain our ways, but it was difficult. Only if I used the example of all mankind's progress towards Paradise was there any meeting of minds. I remembered John Bunyan's *Pilgrim's Progress* and, after explaining the story briefly, said that we all went through a Slough of Despond at some time, but God led us out. So it was with customs which were not correct. With prayer we would be brought out of them.

'This is true, this is true. Thanks be to God,' they answered.

Then Hussa began a startling conversation. 'Tell me, Um Yusef, they say a man walked on the moon. What do you think of this?'

I replied that I had watched my television all day when the first man stepped on the moon. I thought it was the greatest adventure of our age.

'Ha, you can't believe this, Um Yusef,' she said. 'It is of course a trick.' And all the others nodded their agreement.

'A trick? No indeed. You have seen the pictures. You have seen the television pictures and heard the words of the men from space. It is true, my friend,' I explained.

'Now, Um Yusef, you know it is very easy to make stories. Look at all the nonsense on the television. It is all made up. This is made up too. The moon. What nonsense. Next you will tell me they are sending aeroplanes to the stars, just like to London.'

I looked to the Sheikha for help. Her eyes were busy with her sewing. She did not look up. What did she believe, I wondered?

118

All agreed that it was a trick and that it was very silly of the people who made it. Their arguments were faultless and after a few moments I felt myself drowning in doubt, drowning in the time trap surrounding the area. Had Neil Armstrong really walked on the moon or was it a magnificent hoax? I shook my head and felt enormously grateful when the topic of conversation changed.

'They say that the English cannot stay with their child or friend or family in the hospital. Is this true? That only at certain times you can see them? Why is this? It is so cruel. Who will comfort them and watch over them?'

The conversation turned to illness and the old days.

'Today, everyone is sick. We had no malaria before.'

'It is brought by the workers.'

'Before when you were sick - which was not often - you got well or you died. God's hand is in all things. His will be done.'

'His will be done. Praise God. Thanks be to God.'

'Today there is much sickness all the time. Colds and stomach and much cancer. We had this before, but not so much.'

'I do not trust these doctors and all these pills. I do not see them at all. How do they know what they say is true? What are these strange drugs? I think they know less than they think. It is all look, look, look. Pictures, blood, injection, and do they cure you? No.'

'They cure some.'

'Some. But the worst still die.'

'As before.'

'As before.'

'What happened before when you were sick?' I asked.

'How sick? A little sick or badly sick, sick with something you can catch or not catch?'

The Sheikha looked up. 'Well, Um Yusef,' she said, putting down her sewing, 'first, of course, you must pray, for prayer to God makes the mind quiet, reminds you that your life is in His hands and that all is well, truly, thanks be to Him. When the mind is quiet of course the body is quiet and whatever illness you have can be healed more easily.'

She put down her needle and thread and went on, her voice calm with conviction, 'Of course we do not know what God plans for us, so we must be ready to accept His will in all things, but sometimes prayer alone will heal the one who is ill and this is the best way.'

'It is, it is, praise God. May His name be praised,' chorused the ladies around me.

'In the old days,' said Hussa, 'if you had a bad thing like the smallpox,

119

or something others could catch, you were put far away from people in a small hut where things were brought to you and left for you. Sometimes such poor people died, but sometimes they lived. It was all in God's hands.'

'But we were not sick so much,' said the Sheikha. 'We ate very little. Sometimes only dried fish and dates and a little rice. Many things can be made from dates. Sweet things, drinks, cakes, many things. We were glad to have this food. And were very well eating it. And there are desert bushes which give green things in the spring. You have eaten them, Um Yusef? Yes, of course. Here with us. So delicious, eh? And the milk of the camel or the goat. Yoghurt.' She picked up her sewing. 'One day I will show you how these things are made.' Her eyes smiled a promise.

'Praise God.'

'His name be praised.'

The talk went on and the fruit tray became a pile of peelings, the cottage cheese bowl emptied and all was removed. Our visitors rose, said their farewells and walked off across the court again. They moved slowly, their black veils floating around them. The children continued their playing. The tumbling pigeons rose up and tumbled down, their white wings bright in the sunlight.

The Sheikha looked up to the sun.

'It is time to pray. Wait here while I pray.'

'Yes, you go to pray. I will stay here,' I answered.

Shama, who was lifting herself up on her lame legs, turned with a puzzled expression. Then a broad smile crossed her face.

'That is what Umbarak would say to Zayed. "You go to pray. I stay here." Umbarak said that.' And she moved off to her own prayers.

Umbarak - Wilfred Thesiger - rode with Zayed long before the days of oil. I was to hear his name again and again. How had Shama known him? Where had she heard him say these things? I knew I must talk with her again, but at that moment I was content to have used the words of the last of the great desert explorers. I sat watching as the sun reached its zenith and the muezzin began to call the people to prayers. The sound echoed out of the mosque towers across the town. The morning was over.

14

Sand Storms and Desert Ice

EACH DAY ROSE and fell in the same quiet pattern. Each day was blessed with the same strangely cool weather, until one evening the clear sky suddenly filled with haze and the new moon faded out of sight as though sailing out of orbit into oblivion.

That night I did not open my window to the usually sweet night air but kept it tight shut against the threatening darkness. I closed the curtains, went to bed, pulled the blanket high over my head and slept peacefully until I heard through layers of consciousness that unforgettable sound, the voice of the wind.

The voice of the wind is as different in the desert as the language of the people. I am used to the wind's deep-throated shouts as it tears at the corners of our cottage in Cornwall, as it cracks branches and sweeps up leaves. I know its London shrieks and shuffles as it rushes through road canyons and around the sharp edges of tall buildings. But in the desert it gives a strange moaning sound, low and sensual, accompanied by the singing of the sand as it skates across itself. The moans and songs lie low and gentle, then rise to a wild screaming force of sound as though all the ghosts of time had gathered themselves into one great, explosive cry. They deafen you. If the wind catches you in its path it will blind you. Once it reaches its zenith you can neither see, hear nor stand.

If the dry desert storm rises in the day and you are inside, protected by walls of concrete and windows framed in steel, you watch as the sun changes white to red and slowly fades into nothing. Distant walls disappear in a fog

of dust as dense to the eye as the black fogs of old London. Slowly you realise your house is drowning in dust. The concrete and steel begin to leak. The dust penetrates all man's modern inventions, so strong, so carefully sealed. Soon small eddies appear. Thin layers rise on tables and shelves. Windows have frostings of dust - inside. You begin to taste it, bite it, breathe it, and as in England your heart whispers a quick, deep prayer for all those men caught in gales on the sea, so in the desert your prayers rush to those caught in the sand sea.

Quick phone calls are made to sons and husbands who are planning to drive home.

'Don't start. The storm is here. Wait. Wait.' To drive through the storm would be an invitation to suicide. Even in a light wind, a dust-misted day, windscreen wipers and headlights must be turned on, the clink-clonk of the wipers brushing off dust, not rain. In a storm it is madness to move.

I woke that morning with grit between my teeth. I tasted the storm before I saw it. Through the haze of early half-waking I knew that the dust was everywhere. The screaming, shouting wind, the sand fog would obliterate all sight of trees, walls, houses, cars. I put my head under the blanket, but it was no use. The whole house trembled, shuddered, leaked.

'I must go home tomorrow,' I thought. 'How in God's heaven will I get down to the coast in this mess?' It could last for an hour or a day or days, rising and falling.

I poked my head out. The pillow had an almost imperceptible film of dust. I threw back the blanket and walked to the window. Beyond the porch steps nothing could be seen but a cream-coloured, whirling fog of dust. I stood watching the dust frostings rise on the inside of the window panes. I listened to the storm.

They say that typhoons on the South China Seas are the worst, lifting and cracking the backs of freighters like discarded toys. Then there are those who will tell you that the winter storms sucking through the Magellan Straits are the most deadly. Others talk of blizzards, of cyclones and hurricanes, howling and thrashing, winding themselves up before blowing themselves out. I was in a hurricane once. I was a child. The air pressure forced me to my knees and I watched while the wind screwed great oak trees out of the earth and then dropped them in a mess of green leaves and splintered wood.

Every winter the gales of Cornwall lift granite slabs off sea walls and toss them willy-nilly on to the nearest road. The stone walls of our cottage groan and shudder as if tired of battling with the centuries of wind. We're used to that, though. We're used to the sharp cracks of lightning and the belch

of thunder issuing from the belly of the sky. Rain, fog and mist are the acceptable accoutrements of northern gales. But dust? No. This crying, this wailing, this mass of thick air gathered from thousand upon thousand square miles of nothingness, scooped up, pushed and banked against every object which has the temerity to stand up from the surface of the earth; this was weird, oppressive, invasive.

I watched and waited. It continued. I went into the bathroom. My feet made neat tracks on the tiles. I washed, letting the water rush around the sides of the bath, letting it clean as much as possible along with myself. It was a losing battle, but I tried.

I knew that eventually I would have to walk into that screaming cloud. The pattern of the day must continue. I could stay in the house and be marked as frightened, or I could do battle with the elements, making my way to the family as usual. I dressed and then went to my suitcase, searching for an old, black veil. I found it folded in a corner, still heavy with the perfume of the Sheikha who had given it to me. I wound it around my head so that it covered all but my eyes. An Indian shawl went around my shoulders and I started toward the door.

A sudden, mindless, stomach-twisting invasion of fear slowed my steps. The fear of the intangible. My hand went to the handle of the front door but without my touching it, the handle moved and the door crashed open. Now the wind was inside, whipping my veils and skirts around me, picking up folds of cloth and dropping them, slamming inner doors.

Half closing my eyes, I turned and backed on to the porch. Heaving and struggling I managed to close the door, but it kept opening again, weakened by its storm-fractured clasp. My back strained against the wind. I clung to the door, my hands fisted round the useless handle.

Before a prayer had formed itself, a young brown hand covered mine and I looked round to see the turbaned head of the Youngest Son, his face half covered by his head-scarf, his eyes laughing, his whole figure straight against the storm as though he and it had made some truce. He reached inside the door, found the key and locked both it and the house against the invasion. He took my hand. The storm parted in front of us. We walked to his mother's house.

Once inside he pulled his scarf away from his face, the laughter welling up inside him. He put his arms around me in the bear-hug of a joyous boy who had suddenly become a man.

'Come, Mrs Tea Cup, you must not be afraid of the storm. It comes. It goes. It is a big noise for nothing.'

He drew me into the family circle, laughing, telling his mother of my

struggles, of the broken door, but when I started to take my veil off he wouldn't have it and insisted that I keep it on.

'Now you are truly one of us. You must put on kohl. Why not? Why are your eyes pale like this? Eh? It is a good idea, my mother. Um Yusef should wear kohl and the shayla. Then she will be an Al Ain woman and can stay here.' He stood beside his mother, hugging and kissing her, teasing us all.

The microscopic grit was in everything. In the coffee, on our hands, edging forward from the corners of the room. Sometimes the whole house would shake, then lie quiet again, keeping sentinel for this small group of humans.

We sat and drank our gritted coffee, sewed and read. Prayers were said. Men servants came and went, pushing against the wind, their faces bound Berber fashion, leaving only a gap for the eyes. Food was brought, gritty with dust. The phone rang at regular intervals. Queries as to the state of the storm, queries as to safety. Always the answer, 'No, don't come. It is still very bad. We are well. Don't move.'

The Sheikh phoned. Then the Eldest Son, then an uncle, a great-uncle, then the Sheikh again. Sometimes the Youngest Son would speak, standing in some automatic obeisance when he heard his father's voice. Sometimes the daughter with a gentle, half-frightened tone.

'Yes, my father. Yes, it is very bad. No. I am not afraid. My brother is here. My mother is here. All are in the house.'

Towards the late afternoon, exhausted by its own violence, it began to die slowly and soon the 'great noise for nothing' became a gasping puff. The doors were opened and we stared at the drifts of dust which had banked against houses and cars in much the same way that snow drifts against walls and trees.

Everything, every object natural or man-made, had its film of dust and there was no prospect of rain to wash it clean. It would take days to sweep the stuff away, weeks for the green to grow green again, for the dust to settle and become earth.

In the evening, Hussa and Shama walked over from their house which is battened against the front wall of the compound. We talked of the storm and other storms they had known. Rubbing her lame leg, Shama began to speak in her slow, rolling voice.

'I have seen worse storms than this. More quick to come. More strong. More quick to go. Like the anger of the devil.'

'Where?' I asked, 'Here? Where?'

'Oh, here, there,' she pointed her hands at some unknown place beyond the walls.

I told her of the storms I had known as a child in America, of the sea lifting the paving stones in Penzance, of the ice storms in New England where each twig, each leaf is coated in ice, and of how, when the sun shines, it is as though the world were crystallised, as though nature were encapsulated in a diamond.

'This I will never see. Not now,' said Shama. She seemed disappointed that there was some area of life, some vision she could not experience. She must have been nearly seventy. Her round of days seemed to me to be a drone-like existence, moving from house to compound, compound to house. Yet to her each new day had some new fascination.

Now, as though solaced by the memory she said, 'I have known times when the water went to ice. Yes. This happened. It happened when I went to Mecca.'

'Ice?' I said. 'In the desert? Ice? In Mecca?'

'No, no. On the way. Going. It was cold. Very cold in the night. The water went to ice in the water bag. You have seen them? These skins that hold water? No?' she asked.

'Never,' I said.

'I have some even now,' she answered. 'I will show you. Tomorrow when I come. We used them long ago. In the past. All is changed now. Now it is aeroplane. Then only camel.'

'When did you go to Mecca this way?' I asked. 'Were there many of you altogether? When was this?'

'Long ago. In the past. We were few, not so many. Ten camel maybe. Five men maybe and that time ...' she counted on her fingers, naming long remembered names, 'Three women. Yes, three women.'

She described how they had carried their water in those sheepskins, which they call *jerbah*. Many things were carried in them. Small skins were for milk, camels' milk or goats' milk which they got from bedu camps along the way. Old skins were used to carry dates, the sweet, sugar-running, dried Al Ain dates packed down tight. There were skins for flour, for rice, and small leather bags for salt.

'Did you have a tent for the night?' I had always imagined that they would put up and take down tents. A stupid idea, when you think about it. Bedu tents are huge, complicated structures. Movable homes. Travelling was travelling. The object then was as it is today, to get from one place to the next as swiftly as possible. Bedu travelled fast and light.

'Tent?' asked Shama. 'Tent?' She laughed. 'No, Um Yusef. No. There was no time for this. We were always going, going, going.'

'Did you ride?'

'Ride? Yes, I ride. Up high. On top. And I walk. I walk. Slowly, slowly we get there.'

'At night it was cold? Where was this when the water froze?' I asked.

'In the mountains. In the morning we have to wait for the sun to turn it to water. It took a long time, the waiting.'

'It must have been so very cold in the night. Did you have blankets? What did you sleep on?' I asked.

'This thing that goes over the camel. We had no blankets. Just this cover for the camel.'

'Weren't you cold?'

'Cold? No. We were sleeping.' It was one of those answers that they give sometimes. Answers that leave you hanging in mid-air.

As Shama talked, Hussa added a reminder here and there as though they were stories which she had heard many times before. The Sheikha's daughter sat with us, pouring coffee, translating the words I couldn't understand, her quiet voice occasionally breaking into laughter at my questions, my curiosity.

'Why? Why do you want to know these things?' she asked.

'We must know about each other,' I answered.

It seemed a right time, a right moment to ask Shama another question which had been haunting me. I reminded her that she had mentioned Wilfred Thesiger.

'You said before, another time, before, you had heard Umbarak speak. Did you know Umbarak?'

'Umbarak with all bedu. Umbarak stay with Zayed. He sits with him. He hunts with him.' Suddenly she burst into laughter, her arthritic hands waving in the air.

'They made bread. He and Zayed. They put it under the fire. It went to dust, black dust, very sandy. Then they mix it. Mix this black dust with oil and eat it. Umbarak and Zayed. Umbarak, he made it. They ate it.'

She bent over to show me how they tried to eat this dust. Then she pointed to me. 'When Zayed and his friends go to pray, Umbarak say, "You go to pray - I stay here." You say this, same as Umbarak.' She shook with laughter again.

When I told her that Umbarak was still alive and sometimes visited London, she asked, 'Why does he not come to sit with Zayed?' I told her that he came once but he didn't like the new Al Ain.

'They say that he said he would never come again. I heard this.' I told her.

'Perhaps he sits with Zayed in London,' she said.

'Perhaps,' I agreed but in my heart I doubted it. There were days when my husband and my son, too, had sat with Zayed. When it was easy to reach this man whose spirit was born out of the best of the desert traditions. Today he is surrounded by a court.

I told Shama of the years that Thesiger had spent in Iraq with the Marsh Arabs and then in Iran, that now he had a small house in Kenya deep in the country where he could get away from the towns. I told her all that I had read of him.

'He should sit with Zayed,' she answered.

I said he was over seventy now.

'This is not so old today. Many live past eighty. He should come again,' and her eyes looked into what was past.

'They liked it better then,' said the young daughter.

The following morning as I was packing to leave, Shama came limping to the house with a jerbah for me to see. Made of the whole sheepskin, the legs were tied with rings of woven palm leaf. It was sewn with coarse grass and carefully mended with leather patches stitched on with the same coarse grass. A cloth was tied to one end. It was filled there, at the neck end.

'Life has changed, Shama,' I said looking at the Japanese thermos on the chair by my bed and the round box of Danish biscuits which I had been given 'in case you are hungry in the night'. I looked at her steadily and said again, 'Life has changed.'

She watched me from behind her long old-fashioned mask.

'Yes,' she said and held her sheepskin in both hands as though willing some part of the past to remain in the present. Then, saying goodbye and wishing me well on my journey, she limped out of the house, down the steps and off down the drive.

I left for Abu Dhabi that afternoon. The streets of Al Ain and the highway were still half covered in drifts of sand. Every few hundred yards teams of Baluchistan workers were sweeping it away, sweeping it back towards the desert which suddenly seemed everywhere. One felt the enormity of that dry wilderness and the puny, brassy efforts of man. If left to itself the road would disappear in three months. The new houses, the markets would crumble in the wind and the sun and there would be little left to remind man of this strange blip of civilisation in the path of the patiently creeping sand.

Another Babylon, another Leptus Magna, another Petra? Within hours I was flying over it. I thought of Shama and her camels, her sheepskin water carriers, her dates and camels' milk. She had needed nothing but some rough grazing, a few wells and the hospitality of the bedu to get her across.

To make our aeroplanes and fly them we need steel mills, oil wells, an army of designers, technicians, engineers and financiers, pilots, mechanics, caterers and stewards. She took weeks, we took hours. But we both arrived at our destination. It was only a matter of time. The question was and always will be, what shall we do with the time we have saved?

Part Four

15

A Bride for a Prince

'YOU MUST COME. The wedding will be very soon now.'

The voice of the Second Son was pleading and urgent. I could imagine him sprawled on the floor of the pool room in the boys' house, a long, lean figure in a white kandora unbuttoned at the neck, around him three or four young men waiting to play football, to drive, to beat the drums or follow him wherever he wanted to go.

It was summer. He was at home. Studies were over for a few months. There would be one more year of work before he finally achieved his degree, a hard year, a work-filled year, but nothing could or would postpone marriage plans. If the time was deemed to be right, if the prospective bride had accepted and the parents had chosen a time, he would be married, that was sure.

Now his voice was coming over five thousand miles of air and five hundred years of diverse progress. He was in his world. I was in mine.

'Where are you? You must come. You must come now. It is arranged. The marriage is arranged. We have signed. I will be married next winter. You promised to help me. Where are you? When will you come? Tomorrow? Next week?'

They had signed. This boy, this youngster, this barely grown-up Arab 'son' was indeed to be married.

We had talked about it, of course. They always talked about it. Their dreams of love and marriage are hopelessly romantic, still holding the touch

of Camelot or Juliet or Melisande. He would not see his bride before the wedding night so all sorts of pictures could float in the mind.

It was all a matter of trust. Trust in parents, trust in the hearsay of family and friends. The young people lived in hope and waited with great expectations. After all, it is a small society. Gossip is perpetual. Reputations for beauty, grace, wit, intelligence or for strength, humour, kindness, honesty are made early or never made at all. Everyone knows everyone.

'When are you coming? I will meet your plane.'

'Is it all right with your mother? Does she expect me?' I asked.

'She is not here. No-one is here, but she will be glad if you come just the same.'

The idea of staying in a near empty compound in midsummer was scarcely inviting.

'Where are they all?' I asked, postponing the decision.

'Away,' came the enigmatic reply and I knew I would learn nothing more until I arrived.

'Is everything all right?' I asked.

'Everything is perfect. When are you coming? There is much to do and you promised.'

I had promised, so I must go. A promise must be kept.

A promise is the ultimate seal in that sandy world. It is said that Arabs have no compunction about reneging on a deal, that they will blow hot and cold, use the phrase 'God willing' to suit their own purpose, say 'yes' when they mean 'no' and generally confuse their more direct Western counterparts. Written business contracts can be searched for minute loopholes in the small print, for the Arab is most certainly a past master at the game of delay. The exception to this sharp dealing is the word of honour. To break this is to break the code, so it is rarely given. Once given it is as good as a seal. Better. Those who break their word are considered lower than the dust.

I was now bound both by their code and by my own. My promise had been made long ago. It had been made at one of those long, heart-searching breakfast conversations over pancakes and imported Vermont maple syrup. 'When they choose one for me, when it does happen, you will help me, Mrs Tea Cup. This is for sure? I have your promise? Your word?' I agreed. I made my promise. Now I must keep it.

He was on the airport tarmac waiting for me, his Mercedes sports drawn up to the foot of the mobile steps. As thin as ever without an ounce of excess fat, he had the long face and gaunt look of the true desert Arab. His two Omani friends were with him, their smiles wordless expressions of

hospitality.

I stepped out of the plane and into the Arabian summer heat. It was a tangible experience. You felt, tasted and swallowed it in an effort to breathe. It was like a suffocating embrace. The car with its whirring air conditioning was like an oxygen mask. How had they lived in this suffocation before air conditioning? How had they moved? How had they worked? I turned to look at the young man beside me, his long fingered hands resting on the steering wheel. In the unblinking black eyes were a thousand upon a thousand years of survival. No need for the fetish of sunglasses. The eyes had been bred for the glare, the body for the heat.

We drove down the tarmac and out of the airport gates. He gave a quick, curt nod to the soldiers on duty and turned on to the Al Ain road. He drove as he always drove in those days, well, but far too fast.

'Welcome.'

'Thank you.'

He enquired for my family and I for his.

'Your mother? Where is she?' I asked.

'She has gone to Germany with my sister,' he answered.

'And your brothers?'

'The eldest in Jordan. The youngest with them.'

'How is your young brother?' I asked. 'Is he well? Quite well?'

'He is good. Except sometimes he still itches.'

'When did they leave?' I asked.

'A little while ago.'

It is quite hopeless to expect any news which they are either not ready nor sufficiently interested to share. You just have to wait and catch your moment or piece things together as best you can. We drove on in silence. I bided my time but patience was still not a part of my nature no matter how continually I courted it. So I asked again.

'Is everything all right? Is your mother well?'

He glanced at me, saw the discomfort in my expression and started to laugh.

'Of course they are well. It is only to see the dentist and escape the heat. They don't like it so well as London. No-one of them speaks German. But they were told the doctors were good.'

I could imagine the language confusion, the blank looks behind the masks.

'And your grandmother?'

'She is perfectly well. She is staying with my aunt because my mother is not here. She does not like my mother to go, but my sister's teeth ached

and you know the dentists here.' He gave an expression of agony and groaned, then grinned adding, 'There is a maid left there'. He waved in the direction of Al Ain. 'She will look after you. And you won't have to eat my cooking. Others are there.'

Now, at last, the news was shared and I felt comfortable. Why hadn't he said so in the first place? Why did they always cloak everything, if not with seven veils, at least with one?

'Thanks be to God,' I said and settled back to enjoy the drive. The road was clear, his hands were steady. Neither of us said very much. We were both busy with our thoughts. The only sounds were the clean, well-tuned engine and a tape of the famous Lebanese singer Farouz singing 'My Country'. Dear God. Her country. Shattered, exploded, tormented. A battlefield for every devilish emotion known to man. Though I didn't know it at the time, Lebanon was suffering only the *hors d'oeuvre* of the devil's dinner. I shut my mind to the apocalypse and opened it to the complexities of marriage on the lower Gulf.

'Congratulations. Congratulations. Everything is arranged?'

'Yes, it is arranged,' he answered with a wide smile.

A marriage has been arranged. We used the same phrase once. It had a Victorian charm to us, an Emily Post nicety. To them it still had meaning. While hot-eyed youngsters in the West drifted about like aimless butterflies on summer days, hoping for the long-imagined mate to materialise, in this place the search was cool-eyed and planned with the precision of a military campaign.

The Second Son's bride-to-be had been carefully chosen. She was from the hareem of Um Hamed, a large and powerful hareem dominated by Um Hamed's mother-in-law. Um Hamed was the wife of one of four sons. There were four daughters-in-law in their hareem, all from important Sheikh families. The little bride was therefore a distant cousin. Marrying a cousin was very much to be desired. Marrying a first cousin was considered the best possible arrangement. They seemed oblivious to the genetic dangers this could engender.

'I think your bride is very young. Has she finished school?' I asked.

'No. She stops to marry me,' he said and laughed aloud.

She's only fourteen, I decided and spoke my thoughts aloud, saying, 'She's so young.'

'Not so very. Not so very. You know her. I think you know her. Anyway you know all about her, for I have told you. And you have seen her. Surely you remember her? They say she is very clever and will keep my house well. This is more important than a long nose, don't you think?'

'I think it is much more important,' I said laughing.

I remembered the girl. She had been little more than a child when I first saw her, but no-one could forget her beautiful, lively eyes.

'She is very attractive,' I went on. 'She carries her own beauty. Such a girl would be much admired in the West and we would think her very beautiful indeed.'

'Oh?' he said and drove on in silence again.

I had first seen her in the desert when I went for my first 'bedu' breakfast and the prospective bridegroom's brother had played fox in the hen coop. She couldn't have been more than ten then and by our standards would be scarcely more than a child now. I had seen her a few times since and remembered her lively face, her large, intelligent eyes which were always looking here, looking there as if one moment's rest would deny her some crumb of life. I remembered her laugh. Such a laugh was made for very few. It rose like a peal of music heard from a distance on a clear night. You went toward it, irresistibly drawn, laughing without reason.

Yes, I remembered her.

'Yes,' I said breaking the silence, remembering the laugh. 'We would think her very beautiful.'

'They say she is a very good housekeeper and I want a very good housekeeper because my house will be perfect. You will help me to make it perfect?' It was both a question and a statement and we both smiled, for we both knew the answer.

'Who told you she was a good housekeeper? Did they send a searching woman for you?' I asked.

'A searching woman?' repeated the boy. 'Well, they sent Hussa. You know my mother would send Hussa. It is only polite. It is correct. Besides I want to know how she has grown. Hussa is a good searcher.'

'It seems so strange when it is all settled,' I said.

'It is the way. My mother cannot go. Suppose she is grown up bad. This is very embarrassing. There must be somebody.'

There must be somebody. Yes, I supposed there must be somebody. The searching woman had a unique role to play in these affairs. She was the eyes and ears of the Sheikha. Not a marriage broker. Certainly not. Nothing so barefaced as that. The searching woman was a sort of subtle investigator, a visiting 'friend' who observed and reported. A spy? Well, yes. It must be admitted. A sort of known and often welcome spy.

I settled back in my seat, resting my head against the sheepskin, wondering at the strange minuet of their lives, the complexities of their dance of life. I had watched a marriage campaign once. Not for this boy.

Not for this son of a Sheikh. For Hamed, the eldest son of Um Hamed, who found himself on the shelf quite unexpectedly and yet was ready to marry. It was extraordinary. No NATO general could have organised the strategy so well, for what general can recognise and know by name over a thousand of his troops - even when masked? What general could detail their lineage for at least two generations, name their children and describe their children's abilities and characters? Do they have trusted lieutenants to go into the field armed with such information?

Believe me, the CIA, the KGB, Mossad, MI6 are all a lot of coarse novices relying on schoolboy cruelties and inaccurate hearsay compared to the knowledge and sophistication of the hareem information system. Furthermore, the system is not only trustworthy but all information is absolutely sacrosanct. No-one 'outside' would ever know a thing. No-one would ever defect.

'Do you remember last year when your cousin Hamed was looking for a bride?' I asked. 'With Hamed it was a real search.'

'Poor Hamed,' he answered. 'But they are always looking. Always planning. If it doesn't go this way, then it will go that way. Um Hamed had a lot of planning. You know that very well. You know them very well, now. Better than I.'

Better than him? Never. All I could do was pile up small bits of information hoping it would make an understandable structure one day.

There had been weeks of discussion about finding a wife for Hamed. Whenever we visited Um Hamed or Um Hamed visited us, conversation inevitably turned to the latest news of a prospective bride. His mother and the Sheikha were in constant conference. Others came with suggestions. Grandmothers were consulted. Family histories remembered.

Finally, after weeks of debating the merits, advantages and availability of this or that young daughter, a decision was made to send the searching woman, Um Hamed's first lieutenant, who would investigate two possibilities more thoroughly.

The great advantage in these campaigns is to have the best possible first lieutenant. Of course everyone knows to which general she belongs, but it is her eyes, her ears and her discernment that have to be relied upon.

Girl 'A' was discarded. She was too tall (taller than the boy by a couple of inches, it was judged), too old ('They lie about her age. She is older. Her face and hands say she is older') and she had been 'out' and that was the final blow. As she was from a neighbouring Emirate which had a far less critical attitude toward the participation of women in education, Girl 'A', it was discovered, had taught in an infant school after finishing her own

schooling. Thus her face had been seen beyond the borders of her home, classroom or relatives' houses. She had been 'out'. Not acceptable in the establishment hareems of Al Ain.

Girl 'B' became the target and the game began once more and in earnest. The searcher made a casual visit. She asked to see the daughter of the house. Daughter was sent for. There was a flurry. Sorry. Daughter was not available. She was studying. Next visit she was praying. On a third visit she was visiting her grandmother. The searcher returned another day and another and all this was a good sign. It showed that they were not anxious, that they knew they had a treasure. The more the searcher asked to see the daughter, the more the daughter was hidden until that planned moment of 'chance' arrived when all was revealed, and all was, as my young Sheikh would have said, 'perfectly well'.

The fathers met after considerable visiting by members of the hareems, and a proposal of marriage was made. They told me that the girl's father had been as coy as any nineteenth-century English maiden. He demurred, he asked for time to think, to consult his wife, to put the proposal to his daughter.

I turned to my driver.

'You remember how shy the father of Moseh was when Hamed's father put the proposal? Was it the same with your father and your cousin's father? Surely not.'

'Surely yes,' he answered.

'They have to ask her just the same?'

'Of course. She might say "no" even if it was planned a long time. This happened to my brother. The first girl said it would be like marrying her brother so she would not. She was a cousin, too. Not the same one as mine. Another,' and he named the girl whom I knew.

'Well, that's a revelation. She's not married yet,' I said.

'No, but she will be when she finishes her work. She is studying for a degree,' he said. 'Not in a real university. By the mail.'

'Good for her!' I exclaimed and applauded inwardly.

'Maybe,' he said laconically. 'But maybe she will go outside the tribe.'

A Sowaidi should only marry a Sowaidi, a Mansoori should only marry a Mansoori. And if there weren't enough Mansoori boys of the right age for Mansoori girls then the answer was either spinsterhood or a long wait to become the second wife of an older man. Sheikh families bypass the rule, as do others, but not often.

Once the two fathers had signed, once they had seen their names written in the register of marriages, it was irrevocable. That contract would be the

bride's deed, her licence, her legal proof of marriage in all future transactions. She would not change her name. She would not wear a wedding ring. Only the contract identified her position. It was binding. It could be signed as soon as the fathers agreed the match or as late as the wedding night itself, just as long as it was signed before the consummation.

My young Sheikh's father had signed. Next came the wedding. I knew it would be an elaborate fantasy, a courtship, a serenade. It would be all the courting that the bride would know. I began to think about the changes the coming wedding would bring. But not before I saw the speedometer register over 100 mph and decided to fasten my seat belt.

'Are you afraid?' The young Sheikh smiled.

'No. Cautious.' He teased me a bit but slowed down to 85 mph.

The Farous' lament came to an end and the boy punched the tape out of its slot. Fumbling with a collection of tapes which were jumbled around the gear lever, he called out to the boys behind to ask where they had put a tape of a classic poem set to music. The friends had been remarkably quiet throughout the drive.

I turned to look at them. Their dark faces were wreathed in smiles but there was a certain stillness in the eyes. One of them reached over to search out the right tape and handed it to his Sheikh.

'Soon he will be a husband and then a man of family and all will be serious,' I said.

'This is for sure,' they answered, looking at each other.

'No more drums in the afternoon.'

'No more.' Their eyes were expressionless.

'There is still time before I am captured,' said the prospective bridegroom as he put the new tape into the slot and began to tap his hands against the wheel.

The road had been widened over the years. A centre island had been built to divide the oncoming and ongoing traffic. It was planted with mile upon mile of hibiscus bushes. The long yellow stamens of their red flowers spit out into the hot air, searching for the least drop of moisture. An intricate watering system would eventually replace the army of Baluchistan gardeners who tended not only the road islands but the roundabouts and the young plantations of trees struggling for life under the condemnation of the sun.

There was a marvellous audacity about a ruler who had decided to enter the lists and joust against the elements. King Canute had tried and failed, but he didn't have Zayed's oily gold. The cost would be immeasurable, but there would be green on either side of Zayed's desert highway in his lifetime.

As if in answer to unspoken thoughts, the boy broke in.

'My grandfather had a dream long ago. Long, long ago,' he said. 'Back before the oil.' He made it seem an aeon. Perhaps it was. 'He dreamed one night that the way from Al Ain to Abu Dhabi would be green with branches of trees coming over to give shade. He said this dream would become real. And my grandmother said that it would happen. Now you see the beginning. It will happen. It will be so.'

I imagined his grandfather leading his tribe as it migrated from Al Ain to Abu Dhabi, then on to the Liwa and beyond towards Qatar. I imagined his grandmother riding high on the camel's hump, her veils creating her own tent. To dream of cool and shade was to dream of paradise.

'Your grandmother must have been very young and very brave when she married,' I said.

'Very young. They were all brave, I think, for everything was difficult.'

'Younger than your bride?'

'Younger. Much younger. Mine is not so young. Not really, Mrs Tea Cup. Not so very. She has been to school.'

His grandmother might have married at thirteen, perhaps even twelve. This child might be fifteen by the time the marriage took place. The marriage age was rising with education. Rising slowly.

A good housekeeper was she? She would have to be with this boy. He liked everything in its place, wanted his kandoras or suffras, T-shirts or slacks pristine and neatly folded. He hated a mess and would want the tidiest house.

I made a mental effort to visualise his new house, to create some mind picture, but gave up after a few seconds. The images were too much of a jumble because new houses on the Gulf are a fantasy that have to be seen to be believed. Uninhibited by any tradition of building, they have taken off in a confused conglomeration of tile, cement, plastics, marble and paint that would have taxed the imagination of Disney. Architects with small and large reputations have contrived a scene of staggering proportions.

I closed my eyes against the sun and against the confusion of my thoughts. I was tired. It is a long way from London to Al Ain. The tape played endlessly, winding its bodiless sound around the brain. I half slept, then woke as we sped by the rest house where we had stopped for juice on that first visit to Al Ain. We passed with never a backward look and arrived in Al Ain in well under three hours. Our bottle of water, that remnant of respect for the old days, lay untouched on the seat.

Swinging around a newly installed roundabout, we drove towards the family compound. There the new bride house erupted in ornate concrete

splendour. It dwarfed the modest bungalows of the rest of the family. It was not seemly for the Second Son to outshine the father in this way and I knew instinctively that before a year had passed there would be more building in the compound.

The car came to an abrupt halt.

'What do you think of it?' he asked.

'Splendid,' I answered.

'Come. Come and see.'

I took a deep breath of cool air before diving into the blast of heat and walking the few steps to the house.

So many dreams had gone into that house, so many hopes. It had been planned and planned again, drawn on the backs of kleenex boxes, on torn pages from old copy books, on old football posters and the margins of newspapers. It had been paced off in the sand as he announced the dimensions to the architect. 'This room for me here, the kitchen here, the back door here.' His brown legs had marched along kicking stones out of the way. Now it was reality.

I walked up broad marble steps to a wide front porch screened by pre-cast fretted tiles. A large double door of panelled wood opened into a house which had remarkable balance and grace. We went inside. The young Sheikh went through room after room, helping me over some unfinished bit of floor, speaking quickly and sharply to the building foreman, moving the placing of some light fitting. He turned constantly to me, watching for signs of approval or disapproval. We inspected everything; from the plumbing arrangements to the cornices and architraves, entirely 'new' ideas which he had gleaned from his trips to Europe. From foundations to roof it had taken only five months to reach this stage of construction.

'What do you think? Is it good?'

'It is perfect, a perfect house.'

'It must be the most beautiful house. The best in Al Ain.' He hesitated. 'You think she will like it?'

It was a tentative moment. Too much concern would be un-Sheikhly, but he was young, filled with hopes, with possible and impossible dreams.

'Yes,' I said, without hesitation. 'She will like it very well.'

The house would be his gift to his bride, the ultimate statement of his protection and that of his family. It would be completely furnished, down to the last teaspoon. The cupboards would be filled with linens, the beds made, the kitchen equipped with pots, pans, kettle and toaster, the ashtrays in place in the majlis, books on the shelves and a row of tapes and videos waiting to be played. It would be the realised dream of a little girl who

received a perfect dolls' house and then found herself truly able to walk into it. Every picture, every plate, hers.

I sat on an upturned box, feeling the sweat beginning to trickle down my back. The air conditioning was not yet in place. I sat and began to count the cost in dirhams, then dollars, then pounds to the boy's father.

In their world it is not the father of the bride who digs into his pocket to pay for the wedding. It is the father of the groom. The cost rises with the status of the family until at Sheikh level a marriage involves a fortune - small or large - depending upon the size of the Sheikh's 'box'.

The 'box'? In the days before the oil men invaded the skin of their earth, the 'box' was truly an Arab's treasure box studded with nail-heads, bolted and locked to secure a man's wealth. Today the word 'box' can mean anything from a development bank - Al Sandook Al Naqd ('the box of money', translated literally) - to a reference to a Sheikh's largesse. 'He never once put his hand into his box all the years that I served him,' meaning he never gave me a gift of money, a bonus for service above and beyond the call of time.

In this instance, I knew the young man's father would have to dig deep into his box before the marriage was finally consummated and the bride brought home. But his 'box' was large. It would not constitute an insurmountable problem. It would be discussed with his men of business, arranged, an allowance made. The Sheikha would know what she could spend on gifts for her prospective daughter-in-law; the son would be given a budget for his bride house. There was no strain.

In Al Ain, in this little patch of paradise blossoming lushly from the fertiliser of a world petroleum market, there was no problem. If marriages were made on a bed of gold, here not one would fail, and in this case *noblesse oblige*. Largesse, largesse. I knew it would be a grand affair.

Even so, I don't believe I was prepared for the facts. For the months of preparation, for the finalising of the engagement, for the week of wedding 'fantasies', the great feasts and fabulous gifts. No. I definitely was not prepared.

We walked to the boy's mother's house where I would stay while we worked on the bride house. The compound seemed deserted without the women and children. Although a skeleton staff had been left behind to keep the houses dusted and secure and though there were more of us in the compound than the average Western home would see in a month, there was an air of loneliness, an awful stillness as though the heart had been removed from the body.

Our days were filled with long interviews with the architect, the plumb-

er, the electrician and the foreman builder. Work began at dawn, taking advantage of the hours before the sun grilled the earth and the earth in turn reflected its own massive heat.

It was all an oven to me. All twenty-four hours. I could not distinguish between the nuances of temperature, only the change in light. It was either white hot or black hot. The white hot burned. The black hot suffocated.

The men worked steadily on, taking long breaks at the height of the day. There was no union to be consulted, no time and a half or double time to be considered. The enormous pool of poverty in India, Pakistan, Bangladesh or Baluchistan made such social evolutions impossible. These men were grateful to be working at all, fearful that one foot out of place would end the cash flow that eventually found its way into some remote village on the other side of the Straits of Hormuz.

It seemed bizarre to be instructing a Baluch builder in the niceties of a fitted kitchen when the man would never have seen one, would never use one. It seemed bizarre to select a washing machine and an electric cooker for the use of some prospective young maid who was still sitting with her family in a Karachi or Lahore back street. I tried again and again to explain that an electric cooker needed a more powerful circuit than other equipment, but no-one would accept such an idea. If it worked on thirteen amps, that was all the proof needed. Three years and near a thousand fuses later it was changed to gas.

The balance of electricity was a mystery yet to be solved. Overloading circuits was a national pastime. Often at night that hot summer the new overburdened power plants would give up and die. Having kept too many new air-conditioning units going all day, they would be suddenly burdened by the lights of the night and would switch off, blacking out the whole town. We would sit in the majlis shocked by the sudden blackness, held in the sudden quiet. No AC to beat our eardrums. The peace was like balm. The moonlight welcome. Then the suffocating cloud, the heat would move in, weighing down the air and we would go outside hoping to be able to breathe more easily. Carpets and cushions would be ordered and we would sit in the hot stillness, our voices quiet, the half-English, half-Arabic clear on the heavy air.

Sometimes a little Indian maid would sit beside me, a lonely ghost left behind by the household. The young Sheikh and his friends would stretch themselves on the carpet around us, their white kandoras in the half-light of night making a scene of extraordinary beauty.

Eventually they would change into shorts and T-shirts and set off to run two or more miles around the outskirts of town.

'Why, my son, why?' I would ask. 'Why in this heat?'

'We must keep in condition.' He would smile and move off at a steady pace, his friends with him.

In condition? In condition for what? The tormenting life of the desert was over for him and his family. They would be protected from the heat by each new technological invention for creating a fridge in an oven. They would drive the fastest, most perfectly balanced cars, fly in the fastest planes, live cushioned by every facility purchasable by great wealth. In condition for what? What was he getting ready to battle? Was it a last stand against total urbanisation? Was he taking up the gauntlet against the subtle yet inevitable erosion such wealth would bring to the culture of his people? Or was some other vision haunting him?

As the years passed, I would watch his passion for adhering to the bedu principle remove him further and further from the society around him. His total disinterest in the machinations of money bewildered his brothers, his father and extended family. And yet, the circle of men around him grew. A strange circle - not all of one tribe or one nation, but ever-present, as though rubbing up against him would give them some strength.

Through it all his mother quietly and continually supported him and as the years passed we all began to realise that there were unforeseen, unimagined battles inexorably growing everywhere. We were all being pushed towards an unseen precipice. Had some inner clock warned that young Sheikh to 'come out and be separate' from the subtle softening of the new wealth?

That summer I could only think he was mad as he set off around the town and I dozed in the dark heat and stillness of the garden.

16

Fasting and Feasting in the Tide of Heat

R AMADAN ARRIVED WITH the inevitability of time. It arrived with its
promises of thirst and hunger allied to discipline and prayer. A battle
between the senses and the spirit. Our own son had practised Ramadan on
one of his trips to the Middle East 'just to see if I could do it'. He is always
ready for a challenge. He told me that the first three days were an agony,
thirst being the greatest torture, then slowly the body reversed its patterns
and you got used to it.

The fast is for 'a certain number of days' in the ninth month of the
Islamic year, the month in which the Qur'an was revealed to the Prophet
Mohamed. As the Islamic calendar has fewer days than the Gregorian and
there is no allowance for the imperceptible tilt of our spinning world, their
months are twenty-nine or thirty days long, never thirty-one. Therefore
their months seem to drift backwards through the seasons. An Arab can
never know the exact date of his birth according to our calendar, for if he
was born on 12th January, that day in the Muslim calendar might be 12th
January of the previous year by the time he was twenty or twenty-one,
owing to the shorter months. A birthday is a movable feast as the round
of years is wholly unrelated to the seasons. Indeed, the passage of years is
unmarked and unsung. Birthdays were once non-events. Now they are for
small children to celebrate occasionally. Time is, as always, irrelevant.

Ramadan too moves backwards through the seasons, through the years,
the period of the days depending upon the cycles of the moon.

From dawn to dusk, from the moment that the 'thread of day breaks the

blackness of night' until the sun is once again eclipsed by the horizon the fast is kept.

When the first day arrived, I watched the eyes of the boys grow darker. By mid-afternoon hunger and thirst had begun to plague them. Restless and dry-mouthed, they drove to the market to shop for odds and ends of food and drink as though the act of purchasing Pepsi Cola and crisps would somehow equate with eating and drinking them.

Returning, they piled their purchases against the wall of the family majlis 'for the evening'. A final sortie was made to the hotel for a large bowl of 'Bon Ali', a hot bread pudding. Steaming and giving off tormenting aromas, it sat on top of the television, waiting for Al Iftar, the call to break fast.

I was famished. One of the unwritten rules of non-Muslims who work or travel in Muslim countries is that you don't eat or drink in front of your fasting friends. I was continually with them. I had eaten little or nothing most of the day.

As we sat waiting for the last half-hour to grind away, the young Sheikh lifted the phone and telephoned his grandmother - his mother's mother, not Sheikha Grandmother, who was still on her visit to her daughter.

'Have you a small bowl of harees for Um Yusef?' he asked, after explaining when and how I had arrived, that he, and his family, and I and all the household were quite well. I could hear her scolding him for not having contacted her sooner, not having brought me to see her, asking whether I was safe, was someone with me, who was looking after me. He made monosyllabic replies and then repeated his request for a small bowl of harees.

Within twenty minutes a car drove up to the family majlis and began to unload a meal for us all. Harees was there along with a haunch of lamb, rice of various kinds, date mixtures, a lamb stew gently spiced, two thermos of fresh, cardamom-flavoured coffee and one of orange juice and a row of neat little red jellies, each carefully decorated and each in its own glass cup. I knew that Ramadan was a time for sharing and that shared feasts were not unusual, but the Sheikha's mother had surpassed herself. The fact that it had been brought to the family majlis was out of deference to me.

At that moment in time, in that place, with all the women away, I would eat in the family majlis. I could eat alone or the young son and his friends could join me, but I could not eat in the Sheikh's great majlis with the other men of the household. Not in Al Ain. A point of no return had been reached. How or when, I don't know. It arrived imperceptibly. Somehow, step by precarious step, I had been drawn over the invisible divide and was

145

now truly a part of the family hareem. Therefore I was bound by certain of its manners and rules. Not firmly bound. I was free to move back and forth. It took an almost superhuman intuition to know when it was right and proper to cross the divide. I made mistakes and sweated over them, but tried on the whole to err on the side of caution.

One thing was certain. In Al Ain I could not eat in the men's majlis. It was, in fact, never suggested, never a decision I had to think about.

That summer the maternal grandmother's gift of a Ramadan feast was brought without question to the family majlis, and the young Sheikh, his friends and I sat together for those last painful moments of the first day of Ramadan. We sat impatiently waiting, staring at the television like cats staring at a mousehole. The young Sheikh kept grumbling that the TV was wrong.

'My watch is correct. They are late. Always late,' he said.

Finally the call sounded. The 'Allahu Akhbar' was heard from every tower, on every wireless, on every television. 'Thanks be to God' was breathed through the air of the desert. Prayers were said, water was poured down parched throats, dates were devoured and the first Ramadan feast began.

'*Bismallah. Imshi, Imshi.* In the name of God. Let's go. Let's go.'

Breaking the fast had a sort of Thanksgiving Day quality about it, or a Harvest Supper. We sat cross-legged around the food, eating and eating until the meal was decimated. The Bon Ali, the jellies, the harees, the lamb were a jumbled mess in front of us. When the Indian maid and the house-boy were finally called to remove it all, we were satiated. I leaned back against the cushions feeling too full. The boys went off to say more prayers.

It is impossible for a non-Muslim to appreciate Ramadan. We watch bewildered as they turn night into day, criss-cross between self-denial and celebration. We resent the grinding down of business which is conducted at a snail's pace for twenty-eight days. Everything continues to operate after a fashion. Work carries on, but physically everything moves in slow-motion, like a cine-camera with insufficient power. Yet the spirit burns brighter. There is a friendliness, a companionship and general concern. Does man really need some battle to bring out his best qualities? An unpalatable thought.

We sat up late that night and other nights that hot summer in Al Ain, and the strain of Ramadan soon began to show in my young Sheikh's face. Lack of sleep, food bolted too quickly, the heat and the night jogging gave him a dark-eyed expression of endurance. I longed for the emotional and

social cushion of the hareem which would have softened the impact of the days. One English woman and a pint-sized Indian maid were quite useless.

Sometimes when the afternoon tide of heat reached its high mark, we would go over to the hotel. It had grown less incongruous as the town grew towards it. Even though I still imagined prehistoric fish swimming through its pergolas, the whole place now seemed almost natural, like a well-planned country club.

We would cross the marble floor of the lobby to reach the pool in the garden beyond. There the young Sheikh would swim back and forth, back and forth, in a controlled frenzy. Thin and weary, he would come out and drop exhausted in a chair beside me, his chest heaving.

'Too weak. Ramadan,' he would say and close his eyes as the hot air dried him in seconds and I retreated even further under the wilting greenery. The heat had gradually become an expected body blow which was endurable with certain rules. Don't move too quickly, hug the shade, breathe quietly. Though I'd learned that the black abaya dropped the temperature by degrees, and though I'd worn both veil and coat at various odd times, such as in storms, or in the desert heat, the sight of a European woman in such an outfit on an ordinary day in a compound or town would be more than anyone, including myself, could take. Long skirts in the middle of the day were acceptable when walking through the halls of Al Ain or Abu Dhabi hotels, but a blue-eyed English woman in black veils and coat? No. I didn't have the courage. So when we walked from the pool to the car I felt the whole impact of the sun. 'Next time, I'll bring a hat,' I said to myself. I always said it and always forgot.

The Sheikha's mother telephoned often to ensure that we were comfortable. Phone calls came continually from the hareem in Europe and from the Sheikh, but the family majlis was like an empty cup waiting to be filled. It was the first Ramadan the hareem had spent away from home and would be the last for many, many years.

'It is unnatural,' said the Sheikha when we met some months later. She explained that Ramadan was a time of reunion, of coming together to withstand the fast during the day and to share support during the night. 'It is a time to show God's care for us to each other,' she said. She said that it was a time for prayer and especially for prayers of protection against evil of any kind and, sending for her holy book, quoted me the following passage:

O you who believe.
Fasting is prescribed for you
as it was prescribed for those

before you, so that you may guard
(against evil)

Surrah 11, 183

I saw an example of the results of prayerful fasting when I visited Um Hamed one Ramadan a few years later. For a long time her hands, especially the tips of her fingers, had been covered in dreadful wart-like sores. One Ramadan day she had the sores; the following day they had disappeared. The skin of her hands was like that of a child.

'How?' I asked.

'Allah,' she answered. 'Prayer to Allah is always best, always the perfect way.'

In the hareem, prayer is as necessary to life as air to breathing, but in Ramadan it reaches to that depth of spirit where the inexplicable lies. It pulls out miracles small and large.

17

The Dower House
and the Dower

I DID NOT STAY to see the Eid - the Eid Al Iftr, that great feast of the breaking of the fast, the days of celebration when everyone dresses in new clothes as though the sackcloth of fasting has lifted and life has renewed itself once again. Leaving the heat and the nearly finished bride house, I returned to soak up the last of a cool, green English summer. Yet before the leaves had left the trees, I returned to Al Ain. The bride house had to be finished. It had to be furnished, decorated, equipped.

'But surely your mother would like to do these things for you?' I said on one of the many phone calls clogging the satellite links between the Gulf and London.

'No. She wants you to do it. You can shop. She cannot. And you promised.'

I had promised thinking it would be easy to order everything in England and ship it out. But there was no time. The Arab world is much like war. All hurry up and wait, hurry up and wait. This was a hurry up time. The wedding was only three months away.

So I returned.

'You will fix this house, Um Yusef?' the Sheikha asked as we sat in the family majlis, the small children tumbling over her lap like puppies, pushing themselves up for kisses, or simply basking on the warmth of her body.

'Surely this is for you,' I answered. 'It is a thing you would enjoy.'

She threw her head back both in laughter and to avoid a bump from one

of the children. I could see again her broad smile under her burgah. She quieted the children, offered me another coffee, then said, 'Come, Um Yusef. You know our ways. There is now so much work for me. And you can go here and there.'

I knew their ways. I knew her husband was away on one of the seemingly endless 'summit' conferences governments of the world, and especially the Arab governments, invent to try to keep our human condition in existence. While he was away her duties and responsibilities toward the household increased inevitably, and with the wedding growing nearer, she did indeed have 'much work'.

It was true that she would not enter a shop in her own country. Everything had to be brought to her. Catalogues of furniture, samples of carpets, of curtaining. She bought from pictures, hoping things would match. They rarely did. Drivers were sent for this or that and returned with something else. Sons would volunteer and rush off to the village to bring back a 'set of couches', proudly waiting for the praise which she would generously give, though they might not be quite what she expected.

'I will help you, provided you approve what we buy,' I said.

She agreed, so we began.

Furnishing the house was like a game of hunt the thimble, for the days of the fine shops in Abu Dhabi's Hamdan Street or in Dubai were yet to come. The furniture stores in the area at that time sold styles which were a cross between Blackpool and back street Soho.

The beds had to be seen to be believed. I shall never forget one which was proudly displayed in a dusty shop in Abu Dhabi. It had everything conceivable attached to it. Equipment was crammed into every corner. Television, cameras, telephones, flashing lights, mirrors, a round, fur-covered mattress. It was upholstered in red velvet.

'One night on that, my son, and you are in danger of electrocution,' I said to the young Sheikh as the unctuous Asian salesman waited.

'You think so, eh?' said the prospective bridegroom. 'I think it is lovely - very perfect,' and he took my hand to lead me out, rattling off some Arabic which was too fast for me to catch but not too fast for the friends with him. They burst into laughter and we piled once again into his car for another search.

We must have driven several thousand miles back and forth between Al Ain, Abu Dhabi and Dubai. Every warehouse, every shop, every market in the area was visited. Rumours of something new would send us rolling down the ever widening highways. Crates were opened, back rooms of small shops were searched, new rolls of carpeting unpacked.

The boy ransacked his father's stores for old guns, shields and spears which we hung in the entrance hall. A fine old wooden chest covered with intricate brass, nail-head designs was discovered, cleaned and placed in the hall. It created a flurry of disapproval among the women.

'It's too old, Um Yusef.'

'Have you seen the old *sandook* Um Yusef put in the entrance? We don't like these old things. That poor time is past.'

'You can't leave that old thing in the entrance, Sheikh. People will think we are poor.'

But slowly they began to reminisce.

'I had one like that when I married.'

'Mine was bigger, of course, and much more beautiful.'

'Look inside, Um Yusef, this is where the perfume was kept and the sandalwood. And I had a little silver box for my jewels.'

'And the dresses here and the abaya here. My abaya had more gold then than now.'

Eventually they got used to it and allowed it to stay. Today a chest like this costs a small fortune if you can find one.

As the rooms filled, the Sheikha came to give her approval, to suggest a need or bring some treasure. Her personal wedding gift to her son was a magnificent carpet which was spread in the small majlis, a room in the tahat or sitting down tradition with cushions lining the walls. His father brought home his own gift of another fine example of the natural, undyed wool carpets of Tunisia.

These were their personal gifts to him, but the bride dower, without which there would be no wedding, plus the week of celebrations were a family affair. They were a display of one family's ability to look after the treasure of another family, treasure as represented by one carefully protected, carefully prepared girl.

Steeped in the Qur'an and its disciplines, filled from early childhood with tribal traditions, with the manners and morals of her heritage, she was indeed like the green pod of the date palm, a promising treasure, and a valuable asset. She had left school now, relinquishing her top place to the number two in the class. She left without a murmur although she had only a year and a half to go to complete her secondary education. In the West, she would no doubt have gone on to pass 'A' levels or the baccalaureate with enough marks to ensure a place at university and then perhaps a career in law or medicine, banking or politics. She had the neat, clipped mind of the good student. In Arabia she would obey the wishes of her father and marry at barely fifteen. She would be a mother at sixteen. Extraordinary?

Not in their life.

Did the prospect of such an early marriage, of leaving school and cutting off her education disappoint the Al Ain bride-to-be? Was she unhappy? Not at all. Indeed she had an air of conspiratorial joy. Her generous, rather humorous mouth and heavily fringed eyes held a scarcely hidden excitement. She was the centre of attention - like all brides. Her mind was filled with all sorts of romantic images - like all brides.

The fact that she hadn't seen her prospective husband since she was ten was neither here nor there. She had known him then and she knew his reputation now. He was handsome, she was told. In fact, she knew it, for a picture of him had been smuggled to her.

This smuggling of pictures is done by some close friend or relative. The women turn a blind eye. The picture is kept secretly and shown only to those who have a close heart and mouth. Now they each had a picture which they examined and re-examined, trying to breathe life into the two-dimensional image.

Her mind was filled with fears and hopes, the principal one being the same for her as for him. Would they 'go together'? Here was the gamble. Here was the game of chance in a society forbidden such games. Would each have the patience to continue the play, the will to make it work for them? Would they be willing to lose a little as well as win a little as the days added up to years? The odds are scarcely different in their world from ours. Even though the custom of parental arrangement seems so strange, so disaster prone, to them it is the only way. For the girls it is an unassailable tradition.

If a girl married without her parents' consent, she would risk abandonment by family and tribe. In some parts of Muslim society she would be in danger of her life.

In Al Ain, where the women have their own unique, independent spirit, there is little temptation to break the bounds, especially among the Sheikh families. They are secure in their roles and the young are generally simply marking time until they step into the marriage shoes waiting for them.

Among the tribes there are exceptions. I know girls who vow they will never marry. Their devotion is to education. They will not move out of the tradition in manner or moral, but will only marry higher education and will search for some way to use it. Often brilliant, they live in a rarified atmosphere of books, bewildering their parents and grandparents whose plans for such daughters have to be abandoned. Could they be forced to marry? It has been known, but parents who do such a thing are as disliked as they would be in any society, and such marriages are often barren. The

girl is eventually divorced and will return to her parents and her first love. These are the exceptions, the rare exceptions, for the contract of marriage is still the passport to distaff power and still greatly desired.

The fact that the bride and groom are usually wedded long before they are bedded is considered the height of wisdom. What good businessman would hand over even the engagement dower without signing and sealing a contract? Cold? Calculating? Remember that a fortune can be represented in these brides and they themselves are very conscious of their own value.

It is at the handing over of the engagement dower that the mothers finally meet face to face - or burgah to burgah. Not that they haven't known each other usually for years, but such formality has its necessary place, for there are again the exceptions. There are instances when tribal nation will marry outside tribal nation, when a Baniyas will marry an Al Thani, or an Awamir will marry a Manasir. The mothers may not have met in years, if at all, in spite of their knowing each other's family history.

Therefore this first formal meeting of the mothers is most important. It sets the standard, welcomes the bride into a new hareem and displays the promise of wealth the groom and his family have to offer. The mother of the groom may also ask to see the bride and she will be taken off to a remote room in the bride's house, away from the eyes of other members of her hareem, for the bride is in strict purdah for the coming wedding.

Before these meetings of the mothers, there will have been a party at the home of the groom. A party for women who are close friends and relatives of both mothers. Though I missed the engagement party of my young Sheikh, I attended another a few years later. It was a happy affair. Long rolls of oil cloth had been laid on the floor of the women's dining majlis the previous night. There was room for about fifty women sitting comfortably on either side of the cloth. Plates of fruit and bowls of fresh dates edged the 'table', boxes of kleenex were placed conveniently every few feet along the carpet.

'Napkins,' laughed a young wife to me the following day. She had helped to prepare the table.

By ten o'clock on the day of the party the 'table' was loaded with food. Round bowls full of thareed were interspersed with platters of whole mashwi lambs. There were bowls of harees, of bilaleet and platters of the big, round, paper-thin mahala pancakes. Stacks of cinnamon bread, bowls of butter and honey, glasses of buttermilk. It was a breakfast to end all breakfasts.

The hareems, including ours, started to arrive about 9.30 and we drifted

into the women's majlis dressed in our best. The glint of diamanté or pearl-embroidered dresses could be seen under black veils. I watched as my veiled friends chatted busily to each other or rose to greet some relative, touching burgah to burgah, then fluttered down again like so many birds of paradise. Coffee was passed. The smoke of a dozen incense pots filled the room. Perfume was offered, the long gold dipsticks wiped on veils and thumbs, skirts and wrists. Glasses of fresh orange juice appeared on trays and then more coffee. Finally the last expected guest had arrived.

Then came the procession. Down through the garden came servants and foster daughters carrying the cases of engagement presents and the engagement jewels. They ulayed the whole way, that strange, high, trembling sound filling the compound and filling the heart with an eerie excitement.

They arrived with a flourish, laid the cases on the floor, opened them and dragged them around the room to be oh'd and ah'd over by the guests. The engagement jewels were displayed in a case of red velvet, a magnificent set of rubies. Beside them was a thick wad of thin notes. At a guess the bundle was about six inches deep. I didn't look at the denomination but there was no doubt it would have been high. Other cases held length after length of cloth which would be worked into dresses, over-dresses and the embroidered underpants of the bride's trousseau.

After this grand display, we all drifted towards the breakfast 'table', and as at any good party, the guests sat at table for a considerable time. Then back to the majlis for coffee again, and home in time for noon prayers.

The hostess's work, however, had only begun. The remains of the feast, which were considerable, were then packed into bowls and on to trays, covered with foil and distributed to another thirty or so houses. The drivers piled them into cars and drove off to return shortly for another load. If those who have been to Arab feasts ever wonder what happens to all that food and 'tut-tut' over the waste, forget it. Not an ounce is wasted. Everyone in the immediate area gets a present of food and the following day other little presents of cake or Arabic sweet are often sent in return as a thank you.

Shortly after the breakfast party, perhaps the same evening, perhaps the next morning, the bridegroom's mother would make her way to the home of the bride carrying the first load of treasure. In the past, the engagement jewels were often bracelets. For the wealthy there were gold bracelets weighed by the market gold merchants and purchased according to weight and the going price of gold, not according to design. For the less wealthy, there were silver bracelets, often wrought and hammered from the large, heavy, Maria Theresa silver dollars which once flooded the area. These

Austrian coins first entered trade in the mid-eighteenth century. Beautifully designed and minted, the silver pieces were used as the preferred exchange in southern Arabia and down the East African coast until as recently as the 1970s. They often found their way around the Gulf, worked out of recognition, into coffee pots, jewel boxes and jewellery.

Jewellery has always been the Arabian woman's cash box. They are her insurance, her financial independence, so they are worn in abundance, discussed without shame, admired or discarded, and sold. Imitation jewellery is regarded with disdain. Better coined silver than imitation gold. Better no pearls than imitation pearls. Many believe that because foreign women wear 'fashion' jewellery they have no knowledge of precious stones, true gold or silver. Jewels are a woman's deposit account.

The engagement jewellery of our bride was to be a set of emeralds. The necklace, bracelet, ring and earrings were displayed in a tan chamois leather box. They had been selected from a pile of 'sets' which the Second Son had gleaned from the finest merchants in Abu Dhabi and brought to the Sheikha. She had examined each one carefully, discarding then re-examining until she was satisfied that the gift was rich enough without being ostentatious, that the stones, the colours, were right for the girl. This set would be just a taste of what was to come in the wedding dower, a tantalising taste of the jewels that would eventually be showered on the bride.

At the Second Son's 'engagement party', the gifts were handed from mother to mother with complete joy and satisfaction. This was a match carefully made. This was a match that had a chance.

There are other stories. Sad stories of fathers making fortunes out of their pretty daughters by marrying them off to antiquated old men again and again as their husbands wither and die, leaving them with fortune after fortune. Because the dower is always settled on the bride and her family either in kind or in cash or both, it has inevitably led to the stigma of 'selling and buying', to stories of a girl going to the highest bidder. Avarice is one of our more disgusting human failings. No nation has a monopoly on it.

What needs to be understood here is the norm. The abnormal can be left, for news of it will inevitably rise like a suppurating boil. In Al Ain, as everywhere, fathers normally look for the happiness of their children and hope for a compatible, genial match. If love eventually grows, so much the better. To us the whole process is upside down. To us the flood of romantic love should be searched for and found before marriage. In Arabia they throw the dice in the other direction. The match is made first. Two unknowns are cast together.

Once her engagement was announced, our bride began to wear very sober dresses, black relieved by the smallest pattern. If she went out it was at night and she would arrange her veils so that they covered her face four times. Her veil and abaya, far heavier than normal, seemed to turn her whole figure into a sort of black pillar which, unless it moved, had neither front nor back. She entered a cocoon from which a butterfly would emerge on the wedding night.

The month before the wedding, she was not only in complete purdah, but was involved in one long beauty session as well. A blue powder was dusted inside the jodhpur-like underwear. Another orange powder was dusted over the upper part of the body. These were to soften and whiten the skin. Her hair was heavily oiled, perfumed and washed again and again in a henna mixture. Henna patterns were made on her hands. The soles of her feet were dyed with henna, making a brown sandal.

As well as powdering herself with the same orange and blue skin-whitening powders which her mother and grandmother had used, our bride asked maids and foreign Arab friends to search out modern creams and perfumes to be tried and kept, tried and discarded.

Most of her purdah days were spent in these beauty treatments, perfuming and powdering. Other days were spent in cleaning and decorating the bedroom where she would receive her bridegroom. The young women of the hareem, her foster sisters, cousins and young aunts scurried around her much as they do in any society, running errands, advising, gossiping.

Dresses made from the gifts of cloth were designed by the bride and her mother and worked swiftly by a local tailor. As the tailor never saw his subject, it always amazed me how well the dresses fitted. Measurements were taken and delivered along with a very roughly drawn sketch. Back would come a creation which could, in some instances, be worn with impunity in front of the most discerning fashion couturier.

All this currying and caring for the body, for its clothing and for the marriage room went on day after day until the wedding night finally arrived. Only then would the bride wash off her many powders and oils with the help of her mother. She would be dressed in a new cotton serwal with its inches of gold and silver thread at the ankle. Her dress, heavily embroidered in traditional design, would be overlaid by an equally ornate *thoab* or over-dress. A bridal cap of gold would be placed on her head, its intricately woven strands of gold dripping down her back as though the weaver had spilled the threads of his loom. These were wound in and out of her long hair. Around her neck would be placed a bib of gold which reached to her waist. There would be gold wrist and ankle bracelets and a gold ring for

each finger and toe, each claiming its own traditional design. She would shimmer and sparkle. She would be a gold-wrapped parcel, hard and shining on the outside, soft and tempting on the inside.

Over all, layer after layer of black veil would be placed, so that the bridegroom would have to unwrap his treasure bit by bit.

In most areas of the Arab world these complex and costly fashions have now been replaced by the white, Western bridal dress. The bride parades in a creation from Frankfurt, London or New York. The veil, the train, the imitation orange blossom are all there and are to me wholly incongruous. Perhaps in the hotels of Cairo or Beirut these Christian customs are not so out of place. But in the desert, a white bridal gown, born out of a Christian church procession, looks strange indeed.

I knew that such modern ideas would not be countenanced in this establishment hareem of Al Ain, however. There, at that time, the traditions would still be meticulously followed. The bride might have been educated, might have travelled, might speak English well, but she would wear gold and henna, she would dress and look the part of an Al Ain bride.

18

The Stage is Set

I WALKED THROUGH THE bride house, checking the rooms. In five days the wedding would begin. The boy had already moved into the house, into the new master bedroom with its white carpets and pale blue couch. The young bridegroom and I had arrived the previous week after yo-yoing between England and the Gulf all autumn. This time we had come loaded down with things for the house. Towels, sheets, pillows, waste paper baskets, kitchen equipment and a Wedgwood tea set, our family's gift to the young bride and groom.

I had brought fine Swiss linen from London for the massive blue bed which we eventually found in Dubai. He never used the bed, though, preferring to sleep on his palliasse on the floor.

'It is too soft. My back aches from it,' he said.

When I packed his clothes for the move, they hardly filled one case. A pile of white kandoras, another pile of the sarong underwear which doubled as pyjamas, a few pairs of briefs, one swimsuit, a collection of football togs, and a pile of neatly folded white head scarves. These, along with one pair of football boots, a new pair of Italian sandals and a navy blue blazer which I had bought for him in London, completed the wardrobe. Now they were carefully resting on the shelves of the new clothes cupboards. They looked lonely and uncomfortable. A monkish, puritanical collection compared to the explosion of wealth waiting for the bride.

As I folded away the new sheets and towels, the Sheikha arrived with Hussa. They brought a large brass tray with an ornate, decorative brass

coffee pot and small brass cups to place on the low table in front of the blue couch in the bride's bedroom. The bridegroom followed with a heavily tarnished silver candelabra and an equally tarnished silver and gilt coffee pot gleaned from his father's stores. Both were fine pieces, but the Sheikha insisted they were not silver because they had gone black. All the silver they had ever known came from those Maria Theresa dollars which no doubt had enough nickel in them to keep the silver from tarnishing easily. No amount of insistent persuasion on my part would convince her. We put the pieces in the kitchen and I made a silent vow to polish them.

The Sheikha and Hussa walked through the rooms, checking this and checking that, commenting on the colours of the curtains, admiring the candlewick bedspreads in the second bedroom, something quite new to them. Finally they settled themselves on the couch in the master bedroom. The bridegroom and I had followed them like children waiting for secret crumbs of comfort. Now we perched ourselves on the foot of the bed and hoped for praise. It came.

'Congratulations, my son, it is a beautiful house and thank you, Um Yusef, thank you. Now it is time for you to move in here to stay.'

Hussa added her words of approval and the boy and I soaked them up like two dry sponges. Then the rest of her sentence caught me.

Move in? Me? I thought she was joking but she wasn't. It was unbelievable. How could I play gooseberry on a honeymoon? It was ridiculous. I pleaded with the boy. 'But you will want to be alone for these weeks.'

He was as amazed at my surprise as I was at the suggestion.

'Why? She will want company. She will be all alone without her mother and friends. She is very young. You must stay with us to talk to her, to sit with her. You must stay to make her welcome.'

All of them tried to explain, bewildered at my bewilderment. Finally the boy added in some desperation, 'But this is your room, Um Yusef. We always said so.'

When I tried to tell them that in the West it would be impossible for anyone, no matter how close, to sit in on a honeymoon, they quietly reminded me that this was not the West. The Sheikha asked me to remember her eldest son's wife when she was first married. Though she was now a most serene young mother, having given birth to a beautiful baby girl, the first days of her marriage had been another story. She had fluttered around her home like a captured bird, not knowing where to settle. The Sheikha had kept her surrounded by her new sisters-in-law, new aunts and new friends in a concerted effort to keep her from being homesick, but it was a long time before that bird stopped fluttering at the slightest move.

The Sheikha and Hussa watched me remembering, watched me as the reality of the position slowly penetrated. No, this was not the West. The boy and girl, the bride and groom would meet as strangers. Though the bride would travel less than half a mile to her new home, it might just as well be a thousand miles. Her whole centre would change traumatically.

Still, I held back, held on to what I knew.

'Come,' said the boy, 'we will ask my grandmother. If she says you must, you must.' Sheikha Grandmother was the final arbiter of all things, so everyone seemed thoroughly content to leave the matter to her wisdom. I felt certain, however, that the whole thing was now a foregone conclusion, and I was right.

When we went to see Sheikha Grandmother that evening, we found her sitting straight-backed on the carpet of her big majlis, a very small person in a very large room with her servant and Shama beside her. Kicking off our sandals at the door, murmuring our salaams, we entered. The boy kissed her forehead and then we sat cross-legged opposite her. Coffee was sent for and with a few preliminaries - remarkably few - the grandson put the question.

Sheikha Grandmother's eyes looked straight into mine as he spoke. With Sheikha Grandmother I often felt the awkward foreigner blundering into forbidden areas. The chasm between her experience and mine was vast. The barrier of language, religion, manner was high. What basis of mind meeting mind could there be between this devout, brilliant old lady and me? She who had never left Arabia. I who never stayed at home. We were phenomena to each other. Respected phenomena, but phenomena.

Her decision was immediate. There wasn't a flicker of her eyes and it landed me squarely in the soup.

'She must. Must. There is no question. She must stay in the house now and for at least two weeks after. A month would be better.'

Judgement had been pronounced. By going to arbitration I had only lengthened the days of my visit. There was no further debate. I moved into the second bedroom.

Watching me unpack seemed to give the boy enormous pleasure. 'This is truly your room now,' he said. 'You will be with us always here. This is your home now.'

Although Arabs are prone to purple passages, to over-generous use of words declaring that this is your home, he is your son, she is your daughter, after a while, as in all relationships, you get to know which have real meaning and which are politeness. This, I knew, was said from the heart.

'And you can have a hot bath like in London,' he added.

Ah. Now the truth was out. When the house was being built he had made a great fuss about the hot-water taps. He had made the plumber pull them all out and replace them so that the tubs would fill well for hot baths.

'Why?' said the plumber. 'You will only use the shower.'

This was true. Neither he nor his wife would ever use the bath, only the shower. It is against the teachings of the Qur'an to 'sit in your own dirt'.

'Fix it,' said the young Sheikh with a remorseless command. 'Fix it.'

It was fixed. A bath was possible. A bath for 'the English'. This had been his plan and I basked in the welcome. Feeling doubly at home, I settled in quickly.

My room was huge by our standards, about twenty feet wide and thirty feet long. Two large windows looked out on a dry expanse of sandy earth which ended in the compound wall. I had insisted on window 'nets' as well as curtains. The flimsy white nylon stuff drifted pleasantly against the windows, breaking the harsh light.

The room was carpeted in a shag pile. Soft, thick and white, it welcomed bare feet. One wall held a long row of wardrobes with their modern fittings. Another had a group of modern Italian chairs and a couch. There was a twin bed unit surrounded by shelves and drawers and between the windows a dressing table with a neat square mirror and cane chair.

I laid out my things. A jar of hand cream, a box of face powder, cleansing cream, a square box of Chanel No 5. Pictures of my family, my books and note pads went on the shelves by the bed. My long skirts were hung in the wardrobe. My suitcase was put away for the first time in all my visits.

This room was to become as familiar as that of my own house. I can see every part of it in my mind's eye, feel the carpet under foot. I know the foibles of the ventilators in the bathroom, the difficulty of replacing bulbs in the high ceiling. Its welcome waits for me sometimes for weeks, more often now for years, but it is always there.

In those first days, when the boy and I were alone in the house, we would spend long hours talking, planning, wondering what the next week, the next year, would bring. Though the wedding occupied nearly every moment of his thoughts, there were other corners of his mind which continually revealed themselves. He saw the eyes of the world focussed on his people, his place; saw the infection of greed, the worship of size.

'We are so small a people. Very few. Like ants that the big birds pluck and eat. They eat us whole and we slide down the gullet, enjoying the view.'

'What can you do about it? You can't just sit there and be swallowed,' I said.

He laughed and grabbed my hand, 'I think you are one of the few who

does not want to see us digested by these birds. What can we do? Nothing. Wait. Be as you have to be and wait.'

'Wait for what?' I asked.

'Time. You don't know us, Ummi, my English mother. We are very good at waiting. Also very good at dying, I think,' and his eyes went dark.

Often these days his eyes went dark from nervous and physical exhaustion. He slept less and less. In the afternoons he would lie down to try to rest, then get up and roam around the house.

'Didn't you sleep at all?' I'd ask and the answer would come back, 'I slept with my eyes but not with my heart.'

We would get into the ever-waiting sports car and drive over to the wedding ground which was directly outside the bride's compound wall. The place drew him like a magnet.

There, all was activity. An area of about twenty acres of dusty desert floor had been cleared and marked out by poles with vertical neon lights. Coloured 'fairy' lights looped from pole to beam. Hewn scrub trees were piled against the high, sand-coloured walls of the bride's compound, their knobbly branches and twisted trunks grey and dry. They were waiting to be chopped for the fires, the cooking fires for the massive copper cauldrons with their blackened outsides and polished insides, cauldrons which were big enough to hold two butchered camels.

Some fifty cooks milled around making preparations for feeding the thousands of expected guests. A wedding is a party to which all may come. There are no gate crashers. The hospitality is complete. Furthermore, the wedding of a Sheikh is something special. It is not only a party, it is an entertainment, a festival, an open air festival of music and dance, a feast for tribe and town.

The entertainers come from the local community, from neighbouring Emirates, from the inner desert, and these days from as far away as Beirut, Damascus, Baghdad or Cairo. Today it is fashionable to fly in at great cost singers whose names are as well known to the Arab as Cliff Richard or Dionne Warwick are in the West.

At that time, in that place, however, the practice of having modern music was in its infancy. Folk musicians, classicists and traditional dancers still performed without adulterating their arts and every facility was provided to make them as comfortable as possible.

As each entertainer arrived with several members of his family, the problems of accommodation and feeding became ever more enormous. Or so it seemed to me. But this was another world. Hospitality on this scale was a tradition. For centuries great caravan trains had arrived, been

accommodated and moved on. The wedding of a Sheikh had always been an event. Now, as then, tents were pitched. Now, as then, the voices of men called to each other as the poles went up and the black wool or the new white canvas unfolded and luffed in the wind. Pegs were driven swiftly and securely, carpets unrolled, small fires made and families settled down. The only new notes were the lights and the stage.

Yes, a stage. It looked incongruous standing out there in the middle of nowhere, nudged by the odd, straying camel, bypassed by sheep and goats, admired by shepherds and traders. It stood in splendour on the far side of the wedding ground. A roofed and backed stage. A small theatre. Beautifully constructed, with balustraded steps, the whole inner back was wallpapered in white regency stripes as if straight out of some Noel Coward revue. It would be the envy of any provincial performing company in the West, but it would live for only one night and then be torn down and discarded. It was built for the final night of celebration when a modern Arabian orchestra would perform, backing a few well-known young singers. When the celebrations were over the whole theatre would disappear. For one night only modern love songs would wind out over a massive crowd, some seated on folding chairs, some - the Sheikhs - on couches and some on the desert floor.

Leading up to this climax were three nights and four days of continual performance by the traditional musicians and dancers. On the fifth day there would be the women's party and on the fifth night the boy would finally go to his bride.

'It's a good stage, eh?' said the bridegroom.

'Marvellous,' I answered.

While he turned to argue with the foreman on some point of construction, I walked back across the wedding ground to the bride's home and pushed my way through a door in the closed gates of the bride's compound. A sleepy guard sat on a chair, tilting back against the wall of his guard hut. His old face was wrinkled with smiles. He made an effort to rise, but I gestured to him to sit still and he dozed off again in a half sleep, waiting for the toot of one of his master's cars. At that sound, he'd scurry around to open the gates which were never normally shut. Now they were shut against the bridegroom.

Inside the compound walls an area the size of two ballrooms was being covered by a sort of pergola. Poles supported cross-beams which were in turn overlaid with fresh green palm leaves. Here the women would meet on the final wedding day. Here the great *maksar*, the ladies' party would be held, the great feast prepared by the groom's mother but held within the

compound of the bride. Here the dower treasure would be displayed and given. I watched as fresh palm fronds created an area of shade and beauty. I felt an urge to visit the bride's mother, but resisted it, knowing that such a visit would only cause confusion on these busy days. They would feel I must see the bride, but this would break tradition. So I turned and walked out of the bride's gate and back to where the bridegroom continued to gesticulate with the foreman.

My old friend and guide Abed had joined them. Abed, who had taken me climbing up the Jebel Hafeet on my first visit, had assumed his role of general major domo to the Sheikh and was busy directing operations. In any other part of the world everyone would worry whether the whole thing would be rained off, but here it would be dry always - nearly always. And if, in this cool, pleasant winter season, God did send a little rain, it would come and go so quickly that it wouldn't matter. Just a welcome blessing for the parched skin of men and earth.

As we stood talking to Abed and debating with the foreman, the bridegroom's father drove up in his big Mercedes, two of his men with him. He parked the car with a neat flourish, got out and walked toward us.

What is there about a true Sheikh that gives him that air of authority? He walked with his straight back, whipping his thin cane against the dust, his men on either side. He wore an immaculate, almost pristine kandora. His black beard was trimmed with the precision of a surgeon's knife. His expression was totally impassive.

His son greeted him quickly. Nose to nose.

'My father.'

The Sheikh greeted me, 'Welcome, Um Yusef. Welcome, mother of Yusef and mother of this son.'

He laughed and his face broke into light. He said that I would now be known as the mother of this son of his as well.

We stood together in the cool afternoon, watching the carpenters and electricians, the tent poles being erected, the trucks arriving with stores, the water trucks. His eyes missed nothing. This was his show. His people, his tribe would gather to celebrate. His peers, the Sheikhs of other tribes would come to honour the son. It was important that they came. It was a seal, a mark of alliance. Such an affair would show the strength of the man. A wedding had a thousand hidden meanings.

After inspecting the stage and settling the dispute with a short sharp sentence - no one argued - he went on to inspect the tents, the lights and even the cooking compound with its newly fenced slaughter area. Giving

a curt nod, he walked back to the car, and drove off, raising clouds of dust. We followed at only a slightly more leisurely pace.

19

Of Fantasy, Waltzing and Drums

THE CALL OF the muezzin woke me. High, singsong, persistent, penetrating the subconscious. It pulled me out of some night dream into
the day, the first day of the wedding.

I padded across the new carpet to the window to watch the sky change
from dark to light and to add my own prayers to those of the women in the
compound. 'Where one or two are gathered together.' I was only one
Christian in this place, but we all honoured the one God, Creator, Mind.
We were all unquestionably thinking one thought - that this day, this
marriage would go well.

I went back to bed hoping sleep would come again but there was too
much anticipation in the air, so I rose, showered, dressed, made my bed and
went into the new kitchen to make a cup of tea. The blue-tiled floor was
cold on my bare feet. The electric kettle was waiting, shining. I filled it
with bottled mineral water and waited for it to boil. Reaching down a new
Wedgwood mug from the wall cupboard, I made my tea adding condensed
milk from a new tin, then placed the tin in the quietly humming fridge.

'Good morning.' The bridegroom stood in the majlis door.

'Good morning. Did you sleep well?'

'No.' His eyes were getting dark circles.

'You will have a cup of tea?'

'Please.'

We sat quietly drinking them.

'My father will want me very early. Later I will come for you and we will

166

go over there.' He gestured in the direction of the wedding ground. 'They are already coming. Some are there.'

He looked around the room, checking each detail with his eyes.

'It is a good house, eh?'

'The best in Al Ain,' I assured him.

He got up and started to pace about the room.

'Stop,' I said. 'You are as bad as my own son. Always walking, walking in the house like lions in cages. Sit, or dress and go.'

My son was a renowned pacer and would walk round and round our kitchen table with tea mug in one hand and newspaper in the other. Now this Arab 'son' was adopting the same dizzy habit. Wordlessly he walked out of the room to return ten minutes later in a freshly laundered white silk kandora, his short hair still damp from the shower. A clean, new suffra was in his hand. He shook it out, folded it in a triangle and placed it on his head, pulling the two ends sharply down in front to make them even. Then he snapped the black circlet over the top, its long tails swinging at the back of his head. He adjusted the front peaks of the suffra so that they were neat and sharp.

Finally, he picked up a white jacket I hadn't seen. The morning was cool.

'Whose coat?'

'My brother's.'

'It fits well. You look very Sheikh.'

He opened the front door and was gone.

A few hours later, true to his word he came to collect me. 'Hurry, hurry, they are starting already.'

As I scuffed my feet into sandals, the deep, urgent sound of drums began. I held on to the door, not quite believing the moment. The courtyard with the servants moving steadily back and forth, the gleaming sports car, humming and waiting, the immaculate Sheikh, the new house which belonged in this other world, which inside and out was as different from their old homes as a kandora from a business suit. And now over all, coming through that endless blue sky, the sound that speaks to the primitive in all of us. Drums. Deep, dark, impassioned drums.

I stepped into the car. As we passed through the gates I saw the flags. All the gates flew flags. The gates of the bride's compound, the gates of the groom's compound. Every truck carrying stores. Every car. Flags of the nation, flags of the tribe. An announcement to all, to everyone that a wedding had begun. Come. You are welcome.

The wedding ground was coming alive. Fires had been lit under the great cooking pots which were now beginning to steam as the cooks stirred the

contents with paddles as long as oars. One man leapt about his cauldron in a leather pilot's hat from the Lindbergh era, its grotesque ear flaps whipping across his face as he danced around his pot.

Store trucks stood by with sacks of rice, spices and vegetables. The newly erected hardboard fence screened a small herd of sheep and a handful of young camels, all waiting for the quick thrust of the knife.

Near the tents were smaller fires. Men sat around heating the skins of their drums, tuning them, tapping them, listening to each change of sound as the warmth tightened them.

In the centre of the area, a tall, thin, dark-skinned drummer sat on a rickety folding chair. In front of him was an upturned, cut-down oil barrel covered in a taut drumskin. His arms rose and fell, muscles tensed. This was the drum that would out-sing all the others and he was its slave. They were bound together. On this, the first day, the sounds were strong but contained. By the last day they would reach a near insanity of passion. Around him moved a piper blowing endlessly into a brass horn with a long, thin shaft. He created the notes of his song with his mouth, rarely stopping to breathe, pulling the air into his lungs through his nostrils, storing it in his cheeks as a squirrel would store nuts, then pressing it out into the horn all in one continuous movement. His song was pleading, haunting.

Behind him a row of male dancers moved, undulating. Around and around the drum they moved, making a central whirlpool of sound and movement about which other dancers and singers would make satellite circles with their own traditions. The drummer, the piper, the circling dancers were the Lawa.

By the evening the whole area was a mass of movement. At the far end, a group of Manahil had arrived. Their leader was an elderly man with a long, half-hennaed beard which gave him a piratical look. Their traditional dance was a strange waltz. A woman with a dark green velvet dress was invited into the ring. While the men clapped and sang she moved forward, her skirts blowing in the wind, her masked face covered with a costly, gold-embroidered veil. A relative held one of her hands and they circled together in ever swifter steps, around and around while other couples joined them. If the man was not a relative he would move with her without touching her. They would waltz together but not together, steps matching, facing one another, two faintly magnetised beings.

In another area long lines of men faced each other. Arms around each other's waists, they moved in slow, unified steps, singing together. Suddenly they would bow, bending in complete concord, then the song would continue. An answering song. First one side then the other would take up

the theme, praising God, extolling the virtues of the Prophet, repeating verses of advice from the Qur'an. Was I watching a stem from the same root of the great answering Psalms? Probably.

Beyond them, near the door of the bride's gate, an old man sat on the desert floor strumming a primitive harp. Heavily decorated with silver and gold thread and bobbles of coloured wool which shook when he played, the harp had a round leather sound box at the bottom apex of its triangle rather than at the side. Its five strings were made of finely cut skin rather than gut. On either side of him were drummers, one a man, one a woman. They sat on the sand, their drums tilted and half buried to muffle the sound. A fourth member of the group had tied a strange girdle around his hips. It was covered in dangling, dried sheepskin cups cut from the joint just above the hoof. As he moved his hips in rhythm with the drums, he made a tympany sound. The drummers began their muffled beat, the dancer shook his tympany cups and the old man at the harp began to sing as he played, his thin voice reaching cleanly into the air.

In a far corner of the ground was the strangest group of all. A group of men called the Dan who came from nowhere and went to nowhere. They gathered out of the desert to attend great weddings, for their role was unique. In their half and half world they were the only men trusted to enter the women's wedding party. These men would guard the bride's treasure, display it and dance for the women at the maksar, the ladies' party. In the days preceding the maksar, they would dance sensuously, endlessly, here in their corner, drums beating. They never wore the black braided circlet above their head scarf. Most were large men but their black faces had a soft, feminine look. There were several women with them, masked and veiled. To care for them? Or were they in turn daughters of Lesbos?

A man stepped on to the coconut matting which made their dance floor. He began to move up and down holding his head-dress like a woman, rolling his hips and eyes. A young Sheikh standing with his men, watching, gave some money to a servant and sent him on to the 'floor'. He moved around the dancer mocking, laughing, the money held in his teeth, defying the dancer to come and take it. They moved together, shouts from the spectators urging them on. The dancer lunged and took the note in his mouth, the servant leapt out to hilarious laughter and the dance went on.

Near the rows of tents which had been erected to house incoming tribes, another tight circle of singing, clapping men held protective guard over a group of little girls, all in their very best dresses, all carefully washed and polished, all without veils, their unbraided hair brushed to shine but still retaining the wave-marks of their normal daily braids. Now it flowed over

169

their shoulders, thick, black as kohl. They danced. They danced slowly, slowly, their hands lifting their dresses as daintily as Victorian belles, their shoulders and hips moving in a childish imitation of adult flirtation. Then they began to swing their heads, the long black hair whipping around them. Here was the origin of what was to be seen again and again on future Gulf television as this traditional folk dance was adopted by professionals. I stood, fascinated, held by the innocence of the little child-women. Their ages ranged from perhaps six to eleven. None had reached puberty. They were 'allowed' to be seen. They were the daughters of dancers who were the daughters of dancers and so on into some distant past.

The young friend who had been assigned to care for me while the bridegroom attended to his duties laughed at my almost gaping interest.

'It is good, *zein, la?*' His English was littered with Arabic.

'*Zein*, good, marvellous,' I answered. My Arabic was littered with English.

A sudden commotion stirred behind us as the crowd parted good-humouredly to calls of 'Where is the English? Have you seen the English one? The English mother?'

The familiar figure of the bridegroom's younger brother, the Youngest Son, made its way towards us.

'You must come. You must come quickly with me. The Sheikhs have come.'

He caught my hand to lead me toward the centre of the ground. The Sheikh, the host of this fantastic affair, was welcoming carloads of men, his bridegroom son beside him.

They came, these ruling Arabs, like princes out of an Arabian legend. Some with rifles, some with small sub-machine guns, all dressed alike, all moving with indefinable elegance and pride. They were escorted and surrounded by their friends, equally armed, equally dressed, men who grew taller in spirit by being close to their mentors. The Sheikhs in that place at that time manifested indigenous power. Their men ranged around them, waiting, ready for the smallest gesture.

They moved to greet each other, calling each other's names in their deep guttural Arabic. They saluted each other with the nose kiss, smiling, calling, recalling. The fires burned. The drums called. They moved from group to group, looking, moving on, laughing.

Finally, they came to a circle of tribesmen, singing and moving in a slow pavane around two drummers. Slowly the circle grew larger. Rifles were tossed in the air and men pirouetted as they caught them. An old man joined, drew a long, heavy sword from its scabbard, threw it high in the air

and caught it by the handle. One slip and he would have cut his hand off.

Now the Sheikhs moved in, stepping sedately, dipping, turning, dancing, impelled by the drums, their suffras wrapped in the turban style of the old days, their guns held with casual familiarity. This was their place. This was their way. They circled the drummers, faces set in the seriousness of the act, then breaking suddenly into a smile. Around and around as the circle grew larger and the watchers became a crowd, all calling, all singing in that black, star-filled night.

And tomorrow? Tomorrow they would sit in their new offices in the new office buildings as bewildered supplicant businessmen from the East and from the West tried to break their impassivity, tried to secure contracts, tried and tried and tried to get paid for work long since completed. They would sit juggling the figures of ever-mounting bank accounts, studying the price of gold, watching the price per barrel of oil, while the commodity markets of the world waited to see which way they would move.

These same men would move out and away from the centre of their lives, the centre of their history which their dancing reflected and would sit in a foreign environment, wary, without trust, tempted by every sweetener, devouring pleasure, hypnotised by the sight of rising bank statements, caught in the beautiful traps which millions, billions create.

The edges of their minds knew that their life was eroding and they were as powerless to stop it as King Canute had been to stop the tide. They knew their sons' sons would not dance like this, would not hear these drums, would dance as the West danced, imitating another world. I stood swallowed in the crowd, while a corner of my own mind wept, knowing I was watching the end of a time.

The days of the wedding passed in a haze of drum beats, singing and feasting. In between rounds of entertaining, the young wives and daughters would ply with me with questions about what was going on 'over there'. The Eldest Son's wife compared it to the sounds she had heard as a bride from her own compound.

The inevitable gathering in of the tribe had brought many visitors from other hareems, some from as far as Qatar, Dubai and parts of Saudi Arabia. They stayed with us, sleeping in the majlis of Sheikha Grandmother.

Those who lived nearer came for a day, a meal, or just for fruit and coffee. The catering reached gigantic proportions as our normal household of around fifty was often doubled and everything had to be especially fine. Lunch was now a feast of fish, chicken and lamb often barbecued whole. All those tales of feasts with whole roast lambs served on top of mountains of rice began to come true.

It was not just a business of primitive roasting on a spit. Not at all. To make proper *mashwi* lamb requires as much culinary excellence as that required by any classic cuisine. Washed with lemon and spices, stuffed with sultanas, raisins, rice, chickpeas, onions and whole hard-boiled eggs, trussed, wrapped in foil and baked in a pit much as New Englanders would make for a clambake, it is indeed a dish fit for kings. Delicious. Spectacular.

This dish was to be prepared and served many times during the wedding week for both the household and the house guests, but the feasting inside the compound was modest compared to that on the wedding ground. The sight of those massive vats steaming on open fires through the night was like a scene from Dante, though not an inferno. The cooks, using their long paddles instead of spoons to prod and stir their concoctions, danced around their fires like so many genies. It was the feeding of thousands.

At this time, a new face joined the household. Leah was a cheerful soul. She had a thin, wiry figure well covered in gold chains, a mark of her independent wealth. Always smiling, she gave an air of having been with the family for years and years. In a way, she had. She knew them all, knew their lives, their ways, their children. She was both friend and servant. Having once 'belonged' to someone, she was now independant and went from party to party. She had started a catering business, no doubt with the backing of her former employers, and she had done well. She was the number one cook in the area. She came when there was too much for one Sheikha to oversee. She left at the end of the affair. Watching her prepare the meals was an education. Her gold bracelets glinted in the sun as she rolled up her sleeves to season the lambs. Her thin body shook with the vigour of her work and her tongue was sharp as she ordered the cookhouse servants about. But her smile was quick and her laughter as rich as the dishes she prepared. Leah was a treasure.

Throughout the week the hareem remained remarkably self-contained, if continuously busy. They reinforced their henna for the maksar, entertained one another and planned their wedding outfits down to the last jewel. The Sheikha and Leah went through long lists of stores needed for the coming feast, then started all over again on the plans for the bride's homecoming dinner which would be attended by everyone - except the bride, of course.

Each day the Sheikha and her family dressed in new and ever more beautiful dresses. The best jewels were aired. The tall rose-water shakers began to appear and incense seemed to be everywhere, for all the men were at home and in constant need of freshly aired and scented kandoras, to say

nothing of the ladies and their visitors. It was a grand house party, with servants moving in and out, pouring coffee, carrying freshly ironed dresses, or rescuing a child from imminent danger of becoming overstuffed with nougat.

On the Wednesday night I went for the last time to the wedding ground. By now, thousands of people seemed to be milling in and out of the circles of dancers. I saw for the last time the waltzing of the Manahil, the formality of the religious singers, the sword throwing Qubaisat. I watched the Dan mincing and winding, and listened to the thin thread of song sung by the old harpist, his face lifted in some quiet longing. I watched the innocent girl children tossing their hair. But most memorable of all was the Lawa drummer and his piper. Every time he raised his thin, taut arms to pound the huge drum, he lifted his whole body from the chair. He was a dancer, a drummer, a musician. Sweat poured from him, covering his brown skin in a salty sheen. There was passion and life in every gesture. Resources of strength came from some inner source. Around him moved another drummer with a small, hollow-ended hand-drum. He whirled and leapt as though lifted off his feet by the phenomenon of sound. And the piper blew. He blew and blew, his long, thin pied-piper's trumpet issuing impassioned cries. His cheeks puffed out, his nostrils flared, he drained his body of air, drew it in and drained it again, all the while calling the crowd with his pipe. Finally, his legs gave way, buckling under him. He fell in an attitude of prayer, still blowing his pipe while the tenor-drummer leapt over and around him, whirling, dancing, and the bass drummer lifted his thin arms in the gestures of a praying mantis.

Every ache of the soul, every desire, was laid bare by the music of those three men. Those who understood it wept. Those who did not stood mesmerised.

Around them, circling them, protecting them, impelled by them, were the Lawa dancers. Strong, dark men who moved in a contained two-step, singing, calling, suddenly turning. Others joined them, then moved away, but they were a continuum, a circle of definition.

The fires burned hot in the cool night air. The drums, the singing, the swords and guns thrown high, the smell of spice and curry cooking, camels gurgling and sheep bleating, the white of a thousand kandoras moving from place to place, calling, laughing. It was a time beyond time, for waiting on the edge were the cars, the microphones, the electrical sounds, the power which would eventually swamp the indigenous rhythm of life in that place.

When that new stage was set, the musicians seated and waiting in their tuxedos, the audience packed in anticipation, the soloists in their immacu-

late dinner jackets ready to perform, the magnified, metallic voice of the announcer drowned the air. The music of the technological age smothered the music of the previous thousands of years.

The break was too sudden. I went home to my new bedroom, closing my ears to the new world and the modern sounds, but appreciating modern comforts. A hypocrite.

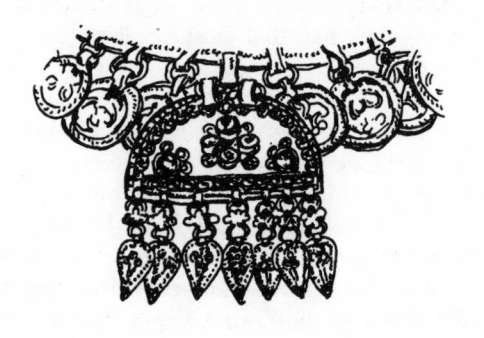

20

A Henna Party and a Declaration of Allegiance

IN OUR OWN compound the wedding cleaning was assiduous and continual. Morning and afternoon, maids squatted on their haunches moving slowly, crab-like down the paths, a whisk of thick reeds in their hands. Chuck, chuck, chuck, chook. Their stickless witches' brooms sounded a rhythm on the concrete. Chuck, chuck, chuck, chook. First one side, then the other. Dust, sand, sweet wrappers dropped by sticky-fingered children, dead leaves and twigs moved in front of them. The pile of rubbish grew while the big rover ants with their thin, wiry legs scurried to get out of the way.

The paths were swept, the houses were swept. A hoover was tried once, but it got clogged with new carpet fluff and no-one could fix it. Besides 'the broom is better and there are plenty to use it', so the hoover stood dejected and discarded in a store room, and the maids continued their crab-walk in the houses. Chuck, chuck, chuck, chook.

Again and again the paths and carpets were cleaned. Every grain of spilt rice was plucked by hand from the dining majlis carpet. Every cushion cover was washed, ironed and replaced, every brass della burnished and polished.

The maids moved on to the bathrooms with their whisk, the all-in-one tool which was never far from hand. Skirts tucked up around their waists, barefooted, they poured bucket after bucket of water across the tiles, their brooms swishing and sweeping the water down into the hole of the Arabian toilet, that remarkable invention which must have grown out of custom. It was an elliptical pan set in the floor with concrete grip pads either side

for your feet. You performed your toilet and ablutions squatting. It flushed away with a heavy, noisy rush of water from a cistern high against the ceiling dangling a long chain. All modern Arab bathrooms had these strange contraptions as well as ordinary Western pans and bidets. Jugs and bottles sat beside a low tap for washing. They considered our use of toilet paper not quite clean.

While the maids swept and dusted and washed the tiles, across the court drivers polished and repolished the cars. It was an endless task in that world of sand and dust, but no household would countenance a dusty car. It was definitely *déclassé*. Now, with the wedding visitors arriving, the collection of Mercedes had to have a special brilliance. Once satisfied with their polishing, the drivers would sit in each car, turning over the engine, warming it for a stipulated five minutes so that anyone could get in and drive off with a fully warmed and tuned vehicle.

I was always in too much of a hurry for this ritual. When the sons visited me in London they were appalled at the way I mistreated our car.

'You must not get in and go. It is very bad. And for the long drive you must change the oil. I change the oil every time I go from Al Ain to Abu Dhabi,' said the Youngest Son. He came to see me in the bride house one afternoon, to offer his praise and a warning.

'Um Yusef,' he said solemnly, 'you go too fast on the Al Ain road. My cousin Hamed saw you. You went by him - zip. He saw you. You were gone. You didn't see him. This is too fast for you, Um Yusef. It is all right for foolish Sheikhs, but not for you.'

His earnest young face looked at me like a grandfather, the big, wise, young-old eyes giving promise of a future judge. I was suitably chastened.

The bridegroom occasionally allowed me to drive his car. There was so much to do, so much to collect, arrange, search for and deliver that I would get in the camel-coloured car and with one of his 'friends' at my side, off we'd go. Speed seemed irrelevant on that long, desert road. You lost your sense of time, motion, space. It was devilish and dangerous. I took the boy's warning and gave my promise to be more careful.

One particular day of the week-long wedding festival was most important to the hareem and became special to me. I had walked across the court, picking my way around the sweeping maids, gathering up my skirts to avoid the brooms, the dust and the ants. As I entered the majlis of the Sheikha to pay my usual morning respects, I found her directing cleaning operations from an incongruous position. She sat on the carpet, her back against a hard pillow with its ruffled white cover, her legs resting on a low wooden

stool, her bare feet warming at a slowly burning charcoal fire on a brazier. The soles of her feet were plastered with a red-brown putty which went up the arch in a fine curve and around the big toe. She sat drying the muddy putty, anchored for once to one spot, directing her hareem who were busying themselves about her.

The day for henna had arrived. It was the hareem's beauty session, a communal affair where all helped each other. The young daughter sat mixing the powdered henna and water to the right consistency in a small mortar with an even smaller pestle. Hussa walked about, one hand heavy with henna, the other holding the day's newspaper which, as usual, she perused as soon as possible.

Abed's wife had arrived. As a Palestinian she was renowned for her excellent patterns and had brought her drawings for the young to look over. On the Levant, the tradition of henna-painting had developed into a fine art with delicate designs of leaves and flowers covering palms, fingers and feet. On the Gulf the patterns had remained bold and simple. The tips of the fingers were covered to the first knuckle. The palm had a large circle in the centre with a small circle or star orbiting. The moon and the north star?

Another pattern had the palm completely covered with lines leading up the inside of the fingers, the whole resembling those stylised patterns of Fatima's hand which are found in all Muslim art. Many believe that there is some great protective power in the handprint of Fatima, the Prophet Mohamed's daughter.

Now, new ideas and new fashions were rapidly taking over, as they do in any culture once it's been invaded. The young wives preferred the delicate designs of the Levant tradition and Abed's wife was an artist when it came to henna. She had a copybook full of drawings and shared them out among us while she herself sat cross-legged on the floor next to the Sheikha, sewing up henna bags. When filled with henna paste, they looked exactly like miniature versions of the icing bags used by chefs to decorate cakes.

In the past the leaves of the local henna trees were plucked, dried and crushed to powder in a mortar, then mixed to a thick, smooth paste with a little water. Now both natural and 'black' henna could be purchased in neat packets with a manufacturer's seal from local Indian or Pakistani merchants even though the henna trees were still grown. Perhaps they were a sort of insurance.

'Come, Um Yusef,' said the Sheikha. 'You must have henna for the party.'

At the insistence and chiding of the hareem, I agreed.

'Something small,' I said to Abed's wife, 'or people will think me foolish.'

'Nonsense,' said the Sheikha. 'They will think you are one of us.'

Abed's wife smiled with understanding and, after rubbing some oil into the palm of my hand, she drew a small flower with a long stem and leaves. She drew it with the tube itself, like a master pastry chef. It was just right. A secret to be displayed on request.

What patience was needed! What a long time it all took and I am about as patient as a cat on a hot tin roof. There you are, one hand useless as it lies open, palm up waiting for the paste to dry. If it cracks by moving about you might blur the pattern. So you're helpless. Then when it dries you start all over again. And again. And again. You keep going over and over the pattern until it's finally declared dark.

Hennaing the hands was enough of a problem, but getting henna to dry on the feet was endless. The process could take a couple of days as it had to be layered on quite thickly. So there they sat, my beautiful hareem, their legs on stools like milking stools, their backs against the hard majlis cushions, their feet at the charcoal braziers.

Of course we all had to be waited on hand, foot and finger, so maids scurried in and out bringing coffee and warm drinks, and children ran errands with an air of importance.

As we sat there drying, talking, planning for 'the day', for 'the days' of the wedding, the idea of my being one of them seemed to expand. It was decided that I must have a 'proper' dress for the wedding, one 'like theirs'. The Sheikha sent her daughter to her cupboard to select a length of purple silk which was woven with silver thread into a Persian pattern. There and then, with my henna half done, the bridegroom was summoned and ordered to drive me to a tailor for measurements. Towering over his mother as she sat with her feet toward the brazier, listening carefully to her instructions, his face broke into that slow smile of his as he gathered up the purple cloth.

We got into his car and drove out of the compound toward the town, the ever burgeoning town of Al Ain. There were many paved streets now. It was beginning to look like a suburb of Miami or Pasadena with its hedges and hibiscus bushes and palm trees, its new villas and expensive cars. Kentucky Fried Chicken had joined Wimpy. Behind the new buildings with their supermarkets and video shops were the old buildings - five or six years old - already displaying that air of crumbling decay which sets in where sand, sun and wind blast away continually. A broken sign, chipped concrete, faded paint, pavements that crumbled into unpaved roads which had been forgotten in the haste of construction.

The tailor was on one of these forgotten alleys. He had a small shop, no more than twelve feet square. A rack of finished dresses stood along one wall. Opposite was a counter covered in a confusion of cloth and at the back was a fitting room hardly big enough to turn around in. Upstairs the work room whirred and buzzed with such earnestness that the ceiling shook. When the young Sheikh and I entered, everything stopped and a worn-out Pakistani woman was called down. Measurements were taken and the style demanded by the Sheikha was drawn on the back of an old invoice. It was to be quite plain. A fitted bodice, round neck, long straight sleeves and a circular skirt. As the fabric was so elaborate, the design needed to be simple. With admonitions from the young Sheikh that it must be ready tomorrow, we drove off in the usual flurry of dust.

'How can he do such a thing without a fitting?' I asked.

'Fitting? What fitting? What for a fitting? It will be good. You will see,' he answered.

And it was good.

I was invited to parade the dress in front of the Sheikha while the Sheikh sat puffing his miniature pipe. His bridegroom son walked around me, discussing the dress. The children bobbed up and down, laughing and shouting. Finally the Sheikh pronounced it very good, his eyes smiling at the sight of his English guest, the wife of his English friend, dressed as the hareem. The Sheikha suggested one or two minor alterations - a stitch here, a stitch there - which were accomplished within an hour and the dress was hung in my new cupboard to await the coming maksar, the women's wedding party.

The hareem would not attend the wedding ground. They would not walk among the milling, madding crowd. They might make discreet visits. They might sit in the back of limousines, bodies and faces covered in layers of black, seeing but unseen, watching from behind their black scrim. Only at the maksar, or in the big formal women's majlis which was now open for the constant flow of visitors, would the women let the black abaya drop from their shoulders. The head veil would rest casually, revealing dresses of silk woven with silver and gold, or appliquéd with silk flowers, or studded with diamanté; revealing necklaces and bracelets of every precious stone. It was at the maksar that I would wear my new dress, a dress which would declare that I was something more than just an English friend, that though a foreigner and a stranger, I had declared my allegiance.

21

Parades, Parties
and a Gold Cap

A LL THE JEWELS of Arabia, an Aladdin's cave revealed by the genie of the lamp, were there in front of me as I walked into the Sheikha's room in the early morning of the day of the maksar. There, in front of me was the dream of an Arabian prince's wedding. The silks, the pearls, the diamonds spilt around the room like a Hollywood scriptwriter's vision in 1934. The smell of perfumes, the smoking incense, the oils and hennas, the cases being packed while maids folded yard after yard of diamanté chiffon. There were encrusted veils each with a price tag of five, six or seven hundred pounds; gold and silver sandals from Italy, cases of fine sandals in every shape; gold-trimmed abaya and gold-trimmed jewel boxes; boxes and boxes of jewel cases, chamois cases, velvet cases holding diamonds, rubies, emeralds, ropes of pearls and rings of gold. There was white gold for blue diamonds, red gold for rubies, yellow gold for topazes and emeralds. There were turquoise and seed pearls from Gulf oyster beds, set in classic Arabian patterns, or designs from Paris or Rome. This was the Sheikha's room as she prepared the treasure for her son to give to his bride.

For weeks fabric merchants had been invading the compound. Every day had seen Egyptian or Syrian women showing samples of fabric which spilled out of cases or bundles. Amazing fabrics. Silks from Japan, chiffon from France, sarees from India, silver- and gold-embroidered voile from Switzerland. The hareem had sat around fabric samples day after day, selecting and discarding, selecting and discarding. Now large Samsonite cases were being packed with lengths of precious cloth, which would accompany the gifts

of jewellery. It was an unbelievable display. The bird of paradise presenting himself to the one, he must win, sight unseen. It was a burst, a flash, an explosive announcement of suppressed passion, a fantastic gesture of romantic hope.

All the dreams of love, all the years of looking for love, for reciprocal passion reach a nova in the wedding display. Sometimes it can take years to arrange, sometimes months, sometimes weeks. It is not a ceremony. It is a serenade, a courtship made outside the walls surrounding the bride before the suitor is allowed to enter. It is a fantasy. A dream which could become a nightmare, or a joy, or an accepted contentment.

It was well before eight o'clock in the morning when I received a message to come and see the treasure packed. I watched as case after case was filled with fabric, as bundles were finally rolled, roped and tied as if for a pack camel. Palliasses and quilts, still with the sheen of newness on them, had been piled with suffras for the men of the bride's family or layered with cloth for the men's wezaar and the women's serwal. When each had been pronounced properly loaded by either the Eldest Son's wife, Hussa or the Sheikha herself, they were rolled and bound with thin, strong, hemp rope. There must have been thirty or more of these bundles. I sipped an 'English tea' and tried to be useful by preventing the small foster daughters from jumping up and down on the luggage.

'We must hurry. They will be here,' said the Sheikha and as if seeing my clothes for the first time, added, 'Where is your kandora, Um Yusef, you must wear your new kandora.'

Somehow I had thought the maksar would be a lunchtime event.

'Now?' I exclaimed.

'Yes, now. Hurry. Hurry. They will be here.'

Feeling completely mystified as to who would be where and when, I ran back to my room to change, getting tangled and bothered trying to do up the long back zip.

In order that I should not look under-dressed in this display of silk and silver, gold and precious stones, the Sheikha sent over by the hand of the Youngest Son one of her magnificent antique pearl bracelets. Gulf pearls, small, irregular, row upon row. Some three inches of them. I felt honoured. Then the wife of the Eldest Son loaned me a beautiful shayla covered in diamanté. 'It is for your head,' she ordered, but I wore it round my shoulders.

I heard someone come through the door and turned to see the bridegroom's sister. She would not be allowed to come to the maksar. Only married women would attend. But she was beautifully dressed all the same. She could hardly contain her excitement and shouted at me in Arabic as

if I'd been on the other side of the compound.

'Hurry. Hurry, Um Yusef. My mother is waiting for you. It is time to go.' She caught my hand and we ran into the glare of the morning.

The courtyard had become as busy as a town square on market day. Two lorries were in front of the family house. In one were the Lawa piper and drummers. Around them and in the second lorry case upon case of the bride's treasures were being stacked. The Dan whom I had seen on the celebration ground were doing the job of packing. They suddenly looked amazingly strong. Their black faces were wreathed in smiles. They had dropped their sensual teasing and were now impeccable guards, ordering the care of the treasure, adjusting the flags on the lorry and on the Sheikh's cars, which had begun to draw up in a loose line. A banter of conversation was kept up between them and the drivers but it was not the conversation of the night. It was the talk of people involved in the same job. The atmosphere was fresh.

It was now about 9.30 and the hareem began to gather. The Sheikha's magnificent purple dress was embroidered with gold. We were all in different patterns and shades of purple decorated in silver or gold. Even the maids were specially dressed and Selma was resplendent in her gold jewellery acquired through years of service. Only Sheikha Grandmother wore the old traditional dress, but it too was of silk with a fine, heavily embroidered thoab over all.

Hussa inspected my henna-flowered hands to see if the pattern was dark enough. The incense pot was passed under our skirts by the maids and they shook rose-water containers over our clothes. Finally, satisfied with her brood, the Sheikha ordered us into the cars.

I had thought we were to go directly to the maksar area inside the bride's compound. Not at all. The cars lined up like a parade. In the front lorry were the Lawa musicians. The treasure and its guards were in the second lorry. The bridegroom came next, riding quite alone in his immaculately polished car. Then came the Sheikha's car with Sheikha Grandmother and the Eldest Son's wife. I was in the third car with the Sheikha's small foster daughters and Hussa. (Small daughters not having reached the great divide of puberty were allowed to attend.) At least three other cars followed us with the rest of the hareem. The piper began to play, the drums began to beat and we were off, a bevy of women dressed in a fortune of silks and jewels hidden under the discreet black of the abaya, led by the pleading piper and a young bridegroom with his gift of treasure.

We did not head towards the bride's compound but instead turned in the opposite direction, towards the end of town. I was bewildered.

'Where are we going?'

'To collect my mother's mother and her sister,' piped a small voice.

'Oh,' I said and turned to Hussa. 'And then to the maksar?'

'No, no,' laughed Hussa, her eyes crinkling in amusement as one of the children hugged me in excitement. 'No, no. We go everywhere around the town to collect all the friends and family.'

So it was indeed a procession. The bridegroom was gathering all the hareems of his near family and hareems of the Sheikha's friends and the Sheikh's allies to come to the bridal maksar. By the time we finally reached the bride's compound, we were a procession of cars that stretched for half a mile and others, many others came on their own.

The maksar area had been richly carpeted. A few cushions had been placed against various poles and the palm leaf roof allowed the occasional shaft of sunlight to break through the shade. Women began to congregate and cluster into family groups, the largest around the haughty, ample figure of the wife of a former ruler. The Sheikha placed me firmly beside a rotund, elderly woman who nodded and smiled with welcome, pointing out that my shayla was in the wrong place. It should be on my head. She herself was dressed in as traditional a way as Sheikha Grandmother, but with an added display. The jewellery on her hands and on her toes was a complete set of antique gold finger- and toe-rings, five different patterns for each of the five fingers and toes. Square, arrow- or spade-shaped, diamond, circle or stemless club. Did they take their shapes from playing cards? Or did playing cards take their shapes from them?

Her chunky, smiling figure settled itself on, rather than against, a cushion and another was hurriedly found for her back. Gold discs linked like gold atoms swung across her wide bosom. Their weight must have been considerable. But the most memorable thing about her was her personality - her welcome, her smile. It was so strong, so radiating that even today I seem to see her whole face, unmasked, natural, smiling and talking - and yet I know for certain that she wore an old fashioned, rather long, burnished gold mask. I see her in her veil, sitting on the cushion, her fat little feet crossed in front of her, a benign grandmother bedecked in gold, her round face nodding and smiling - and yet she was masked.

Coffee was served again and again from every conceivable shape of pot, from the most ornate antique brass to the modern thermos. Maids, proud in their new dresses, sprinkled rose water and jasmine water over us. Incense was burned in large, stemmed containers decorated with coloured stones.

Women greeted each other as they do all over the world.

'Welcome,' 'How are you?' 'How is your husband?' 'What is your news?' 'I haven't seen you for months.' 'No, not since Ahmed's wedding.' 'How is Leila's foot?' 'What is the news?' 'Were you at Hamed, son of Khalid's wedding? I didn't see you.' 'Welcome. My house is yours in God's name.'

The crowd grew, the maksar filled. A group of Wahiba women arrived, their long cloth masks looking strange. Their ankle bracelets jangled as they walked barefooted. They were made doubly welcome and were seated near the centre of the floor where the Sheikha could watch over them personally. From the Liwa, an oasis far to the north, tall, graceful, slender women arrived. They were staying in the compound of the bride. The wives of the Manahil Sheikhs arrived, their rich heavy dresses sweeping the ground. The Sudan, the Qubaisat, the Awamir, the Manasir, the ruling Nahayan, and more, many more. The list was long. They were all from the hareems of the tribes allied to the Bani Yas.

Then there were the wives of wealthy merchants and of foreign Arab civil servants who needed to be seen. Some masked, most unmasked, all veiled. They sat belonging, yet not belonging, knowing yet not known. Three Egyptian teachers arrived, disdainful in short dresses. They kicked off their shoes and sat at the edge of the area talking among themselves, pulling their straight short skirts uncomfortably around their knees. They were made welcome. All were made welcome.

The Sheikha came up to me. 'Watch our shoes,' she whispered and I quickly tucked several pairs around me. Small hills of sandals were growing here and there. I grabbed as many of the family's as I could see, gathered them around me and then, on the instructions of my rotund, smiling companion, tucked them under my skirts like a hen sitting on her eggs.

Suddenly a bolt of oilcloth was unrolled between us, putting my new friend on one side of the 'table' and me on the other. Rivers of oilcloth ran the length of the area like so many banqueting cloths. The Sheikha, Leah and Selma had positioned themselves at various vantage points to oversee the whole affair. I never saw them sit at any time. A quick gesture, a welcoming smile, a word here, a nod there, the Sheikha never stopped moving.

As steaming bowls of harees and thareed began to arrive, the music and singing of the homosexuals began from the back of the maksar where they had positioned themselves as a musical guard over the wedding gifts.

Bowl after bowl of a variety of breakfast dishes were followed by fruit and coffee and then massive platters of rice topped with the mashwi lamb, or with barbecued camel. The feast ended with more coffee and dates, every dish having been carried by women, every bowl, every platter, every coffee

pot, every cup carried and served by women. The only men allowed were the singing treasure guards.

As the last dishes were removed, the scented warm water poured over our hands to clean them, the kleenex passed to dry them, the coffee served again, so began the display of the gifts. The jewel boxes were passed down the tables, inspected, admired, passed on, the cases of cloth lifted high on the shoulders of their guardians, displayed, put down, displayed again, put down again.

All through the party the bride's mother and grandmother and their hareem had been a centre of attention, watched over, cared for and cossetted. They were a large group and sat resplendent in their jewels and fashionable dresses. Attractive, well-travelled, yet entirely conservative, both young and old had an aura of chic, an air of beauty. Of course Um Hamed was there, serene and lovely as ever.

The bride's family compound was planned entirely differently from the Sheikha's. It was like a modern estate with cul-de-sacs around which ranged two or three bungalows. Palm trees and flowering shrubs were everywhere, the concrete drives were well laid and the curbs well tended. Each bungalow had a broad porch with the familiar short rise of steps to accommodate the customary lift of the house off the ground. The whole gave the impression of a pleasant suburb surrounded by a thick, high, sand-coloured wall with its own round, bulbous lights much like ours. I had often walked to visit them, entering by a small short door in the back wall, stepping over a high foot-guard and ducking under a low lintel.

They now sat serenely, accepting all the attention with grace and gravity, tinged with the sense of humour indigenous to the area. Now that the gifts were given, the whole treasure was taken to the house of the bride where she remained closeted with her cousins and friends. No-one would see her until the following day when, having been claimed by her husband, she would parade before an intimate group of invited friends and family in all her wedding regalia. Everyone was at the bridal party, the big maksar, except the bride.

My companion across the table looked at the sky and the shadows and decided that it was time to leave. The sun was reaching its zenith and at the height of day there were prayers to be said.

'It will soon be time to pray,' she reminded me, and, reaching her hand towards me, asked for a lift up. Several women around her hurried to her aid as I held her hand to steady her. She admonished me once again to put the shayla on my head where it belonged and, smiling widely, moved toward the Sheikha who was already on the way toward her. I learned later

185

that this memorable woman was a sister of the ruler.

All the women now began to rise, cars were called and within half an hour it was over. There was only, as always, the mess to be cleared. A good many women seemed to have gone without their shoes, as a large collection remained piled in the centre of the floor. Our hareem had fared reasonably well, due no doubt, to the Sheikha's note of caution and my companion's advice. Only one of the children's sandals was lost in the shuffle. We went home to flop exhausted on our beds and palliasses, too keyed up to sleep, too tired to sit up.

After an hour or so of body rest, I walked into the new tahat majlis to find the bridegroom restlessly pacing about, moving ornaments and putting them back. He made me a cup of tea and we talked about the day, about what I'd seen, who was there, how it went.

He had become more and more restless as each day passed, prowling about the house, trying the lights, rearranging a piece of furniture. A few days before we had gone to the local agricultural station to buy some houseplants. Wildly costly, he watched them each day, sure that they would never live inside the house. Then he would accuse himself, saying that they were a waste of money.

'She will never know what to do with them. They will die.'

A maid had arrived to sweep and dust yet again. She was Sri Lankan and had a disconcerting habit of shaking her head when she meant yes.

'If my mother gives me this one for a servant, I shall go mad,' said the bridegroom as he settled back against the cushions. He stirred three generous spoons of sugar into yet another cup of tea.

'Tonight you must come with my mother to push me in the door,' he said.

'Push you?'

'Yes, you must know everything. See all our ways. The women of my house, my mother and my grandmother, must take me to her house. Surely you can see that my father cannot do this. He cannot go where their women are.'

'Yes. I see that.'

'So my mother takes me there. And you must come.' His eyes were dark with tiredness, bright with anticipation.

'I will come if you wish and if she agrees.'

'She will agree, of course.'

So we talked again, walked the house again, planned again. He scolded me for not coming to hear the modern music the night before. I chided him for liking the modern music better than the classic. Then suddenly in

186

a burst of memory he said, 'I forgot. You must make her a cake, a wedding cake for when she comes home.'

My mouth dropped. 'I can't, I haven't the things, the tins, the ingredients and everything. And I couldn't possibly ice a wedding cake.'

'That's all right. Make her a spicy one like you make for me and decorate it a little.'

'It won't be big enough.'

'It will. It will. You must. A wedding must have a wedding cake.'

With a sigh I agreed to try and he was all at peace again.

That evening I dressed especially carefully in a long-sleeved taffeta evening dress I had brought with me and a velvet hand-embroidered Syrian coat. The Sheikha, Sheikha Grandmother, the bridegroom and I were driven to the bride's house.

The bridegroom was received on one side of the house by the bride's father, grandfather, uncles and brothers. We were received in a family majlis. A small group of distinguished visitors were there, along with the bride's immediate family. It was considered a special honour to 'dress' the bride.

We drank coffee and ate sweets and fruit until a knock on the door announced that it was time. The Sheikha gestured to me to come.

Our bridegroom walked in the front door with the bride's grandfather. At the invitation of the bride's mother, we grouped behind the bridegroom and walked the few steps to a closed door at the far end of the hall. No 'pushing' needed to be done. The boy walked straight to the door, gave two sharp raps and flung the door wide. There, on the floor, on a white palliasse was a triangular bundle of black. A heavy waft of incense came into the hall. The boy turned, smiled at me to make sure I had seen, then entered the room, and shut the door sharply.

He told me months later that the culmination of all those days of serenading was to find his child bride shaking all over as she sat there. After having worried for days as to what would be the first words he would say to her, all he could do was comfort her as he took off her veils. 'Don't be afraid - just pretend we have been married for two years, not just now.'

Friday morning, the first marriage morning, the Sheikha and I drove to the bride's house to pay our first visit. Their majlis was already overfilled with an assortment of visiting women. Indeed the whole bungalow seemed to be spilling over with women. They stood in the halls, at the windows, on the porch, all chatting and laughing, gesticulating with their henna-painted hands.

The bride's mother took the Sheikha and me to one side and led us to

her own bedroom. It was a simple, comfortable room, not overly large, furnished with a suite of modern Jacobean style furniture - bed, wardrobe and dressing table. It was the room of a modest semi-detached in Surbiton.

At the foot of the bed, on the floor, on a flowered palliasse, the bride sat cross-legged. She had been transformed from a black triangular parcel into a golden, Eastern doll. Her hair dripped gold. It fell over her hair and down her back. Her ears dripped gold. Her breast lifted under a bib of gold.

'Speak to her in English,' said the Sheikha.

I sat in front of her and looked into her eyes with their long, thick, heavily kohled lashes. I held out my hand.

'Hello,' I said. 'I am Um Yusef. Do you remember me?'

She smiled. It was a good smile but her hand was cold and damp with nerves.

'You look very beautiful, but all that gold must be very heavy.'

A hint of that never-to-be-forgotten laugh. 'Very heavy,' she said, dwelling on the words, 'but it is the custom here.'

'I know, and it is so beautiful to see.'

Her dress under the gold was creamy white silk with white silk appliquéd flowers. Very simple. Very expensive. We talked for perhaps ten minutes before she was led away to parade in front of the visiting women. This performance was to take place for many days, each time in a different dress, each time in her weight of gold.

Every day the bridegroom came back to his house to check it, get fresh clothes, see his mother, then return to the bride room. He was uncomfortable staying in her house. He was out of place and only endured it for her sake and that of custom. It is the only occasion in their lives that men visit in the hareem of another house.

He invited me to visit the bride room. I went with some trepidation but could not disappoint him in anything at this time. The room was filled with flowers from well-wishing foreign Arabs who knew the family. There was a wedding gift or two from European families with whom her father had been associated, but one of the strangest sights was a collection of unmarked trophies for golf, cricket and horsemanship.

'Where did you get these?' I asked.

'From my father.'

'Is he a competitive sportsman?' I asked.

'Oh no. Someone gave them to him.' I imagined how some Englishman might have parted with his beloved trophies when her father either won them or admired them.

Everything was neat and tidy. I was served a cup of English tea with great

care, the first of thousands I would have with this child. We sat on the floor. A large palliasse had been unrolled next to the double bed and I knew that the boy had already made his preference known.

I told her that I had seen her for just a glimpse, a black parcel on a white sheet.

'The white sheet,' she exclaimed and they both broke into secret laughter.

In the past, a bride who has just been bedded must bleed on a sheet which can be shown to the groom or to his family on demand as proof of her virginity. In parts of rural Egypt, this 'tearing of the veil' was sometimes done with two women sitting back to back on each spread-eagled thigh, the bridegroom performing between them.

In this oasis community, the practice of showing the sheet was allowed, even offered, but rarely demanded. In this marriage it had been ruled out of court. 'Barbaric,' said the young Sheikh, and their secret laughter held the promise of a shared incident which belonged exclusively to them.

22

The Bride Comes Home

WE WAITED A week for them to return. They could have returned the moment the marriage was consummated, but she was a much loved daughter and granddaughter, so out of courtesy to her parents they stayed in her bridal room a full week. By custom, a week is the maximum time allowed to woo and win a bride. To stay in the bride room less than two days is impolite, more than a week, impossible.

On the last possible day, it was announced that they were returning.

The bride would be brought to her new home escorted not only by her husband but by all the women of her family. To celebrate the homecoming, the Sheikha would give a large dinner party inviting perhaps one hundred women. A more intimate affair than the maksar.

She planned the dinner with care. It was to be a 'set' table. The long rolls of oilcloth were spread in Sheikha Grandmother's dining majlis. At each place a small bowl of fruit was arranged, an entirely new conception. There were small dishes of salad, yoghurt and dates. The great platters of rice with their whole mashwi lambs would go in the centre.

'It looks good?' she asked me.

'It looks perfect,' I answered.

'It is a new idea. They may think I am ...' Her voice trailed off. She wanted perfection and innovation combined. Difficult in any world

'Everyone will enjoy something new. They always do,' I said. She smiled and we walked over to the bride home. Selma came with us carrying rose-water and jasmine-water shakers. The Sheikha's daughter joined us.

The Sheikha went into all the rooms, placing incense pots and shaking the perfumed water. She opened the bride bed, newly made with the sheets I had brought from London. Rose water was sprinkled between them. Then we sat together for a moment on the new blue couch, surveying the room with the eyes of inspectors searching for some speck of dust, some ornament out of place.

The Sheikha leaned back against the cushions and turning to me said, 'In the past, Um Yusef, we would make a bed of jasmine flowers. We would cover the palliasse with the flowers. Just the blossoms. Then we lay a veil or piece of material over. When we lay down the smell from the crushed flowers was beautiful.'

Her daughter laughed with delight at the thought and I realised once again the romance embedded in each Arab's soul. I caught the Sheikha's eye and there was another moment of inner recognition between us. In seconds it was gone and we walked out to the porch to wait for the cars.

They came, the bride's hareem, in a group of big, black Mercedes led by the bridegroom and his bride in his sports car. She stepped out of the car with care. She was heavily veiled and equally heavily weighted with her gold. He led her up the steps and into the house, then disappeared, leaving the house to his bride and the 'oh's' and 'ah's' of her relatives. She went from room to room, touching, looking, followed by her mother, grandmother and her aunt, Um Hamed. Um Hamed and I escaped together to the dining room where she saw that I had made the promised cake. Not a wedding cake, I hasten to add, but a cake with icing and modestly decorated. She promptly cut a piece, pronounced it delicious and went to get the bride to sample it.

Other women began to arrive, drawing up in their huge cars, stepping out in their best jewels, talking, laughing, complimenting, moving in and out of the new house. The bride had now removed her veil to reveal her gold bridal cap with its strands of gold woven in and out of her hair, the long gold earrings, the fringe of gold on her forehead, the bib of gold coins that spilled to her waist. She would not attend the dinner. She would sit with her aunt Um Hamed in her new living room in her wedding costume, waiting to receive the guests after they finished their dinner. I decided to wait with them.

It was a long evening. Her young head strained under the weight of the gold. It was the last time she would wear it. Her husband put his foot down now that she was in her own home. 'Have you felt the weight of it? Ridiculous. No more of that nonsense. It gives you a headache now. This is enough.'

Finally the last visiting car left and the Sheikha, Um Hamed, Hussa and I kicked off our sandals and sat on a couch in the new house, wiggling our toes and stretching. The bride had gone into her new bedroom to change.

'She said the food was late,' said the Sheikha.

'Who?' asked Um Hamed.

A Sheikha was named.

'Ah. She always complains.'

'It went well,' said Hussa. 'Very well.'

'Of course,' I added.

'Why did you wait here?' the Sheikha asked me. 'I wanted you to see how it went.'

'I knew it would be perfect as always, and she was so new here,' I answered.

'Um Hamed was here.'

'Yes, but they were alone.'

We talked as women always talked after the guests had gone. We talked until the bridegroom arrived and a car was called for Um Hamed. It was over now. Something new would have to begin.

As I lay in my bed listening to the night I relived the evening in my mind.

A strange evening. Strange to me. The house had been filled with women I had never met. They had been impressed with the dower house. That I knew. But I had begun at times to feel like a fish out of water. Their curiosity was everywhere. Their conversation exclusive.

I realised that it might be days, months or even years before the easy familiarity I had known in this particular house would return. There were new relationships to be built. This little bride was part of another powerful hareem and, although she would eventually settle into this new compound, a part of her would never leave her former life. She was upheld by her own hareem. She was totally traditional and yet had her own independence. I knew almost instinctively that she would be a kitten that walked alone.

23

Palaces are Planned

WITHIN DAYS OF the bride taking possession of the bride house the family gathered in the family majlis. The Sheikh had sent a special message for me to join them. As predicted, the house of a son could not be better or larger than the house of the father. It was unseemly. Now they were all gathered together, each expressing a definite opinion as to which way the rooms should go in a new, huge palace of a place. The Sheikh listened to them all and then called me in to act as secretary and primitive draughtsman.

In spite of the fact that it was a stormy winter's day, they decided to go to the proposed construction ground behind the family bungalows. The wind was howling, the sand was stinging. The Sheikha covered me in black veils and with my dark glasses to protect my eyes against the dust I was more thoroughly hidden than the Sheikha herself. The sons laughed uproariously at the sight.

We marched up and down the area where the great new house was to be built, everyone shouting their ideas above the wind. I held a notebook and pencil in one hand and a sheaf of rough drawings in the other. The Sheikh, oblivious to the arguments of his sons, paced out on the sandy earth the pattern he had in his own mind. Here the big majlis, here a bedroom, here the women visitors' majlis and finally his mother's house which, though separate, would be part of the whole. A palatial 'granny flat'. It was this part of the house that troubled him.

'Now, Um Yusef, write it down exactly the same as her house now or

she will not move,' he said in that no-nonsense way of his. 'Each room bigger, but in the same way as the other or she will never let us tear down the old place.'

'Even the bathroom?' I asked, thinking of the where and how of the pipes.

'Especially the bathroom,' he answered, and one of the boys explained that the bathroom could not be between her and Mecca when she prayed.

There was considerable further discussion about whether or not Grandmother would really leave her house.

'She says no, my father,' said the Eldest Son.

'And you know when she says no that is the end of it, sir,' said the Second Son.

The Youngest Son grabbed his mother round the waist, teasing her and kissing her, while shouting to the wind, 'We'll have one little bump of a house in the middle of the garden.' Then they all chorused that no-one would move at all. The big house would stay empty and they would all live in the old ones until the walls fell in around them. The wind continued to howl as if in general approval of the whole scene.

There was some truth in the possibility of the walls falling in. Given another few years they might, for although the bungalows were barely a decade in age they were already showing severe signs of decay. Maintenance of modern buildings was a new science in the desert and little understood. Houses began to disintegrate quickly in the harsh atmosphere. Paint peeled, wallpaper rolled off the walls, windows stuck, door handles broke, light bulbs were the wrong size or shape. Furthermore, it was the easiest thing in the world for builders and architects to cheat and defraud the people of the area in those early days, for knowledge of new building techniques and materials was nil. There were stories of great new palaces whose ceilings promptly fell down, of fine buildings which became slums in less than five years.

The architect who had been appointed to build this new 'palace' was the same one who had designed the bride house. A young, newly married Lebanese, he had actually been trained as an architect. This was an amazing change, as most of the houses were the designs of builders out to make a fortune. The pleasant young Lebanese was not out to defraud. On the contrary, he had a sincere desire to please, for as his first house had been a success, he was certain that if he could also make a success of this one, his fortune would be made. Unhappily, success for this young hopeful was to be a prize at the end of a tangled and knotted string. He remained in a constant state of confusion as new ideas were added or the dimensions of

rooms were enlarged. Furthermore, he had absolutely no idea of the needs of the household, especially the hareem, and of course the women of the house could have no direct communication with him. Modesty and tradition would not allow it.

'If this house is to be for his wife and the next one along is to be for his mother, I suppose this last one here will be for another wife, or what?' He was standing with his sheaves of plans, pulling out roll after roll to show me so that I could ask 'them', as 'they' were always changing and 'they' were always busy.

I burst out laughing as I realised how ignorant he was of their life, as ignorant as I had been the first day I had met the Sheikha. Turning the plan around, I explained that the 'house' in question was not a house but a visitors' majlis with washing facilities. The little independent bedrooms were guest rooms. The large house at the other end of the complex was the family house. The Sheikh would live there with his wife and children.

'You mean he doesn't live over there?' He pointed to the men's majlis. 'I thought he lived there and just called for his wife when he wanted her.'

'Nonsense. They are a family like you and your wife and children. But their customs only allow the men of the immediate family to see the women, so the Sheikh must entertain his friends elsewhere.'

It was the first time I had ever explained an Arab to an Arab and I realised what a privileged gift of understanding had been given to me. It was given in fragile trust and yet I knew that I had to share it for the givers' sake.

As we reviewed the drawings, I saw how many things the architect had left out. How could he have known that they needed a coffee house, a fruit store, a dairy, a place for the servants to rest? Sketching a few lines on a piece of copybook paper, I took them that evening to the Sheikh for his approval. Finding him with the Sheikha and all their children around them, I showed him the minor changes needed for major comfort. But his greatest concern was still whether he would ever get his mother to move.

'Everything must be exactly the same, or we will have to look at that old house in the middle of the garden forever,' he said. 'You tell him, the bedroom, the bathroom, the majlis. Everything exactly the same. These are the important things. The rest is good.'

He handed me back the drawings.

In the end, Sheikha Grandmother did move, but only with much persuasion and having seen for herself that the rooms were in exactly the same position as in her old house - only bigger, much bigger. The ornamented ceilings were picked out in gold. Her fine old bed with its

embroidered curtains and its mounds of bed rolls still stood in a corner. Her chest was on the floor and her rows of embroidered cushions lined the walls. Her carpets were spread out to their best advantage and the only concession to modern furnishing was the television in the corner, rarely tuned to anything other than religious programmes.

It was to this part of the house that the bride often turned in the early days of her marriage. She would be found sitting close to the old lady, listening to stories of the past, warming herself in her own tribe's history. They formed a strong relationship which would be unaffected by events to come. Events not of their own making. Events which would inevitably, in the name of progress, change all their lives out of recognition.

Part Five

24

Excursion out of Time

SIX MONTHS PASSED. Then seven. Then eight. It was September when I returned to Arabia. The sun, hot, heavy, remorseless was still slowly casseroling the inhabitants of Abu Dhabi. In Al Ain it was at least a dry bake.

The bride house and my air-conditioned room welcomed me, as did the little bride, now heavily pregnant. She greeted me with warmth and a *savoir faire* amazing in one so young, but it was soon evident that her lively mind had become numb with the weight of her body. There were odd moments when she asked questions about England, about me, about my family, but usually she lay about the house, breathless, restless, listless by turns.

The heat imprisoned us. Doors were shut, curtains drawn. We lived in the half light. The constant whirring of the air conditioning and the stale, cold air dulled the brain. Children were irritable. The young women drooped visibly, suffering as severely as Westerners. Accustomed to air conditioning, never exercising, their thin, languid bodies had little resistance to the climate or the plagues of new illnesses. Endless petty viruses seemed to attack them and although Vitamin C was doled out by the Indian doctors as liberally as aspirin, the lack of air and exercise, the continual spraying of the rooms with DDT derivatives in a perpetual war against flies and mosquitoes were enervating.

In sharp contrast, the women whose childhoods had been spent in the harsh realities of Arabia, before the oil deluge, were stronger and healthier. They seemed to attack the heat from a different perspective, bending with

the days, not battling. They were unafraid of the breathless air and moved in and out of their houses to conduct the business of the day with few complaints.

In the evenings, undaunted by the heavy atmosphere, they would take their walks. Slowly, straight-backed, they moved out of the new 'palace', down the new, long, balustraded porch and into the garden, looking like a bevy of nuns pacing a cloister, studying their collect for the day. Sometimes I would join them, suffocated by the artificial inside air.

'Come, Um Yusef,' they would call as I moved towards them and we would stroll together, looking at this and that. A young tree, the tumbling pigeons roosting sleepily in their house, an untidy servant's doorstep whose owner would be called to put it right with a short, sharp command.

The Sheikh's new 'palace' had been completed in record time and was a delight. Gracious, well-proportioned, the various areas of the house were united by a fine, long, marble-floored porch at ground level.

'Steps are too hard for my mother,' the Sheikh had said.

Sheikha Grandmother's house, the coffee house, the new dining majlis, the family house all opened on to the long, arcaded porch.

The rooms of the 'palace' were larger by two to six feet than those of the bride house. This had been achieved with much care and careful measuring. Protocol had been maintained.

The centre court with its dry fountain and equally dry blue pool had disappeared. In its place was a new lawn bisected by the old pergola. The lawn was edged with young bushes, giving promise of a flowering hedge. New date palms and lemon trees had been planted and rose beds were everywhere. Given a few years it would be a fine garden square. It was around this square that we strolled in the evenings.

The young bride rarely joined us. She stayed indoors extending her limpid days into equally limpid nights. Moving from couch to couch, from big majlis to small majlis, she would clap her hands like a small female pasha, commanding her bewildered Sri Lankan servant to 'bring juice', 'bring kleenex', 'bring tea'. The only language in which they could communicate was English and certainly the maid had even less English than I had Arabic.

The Second Son had finished university at last. The results of his often hard-won blending into British university life had just been received. He had passed and passed well. We all rejoiced. Back in Abu Dhabi he was laying plans for his career, but this was made difficult by his patent lack of interest in business. Neither his brother nor his father could understand him. In time he would travel to Jordan to study engineering. Now he

worked restlessly with friends of his father.

Each Thursday evening he arrived to stay until Friday afternoon and then returned to Abu Dhabi. He had joined the regiments of week-end husbands. It was an unnatural life for all of them and created even more marriage hazards where enough already existed. The men compensated with the demi-monde of Abu Dhabi, the women compensated with their children and their children's children, with the work of running the compounds, farms and hareems. The young women and the newly-weds drooped and retreated into their dreams, spending hours watching romantic Egyptian video films, repositioning ornaments in their houses, or buying more and more cloth for more and more dresses to stuff already overstuffed cupboards.

It was a scene I watched with sadness and in an effort to break the mesmerism I encouraged them to study, to learn to cook and to bake cakes for their visitors. Our young bride to my delight eventually took her school certificate with honours, and went on to a higher certificate, packing three years work into two and wearing out her tutors. Others became prolific cooks and delighted me each time I visited with their homemade cakes. But my efforts were puny and I often felt a sense of helplessness as I watched these talented, beautiful young women drift aimlessly about.

Whenever I seriously suggested that they come to England for a summer and take a flat for themselves and a maid, their husbands would round on me with one of their quizzical smiles and say, 'Who would be with her? She would be alone,' and the young wife would nod agreement. 'But this is an impossible way for you to live,' I would cry. And they would agree and we'd all sit bound in our own frustrations.

Once, when one of these conversations took place in the home of our youngest, heavily pregnant wife, her husband said, 'Perhaps my father will build a family place in Abu Dhabi.'

'Will your grandmother leave here?' I asked.

'Ah, that is the question.'

So we puzzled and wondered and made plans which never seemed destined for fruition.

There were other days when the talk would be of the rest of the world, its troubles, its threatening postures, its violence. The guardians of the world's petrol power were always conscious of their own vulnerability. They knew that they were the powder keg at the end of a short fuse and were equally aware that matches to light it were often in the hands of ignorance and fear.

'Nowhere is safe any more,' said the Second Son as we sat looking over

a scene of perfect peace, his eyes turning dark and angry.

It was on a morning following one of those talks that he walked into the house and stood in the door of the 'baby' majlis, as the small, tahat majlis was now called.

'Are you coming?' he asked, looking directly at me. Through the door I could see the sports car. It was waiting in the shade of the house. I never knew when or where he or his brothers were going or when they would return. Plans were seldom made, but ideas brewed continuously.

'Yes,' I answered without hesitation and unwound myself from the floor. It was easy for me to come and go. No coat, no handbag, just sunglasses to collect from the chest in the hall. No 'Where are you going?' Just get up and go. No-one minds. No-one questions and yet my Western mind could not bear it. I looked down at the pregnant little wife and the Sheikha's daughter with whom I had been sitting.

'I will see you later,' I said apologetically.

They looked back, smiling, and said, 'Go with God.' I walked into the sun.

The heat had faded perceptibly as September had moved into October. It was easier to breathe, easier to move.

'Where are we going?' I asked, thinking we were off on some brief shopping expedition or possibly for an ice-cream at the Hilton.

'To Oman.'

'Oman!' I gasped. I knew by his expression that this was not to be another tour through the Omani section of the Buraimi Oasis, a tour I had often taken since that first visit to the market with Abed.

The car wound in and out of back lanes edged with plaster and daub houses, each with its own gate painted more brilliantly and intricately than the last, sudden bursts of brightness in a sand-coloured world. We stopped and I waited while the young Sheikh went inside one of those houses, the red, orange and green gate swinging open to his knock and closing behind him.

I waited perhaps ten minutes as the car heated in the sun. Then he returned with a tall, thin man at his side. An older man, much older, and wearing an Omani turban. The lines of his face were deeply etched but his eyes were clear and direct and his smile was wide when he was introduced.

'This is Shiar. He is Omani.'

I nodded and greeted him, adding, 'I can see he is Omani.' It was the manner of dress that marked nation from nation, area from area, tribe from tribe. The folds of the turban, the angle of a small point of cloth, the off centre tag at the neck of a kandora.

The wheels of the car made small flurries of dust as we moved off.

'Is it far?' I asked.

'A little far, but not far,' the young Sheikh answered. A very Arab answer. Wholly non-committal.

We drove to the western edge of the town. The Jebel Hafeet rose high and sharp against the sky. Veering left on to a narrow tarmac highway, we began to move towards the distant cut rock outlines of the Oman mountains, definitive, peaked and yet welcoming in some strange way.

The young Sheikh's face was expressionless, his eyes fixed on the road ahead. Then he began to talk, his English coming in sudden spurts mixed with the occasional Arabic.

'My father used to hunt here. We came with him. It didn't matter if one place was Oman or one for us. It was all as one. We came, we went. They came, they went. Then one day my brother was stopped by police. Where is your visa? they said. They kept him in a police station for many hours. It was a long, big problem. Why do you have a gun? they said. To hunt as always, he said. Maybe to hunt us, they said. Why, what for? My father was very angry. They never went to the area again.'

He was silent driving. He turned to Shiar quickly and smiled and then fixed his eyes on the road.

'Shiar is our friend from long ago. His family is our friend - my friend. I do not forget them. I still come and go where we went before. No-one knows. I think no-one cares. Long ago I told you of this village. It is full of stories. They are true stories, but I know you do not believe. Long ago I told you I would take you there. Now we go.'

Yes. He had told me long ago. Long, long ago in London when our friendship was new and my curiosity unbounded. He had told me about a place in the mountains of Oman, a place where magicians could turn men into donkeys or chickens or birds or beasts. He had told me about the market where they bought and sold souls; about kings who walled up their daughters - 'You can see the hair coming out of the wall'; about servants who could make carpets fly - 'I saw it lift. I saw it go.'

Yes. He had told me many things, many stories, many Arabian tales of wonder and wizardry, and it was true that I did not believe. I only half believed and that half was because I knew what fear and fantasy could do to the human mind.

He had told me of this place, this village high in the mountains where the men of magic once lived, that it was safe, that armies could never attack it.

'What army? Whose army?' I'd asked.

'Any army. Anyone,' he'd answered. 'But you don't believe.'

No, I didn't believe. And yet, if we can create holograms for entertainment, what is so remarkable about mental holograms? Furthermore the village must be a fact as we were driving towards it.

'Are there men of magic there now?' I asked as the sports car sped down the tarmac.

'Are there any magicians left in Oman?' he asked Shiar. 'You must tell her, for it is your country, your place. We go to your place.'

'Many,' said Shiar. 'But not in my village. Not now. But I know men who will not stand under the market tree in one town, who will not drive through another.'

'Why?' I asked.

'For fear their souls will be sold,' said Shiar.

'You see? You see?' said the young Sheikh and smiled into the sun.

The car slowed and turned off on to a shale track. It climbed, wheels spinning on the unyielding stone.

It never occurred to me that we were defying the law, crossing borders made by men in Whitehall who cared little for the customs of a thousand years and more. Such men had only to consider the mechanics of international politics and draw lines on maps with brazen sweeps of their pens, lines which changed whole areas of life, creating new resentments. I never thought of my passport. It seemed to be the most natural thing in the world to be speeding along a desert road towards a ridge of stony mountains, with a young Arab Sheikh and his gaunt Omani friend. I was wholly without fear. Was I already under the spell of that magical country? I decided to wrap a few prayers of protection around me just in case.

Mile after mile we went, on and on, always climbing until there was no road at all, just a rough terrain of dust and stone. Shiar said that the Omanis walk over it barefoot. How cossetted we were in our air-conditioned, technological carrier, like travellers out of time. The hardy Mercedes went without objection over hillocks and into valleys.

Then quite suddenly in the near distance I saw an oasis thick with palms. It was tucked into a crevice of a mountain. Acres of tall date palms were growing out of a cut in the mountain.

'That's it. That's it,' said the young Sheikh.

Within minutes the car stopped. It could not possibly go further through the welter of rock.

'Now we walk.'

I opened the door and stepped on to the stony ground. I was dressed in silk from head to foot. My shoes were white sandals from a shop in Sloane

Street. We walked.

'Come,' he said and held my hand. 'Look. Look up.'

High above us, on a pinnacle of mountain overlooking the oasis, was a round turret, its castellated top reminiscent of children's toy forts. But this was not a toy. It was in good repair. It was real.

The young Sheikh lifted his arm, pointing up at it. 'Shiar spent months up there in the war keeping guard.'

'The war?' I asked, thinking only of World War II and wondering why anyone should want to guard this unknown, unmarked grove. 'In the last war?'

'Not that war. Not your war. Our war. The long fight. These places have always been attacked. They come from the south. The big raiding tribes. You have seen women with those long masks?' He covered his face with his hands. 'Those long ones. Their women are like that, too. They come raiding and taking. They take women, boys, children, all to sell. If you are high up there, you can see for miles. You can see the dust of them coming and you can warn the village. You can make ready then, blocking every-thing, getting guns ready. You can protect your families.'

I walked carefully, picking my way. The ground was hard, rough, massed with stones and gravel. We moved on to a raised causeway. The people of the place had built stone causeways. You walked on the top as though walking on top of a wide wall. Ruined miniature fields were all around us. Dry, barren ruins, looking much like ruins everywhere.

We walked into the trees and the stone yielded at last to rich earth. Date palms sheltered lemon trees, mango and fig trees. Even grapes grew there. The engineering had been intricate. Each tiny field had had to be cleared of stones. Not rocks like the New England fields, nor the warm pink Cotswold stone, but myriads of stones the size of a man's fist. A labour of eternity. These stones had made the paths, the walls, the canals.

From the car to the village was about half an hour's walk. It was behind the fields, backed up against the mountain. The houses, too, were in miniature. Made of small stones and a mortar of mud, with packed earth floors and barred windows. Carved shutters could be closed against the night. There was no glass here. It was bare subsistence living of a back-breaking kind.

Once, there had been a hundred men in the village, Shiar said. Now there were only ten. The town had pulled them in - the oil-made town of Al Ain. Many houses had fallen in upon themselves, dying structures, starved of care. Only a few were left with children running about.

The roads between the houses were just wide enough for a donkey to

pass laden. The water which spilled out of some under-mountain reservoir was channelled along the side of the village. Beyond the main water channel was a massive drop into a dry valley.

'You see. Good protection,' said the young Sheikh, lifting his arm to point first to the turreted mountain and then to the sheer precipice. 'It is safe here. If it is safe anywhere, it is safe here,' he said quietly.

Was this why we had come? To reassure him that it was still here, still safe? Or was it because he had said he would bring me and had to keep his word. Would he sit up in that fort one day, watching? Impossible. And yet...

We sat on the edge of the canal, immersed in the deep quiet of the place. The only sound was the movement of water and the occasional rustle of a bird foraging for food. Here was peace. This was the magic of the place. The deep, quiet sense of peace. Protected peace.

We sat immersed in the atmosphere for - how long? I've no idea. Shiar had disappeared into one of the houses. We said little to each other. Words were superfluous. Then, breaking a silence, he said, 'Come, you must see this place. It is very old. The people are poor.'

He held out a hand to help me up and we walked into the village. As we walked we were urged from every door to come in. 'Welcome, welcome.' The young Sheikh was greeted like an honoured relative and I was welcome because I was with him. They knew him. They would accept me. Though he greeted them all carefully and kindly, he would not accept their hospitality.

Finally we came to a clean, open space with a low wall which surrounded three sides of a square. A high, painted wall made up the fourth side. The floor was carefully laid with flat stones and cleanly swept. It was the mosque. Shiar joined us and rebuked the Second Son for not accepting the hospitality of anyone and most especially of Shiar's relatives. Was it because the young Sheikh did not want me to see their poverty and compare it to his wealth or was it because he had brought nothing with him and did not want them to share what little they had? I never asked, but I felt the disappointment of the women and my own disappointment. Why? Why not go inside?

'No,' he said. 'Not this time. Thank them. But no.' He had his reasons. I turned to Shiar. 'Forgive us. Ask forgiveness.'

'I will,' he answered and his crinkled face broke into a smile at my disappointment. 'You will come again.' It was a statement.

'God willing,' I answered and wondered if God would ever be willing.

We sat together on the low wall of the mosque.

'Tell me, Shiar. Tell me, were there truly magicians here? Truly? It is

too quiet, too still, too calm for magic. There is nothing malevolent here.'

'Malevolent? What's this?' asked the young Sheikh as he translated.

'Bad. Wicked. Evil.'

Then Shiar began in Arabic to tell the story of a man who lived in his father's day. A man who had had a servant.

'There were big houses here then,' said Shiar. 'More fields. The servant of this man was not good. Always talking. Always shouting. Never working. Never obeying. He did not know his master was a man of magic. This servant shouted too much. He shouted for the last time. His master turned him into a big, big chicken and he ran off squawking into the mountains. Squawk. Squawk. Squawk. He ran and ran and never came back.'

The two men rolled with laughter and I laughed at their laughing. And then it hit me the way it sometimes does.

What was I doing there? How did I get there? How did it all happen? There I was sitting on a wall with a young Arab Sheikh and an old Omani villager, sitting on the wall of an open mosque under date palms growing out of the cleft of a mountain a thousand miles from nowhere. Ten thousand miles from home. What was that song? That American folk song? Ten thousand miles from home? I was living it out. Was I the same person who had once sat wreathed in grandfather's cigar smoke listening to tales of the Indians? Was I the same person who stood watching white clouds scud over a blue New England sky while blonde curls were pulled and tugged and rolled into hated ringlets? Was I the same person who lay disobediently in the dolphin net of a schooner watching the green Long Island Sound cut under the bows? Where was that child? Absorbed? Forgotten? How did she grow older and older and find herself here?

Strange. Strange. What was the touchstone of my life? How was the pattern weaving? Towards what end?

'Come,' said the Second Son. 'You are dreaming. You are always dreaming, Mrs Tea Cup. Always dreaming. Shall I leave you here?' He smiled slowly.

'No, no,' I said, getting up and shaking out my silk skirt. 'I am with you.'

We began to walk back to the car. We walked slowly, my white Sloane Street sandals incongruous on the Arabian stone path. Maidenhair fern grew at the edges of the canals. The fronds of the palms were like green inverted umbrellas keeping off the heat instead of the wet.

Half-way back we saw a bare-headed young Arab who was presumably a man of authority, walking towards us on the path. His face darkened to anger as he saw me.

'Keep walking,' said the Sheikh, 'say nothing.'

'Why?' I said in Arabic.

'Speak in English,' he said. 'If you must speak at all.'

I held my tongue and lowered my eyes as we passed him in silence, never altering our pace. Only Shiar stopped to talk with the bare-headed Omani, whose face continued to be tight with anger. When we reached the car we waited for some ten minutes before Shiar moved out from the trees and down through the dead fields. As he got into the car the Sheikh asked, 'Is all well?'

'All is well,' replied Shiar and we drove carefully back along the way we came.

25

Baby

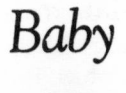

I WASN'T THERE when the baby arrived. It was a hopeless bit of timing. I hadn't been home long and was just beginning to settle into my London routine, just beginning to relax into my normal daily round of home, office, family, friends. The days were good but in the nights I would still wake, hearing in some half dream a child's voice calling 'Um Yusef, Um Yusef, *wein inti*? Where are you?' and I'd drift off in an imbalance of space, not knowing whether I was here or there. With the first light of morning I'd throw myself into a frenzy of work in an effort to cure the disorientation. This time the cure was not to be allowed. The night dreams became reality.

'Where are you? Where are you? You should be here. The baby has come.' Not a child's voice but the message was the same. Then he added, 'It's a girl.'

The disappointment was almost tangible, even over the satellite connection.

'Is she well? And her mother? Is the baby perfect?'

'Oh yes. They are very well.'

'Then congratulations. *Mabruk*. Hurrah. You are a father.' I put as much energy and joy into my voice as I could.

'But I wanted a boy, truly,' he said.

'The next one will be a boy. A girl is lovely. Your wife is a girl. Why in the world do you all always like boys? We are just as happy for a boy or girl,' I insisted.

'Yes, of course, I am happy. But you know how it is. We want a boy at

first. I suppose it is wrong, but I can't help it.' A pause. Then, 'When are you coming?'

Two days later I was back in Al Ain. He drove me to the hospital to see his wife. A collection of long, low buildings stood in a grove of trees beside one gleaming new multi-storey block which had just been completed. This was the only hospital in Al Ain. We drove up to a bungalow where private patients had suites, and walked inside to search for the young wife. She wasn't there. The big room looked very empty.

'The baby isn't feeding well, so they took her to the special nursery. Your wife is there,' said a straight-eyed Sudanese nurse. She wore the long white trousers and white over-smock which is the accepted nurses' uniform of Americans and Muslims. The former wear it for casual comfort, the latter for modesty.

We searched the new hospital block, investigating corridor after corridor. It was so new that no-one knew the whereabouts of anyone else and there was a marked paucity of staff. Eventually we saw a small, rather dejected, black-veiled figure sitting on a chair at the end of yet another very long, very white corridor. It was our young mother. She rose to greet us. Her face was grey and pinched and her eyes were frightened. She wore the vulnerability of her position like a hair shirt. She greeted her husband shyly, worry etching every gesture.

'The baby is all right?' he asked.

'She is sicking up her food all the time,' she said and turned to me. 'Why is this, Um Yusef? Am I not good for her?'

'Of course you are good for her. You are the best,' I answered.

We walked into a room where another white-trousered Sudanese guarded a small dark-haired bundle, sleeping quite peacefully in a high cot.

I admired the baby and took the two exhausted parents by their hands. We walked down to the car and drove the few hundred feet to the private room. The entire time I kept up a patter of what I hoped were soothing sounds, knowing in my heart that the baby's problem was the result of the mother's worry which was the result of her husband's disappointment.

It's a hypocrisy to sit in judgement. Name a Western father whose chest doesn't swell that extra millimetre when his first born is a son. They can't help it. It's in-born, that desire for a male heir, for another pair of hands to carry the load of life.

How does an observer feel when observing nonsense? Sad, mostly, if you allow yourself the luxury, which you can't because the human situation, whether economic, social or cultural, is so full of nonsense that we would spend far too much of life being sad instead of enjoying its wonder.

Both mother and baby were to remain in hospital for another few days while the doctors tested them for every known physical sign of ill health. To me it was obvious that the signals were entirely mental. The Sheikha was, as always, a fund of knowledge and a well of love. She shrugged off any suggestion of despair, delighted in the baby, told her son to pray - the panacea for all problems - and lifted up the atmosphere with a little gentle teasing. This, added to some words of wisdom and scorn from the boy's elder brother, who had himself spawned a most beautiful girl, began to heal the wound.

A flurry of cleaning was started in order to make ready for the arrival of mother and child. I had brought a little wicker carry-cot from London lined with frills and furbelows. It seemed a very small bed for a very small person in my huge room, which would now be the baby's room as well. Cradles had long been a part of the furniture of Arab life, though bedu women often used small hammocks. As for babies' bottles, when a mother found nursing difficult and no wet nurse could be found, a small conch shell was cleaned and used as a sort of bottle. Drops of camels' or goats' milk were poured through the shell into the baby's mouth.

But it was the actual birth of the child which put me in awe of the courage of these women. In the past their stringent rules of modesty left them without even the normal help of a midwife which women in most societies, whether primitive or modern, would have had.

'Do you know how we once had children?' asked the Sheikha the afternoon before we were to collect mother and child from hospital. We were sitting on the new long porch of her new big house. It was an entrancing place to sit. Persian carpets were unrolled in the shade. Big cushions were placed against the wall of the house for our backs, while in front of us was the new garden square with its lawns, hedges and flower beds. The bougainvillaea on the pergola spilled colour for our pleasure.

We sat sipping coffee as always and enjoying each other's company.

The daughter was there beside me, ready as always to tease me about my Arabic. She lorded over her foster sisters as they played hopscotch on the drive. The Eldest Son's wife sat sewing. Hussa, Shama and Sheikha Grandmother were there, but no visitors. Well, I was a visitor, but somehow had dropped into a peculiar role of non-visitor. My very foreignness contributed to that strange role. I believe now that my lack of knowledge of their language was an advantage, especially in the early days, for they could speak above and around me, only allowing such family information to reach my ears as they deemed fit. It was my very isolation which, in the long run, helped to overcome barriers.

'Do you know how we once had children?' repeated the Sheikha as she held out her coffee cup for her elder daughter-in-law to fill. 'It was not as it is now,' she said and tipped up her burqah for a quick sip. Then, settling the mask firmly back on her nose, she leaned against her cushion. 'There was a pole. A thick, strong pole put in the ground. When the pains come you squat down and hold the pole.' She put her two hands in front of her as if clutching an invisible pole. 'Then you push your head against the pole.' She leant forward. 'There are three women with you to help. One held down one leg at the heel and another held down the other leg. The third held up the back. The bottom. This way the child was born. But no sound, Um Yusef. You cannot make any sound. It is not polite. Only like this,' and she made a soft grunt.

She went on to tell me how when the baby arrived and the cord was cut the words 'God be praised' were shouted into the child's right ear. Only then was the baby washed and oiled. But it had had to arrive on its own. Any real assistance would have been impolite.

After ejecting the afterbirth the mother washed herself. If any excessive bleeding took place, she packed salt into the cavity of her own vagina.

How many women lived and bore children easily and naturally, and how many died, God alone knows, but I myself know of one little Saudi Arabian who was flown to London after being allowed to suffer labour pains for three days.

'It was hard,' I said.

'Hard?' said the Sheikha. 'Yes, hard for women who are too small. Thanks be to God.' She held her hands up in prayer as she praised God, then wiped them over her face, adjusted her mask and picked up the coffee pot to pour another round.

Baby was eventually installed, along with a rather beautiful Zanzibari nurse. She and I became firm friends. She was a fund of information. Tall, intelligent, she walked with a certain glamour, especially when she wound her great coat around her. It was a long, black sheath which she whipped about her in a few twists, covering her whole figure and leaving only her hands and eyes in view.

We talked for hours as she washed the baby, rocked it to sleep, changed and cuddled it. She said she would only stay a few weeks as the baby would soon get the mother's smell and she would be of little use except as a maid. That she refused to be. Indeed, after only a week she announced that the baby had already caught the smell and she would surely stay only her contractual month.

She slept in the bed beside me, the only person ever to use it. In future

212

years future nurse-maids slept on palliasses on the floor, the growing child on a palliasse beside them. But my Zanzibari friend used the bed, placing the new little cot on a bench beside her. In the night, I would open one eye to see the young mother feeding the baby on the couch at the opposite end of the room, the nurse beside her. They made a scene of complete devotion centred on the child. I would rise on one elbow to look and they would murmur admonitions for me to sleep, which I contentedly obeyed.

One morning, when the routine of baby nursing was particularly quiet, nurse and I began to talk of Zanzibar customs and those of Somaliland and East Africa. I learned just how emancipated she was, how forward thinking and knowledgeable, particularly when we talked of female circumcision.

In Al Ain, a type of female circumcision was practised until very recently and the fact that young mothers no longer allow it is often hidden from ageing grandmothers. There, when girls were around six to eight years old, the tip of the clitora was snipped off.

'Not like those people,' said the Sheikha when I asked her. She waved disdainfully in the direction of Africa, 'Not that bad business.' In parts of East Africa, I had learned, the entire clitoris is excised, without anaesthetic, when a girl is between five and eight years old.

The Sheikha went on to describe how the mother and aunts would arrange the circumcision of their daughters with the aid of an Arab woman 'doctor'.

'We cut just a little, a little bit off the tip,' and she measured about an eighth of an inch with the tip of her finger.

'But why?' I asked.

Her eyes looked at me blankly. 'Why?' she repeated. 'Why? Why?' She raised both hands to reveal the henna circles in the palms. 'Who can say where this came from? It has always been. It is not in the Qur'an, not a rule, but it has always been.'

My curiosity was not satisfied. 'Some say it is because by doing this you spoil the pleasure of the woman when she lies with her husband and she cannot be vain and have power,' I said.

She burst out laughing, 'Who says this?'

'Westerners,' I replied.

Her eyes again became still and blank, the poker face which Arabs adopt when they don't want you to know what they are thinking. Then she said quietly, 'We cut too little here. Western women think of that bad business over there,' and she waved again in some unknown direction. 'Here it is nothing like that. Never. No, Um Yusef, they do not know us. But why it is done, I cannot say.'

Male circumcision is another story. As there is evidence that the Prophet Mohamed was circumcised himself, all boys born into the Islamic faith are circumcised. In the past, the recent past, boys were circumcised in groups by Imams when they were about eight years old, lining up like so many lambs. If they cried out, they let the side down. Such behaviour was not countenanced by family or tribe.

'And were you so brave?' I asked the Youngest Son when he told me about it.

'Me?' he said and promptly burst into laughter. 'Me?' He rocked back and forth with laughter, his handsome face catching the light. The boy was full of that magnetic charm with which some Arabs are endowed. The stuff that dreams are made of. 'Me?' The laughs slowed just enough for him to say, 'I screamed like a beast. I screamed and screamed. The old man had cut the tip off as well. He had done too many and got careless when it was my turn.' Then seeing my face, he gave me a great hug and said, 'Don't worry, Mrs Tea Cup, it's as good as new.'

He then told me of the great celebration that took place after the circumcisions were done, the feast with singers and dancers, the Lawa drummers and piper. It was a celebration of victory over pain and obedience to their teaching, a religious initiation into the male circle of Islam. But the rite is older than Islam.

According to the book of Genesis, Ishmael, the father of the twelve Arab nations, was circumcised at the age of thirteen, along with his father Abraham who was then ninety-nine and all the male members of the household, including slaves. But there is no Biblical record of female circumcision.

As for whether our new baby would be circumcised, that decision had already been made.

'Of course not,' said the new mother. 'That is an old tradition. We do not want that business for our baby.'

I was heartily relieved to hear her being so definite, for however small the cut may have been in their tradition, it was an unnecessary moment of pain and shock for a little girl. It was equally satisfying to know that boys were now 'done' when newborn babies.

In spite of the meticulous care of the Zanzibari, the life of the house had begun to change perceptibly as it always does when a child arrives. There were frequent visits from her grandmother, great-grandmother and the many aunts. Gifts of clothes were brought by relatives and friends and the oh's and ah's were identical in Al Ain to those in Atlanta, Auckland or Birmingham.

One morning, Sheikha Grandmother came in with a small object shaped like a ring doughnut. It was a *ddaug*, a round ring of packed cloth. The back of the baby's head was placed in the centre of the ring as she lay in her cot. The object was to help shape the back of her head and to strengthen the neck which in turn would keep the back straight. A girl with a weak neck, round back and slouched walk was not 'Sheikh', and this little one would certainly be brought up to be 'Sheikh'.

Is it 'Sheikh'? was the constant query. It applied to shops, houses, cars, clothes, whether the sea was boiling hot and whether pigs had wings. Everything had to be 'Sheikh' and with the tasteless advice they often received from tasteless merchants and tradesmen, much that pertained to their houses was anything but 'Sheikh' in Western eyes.

Behaviour, on the other hand, was another matter. Little girls born as 'Sheikhas' were constantly reminded of their position. *'Inti Sheikha'*. You are a Sheikha. Therefore, sit like a Sheikha, eat like a Sheikha. They use the word almost as we would use 'good girl' and yet, of course, it is different. You have a position, you are the leader. You have a responsibility to your family, you are the hostess, the lady in charge, the central pivot of this group. Be gentle, be quiet, sit straight, walk straight. Oh yes, they are Sheikhas from the day they are born and they are taught to know it absolutely.

They are still children, of course, running around noisily and happily or unhappily, according to who has what at the moment. If one has a car, all must have cars, if one has a sweet, all must have sweets, and this can be quite a problem, as within any household there may be a dozen or more brothers and sisters and cousins, all potential Sheikhs and Sheikhas.

There are friends, of course. The children of servants swell the group, but theirs is a 'give way' role. They must give way to their little masters and mistresses, and little Sheikhas must give way to little Sheikhs, and these little Sheikhs can often be appallingly behaved, as they are allowed their own way in everything. If they want the toy of another child it is given to them. If they want to hit their nurses, sisters, even mothers, it is laughed at, allowed, smoothed over. I suppose I am the only woman who ever spoke a severe word to a male toddler in all the years I've been visiting the area. The fact that I did brought a puzzled moment and I had the feeling that I was forgiven for the breach of custom rather than supported as correct.

The little Sheikhs' behaviour with their elder brothers, fathers and other senior members of the male household, however, has to be impeccable. What is more, after about the age of eight, their behaviour to the female members of the household changes markedly. They seem to go through

some sort of metamorphosis and, on the whole, become charming little men almost overnight. But the system has already allowed the boy to realise that he is special. Segregation has been implanted like a weed and it is difficult if not impossible to pluck out. Its roots are deep. The young Sheikh is segregated not only by sex but by position and he knows it. Only education, travel, rubbing up against other cultures softens the edges of a chauvinism which has been so strongly nurtured; nurtured not so much by their male tutors as by the women.

Yet in spite of this cossetting of and kowtowing to the male, in this area, in this small segment of the Arabian scene, the women maintain an extraordinary independence and strength of spirit and influence. They hold long, strong reins which reach out into the heart of their society. Our baby Sheikha would be no exception, although at this stage her training was confined to the *ddaug* and the attendant belief in encouraging a strong neck, a strong back and a fine head.

Other problems, both new and old, hung like unseen black mists in the otherwise placid atmosphere. The mother's guilt at producing a girl instead of a boy was ever present, if unexpressed by word. It manifested itself in feeding problems. Her milk upset the child more often than not, thus creating colic and sleepless nights for both nurse and parents. Then her supply began to dwindle.

When this happened the Sheikha arrived with a delicious drink to cure the problem. It was made with sugar, water and the red seeds of a flower still unknown to me. In fact, I've asked so many questions about this seed that the Eldest Son or indeed any of the sons when they see me with notebook and pencil call out, '*Habbat al hamra*, Mrs Tea Cup, have you found *habbat al hamra* (the red seed)?' I haven't yet, but it apparently comes from a red flower grown in the area of Al Ain.

This drink of slippery seeds was followed within hours by another speciality, a custard-like substance made of egg, oil and sugar. Then as a special nourishing treat, the maternal grandmother of our nursing mother sent over a bowl of camels' milk every morning. It arrived punctually at seven carried in a small, cloth-covered, enamel pail borne on the head of one of the servants of that hareem. Rich in protein, low in fat, the ideal drink.

Thus with the quantities of camels' milk, orange juice, dates and habbat al hamra, the little mother began to pick up. The feeding problem faded. The guilt was pushed into the back of the mind, there to fester until a boy could finally be produced - God willing.

Over and above these settling in problems there were specific traditions

which had to be observed. The day after baby arrived home with her Zanzibari nurse, I walked into the dining majlis to find a great feast of mashwi lamb and other feast dishes.

'What's all this?' I asked.

'A-sabat, Um Yusef, a-sabat,' was the answer.

A-sabat, the Seventh Day, the seventh day since the baby's birth. She had lived for a week in this dimension of life. It was a moment to celebrate. While the young mother received the good wishes of all, the hareem celebrated by eating too much, as we all do on days of thanksgiving all over the world.

Another day of celebration took place on the baby's fortieth day, called *Al Arbaheen*. Why is forty such a magical number for us all? Noah waited forty days from the moment land was seen before sending off the dove and the raven. Moses led his people through the wilderness for forty years. Jesus wandered in the wilderness without food for forty days. At the end of each period was the reward of life. It begins, as it so often does in other traditions, with a sacrifice. In Al Ain and most of Arabia all the hair of the child is shaved off on the fortieth day of life.

'She will have much better hair,' said the little mother as she snipped away the baby fuzz. 'It will be stronger and so will she.' But when the baby's fine, straight black hair grew back in curls she was not so pleased. While we frizz and perm our hair into all sorts of curls, they spend their time straightening any bend at all. Will man never be satisfied? Must we always think the grass is greener on the other side?

Nonetheless, Al Arbaheen was a happy day. Baskets of nuts, sugared almonds and dates were delivered to all and sundry, along with bowls of helawa, the Arabic sweet. Bowls of sweets and nuts were placed on tables in the house for childish hands to enjoy and indeed, children seemed to materialise from every corner to stuff themselves with goodies. A happy day in spite of our darling looking like a fuzzy billiard ball.

One further custom had to be observed. Painting the eyes with kohl. This had to be done before Al Arbaheen. If such a custom were ignored the child might grow up envious of others, to say nothing of the fact that kohl 'protects the eyes from disease and wards off flies'.

Again it was the Sheikha who arrived with her own little pot of kohl and a tiny brush to paint the lashes and rims of the baby's eyes. After the make-up session, baby looked like a prize fighter. She had two large black eyes, but woe betide the nurse who washed off this special painting. She stayed that way for several days, the kohl dripping down her cheeks if she shed a tear. These extraneous lines could be cleaned up, but not the eyes

themselves.

Whether she was protected from an envious personality or not, and whether she was protected from diseases of the eye or not, doesn't really matter. It was believed to be true and that belief was protection in itself. Oh, they laughed about it and said it was only a belief - 'just a tradition, Um Yusef' - but surely we are the same? Our fear of the number thirteen, the way we throw salt over our left shoulder to appease the devil, the black cat syndrome; all equally bizarre.

It came as no particular surprise, therefore, when one evening shortly before supper the young mother hurried into the bedroom and all but ran to the window. She quickly drew the curtains, making sure that they were completely shut, blocking out any possible view from inside out or outside in. As she usually didn't mind whether they were shut or not, and as I was the one who usually went around the house drawing the curtains, I watched her with amazement.

'Didn't you hear it?' she said.

'Hear what?' I asked.

'The owl ... didn't you hear it?'

I had indeed heard the owl. It had been pleasant and surprising to hear the familiar hoot of the 'wise old bird'.

'Yes, of course,' I said. 'He is a nice, wise old man who is no doubt busy catching some mice.'

'He is not good, Um Yusef. He is very bad for baby. She must not be seen by him. Not at all. These birds, they bring sickness. Sometimes very bad sickness. We must keep baby away from the eyes of this bird,' and she reached up to make sure there was no crack through which the dreaded bird could look.

I watched her with affection and curiosity. Here was a child who was quite brilliant. A scholar. A girl who tried to understand the outside world, spoke English well, albeit with her own idiosyncrasies of grammar, and who preferred to be known as very modern. In truth, the heart of the girl was more full of tradition and ancient custom than that of her sister-in-law, the Eldest Son's wife, who presented the most perfect picture of traditionalism and yet was, at heart, more modern in her approach to real living. More accepting of change. It was a dichotomy which was to prove more and more difficult for our young mother. In her dreams she was only waiting to leap over the wall, to be 'Westernised'. Given the chance, however, she would retire behind her customs, fearful of the consequences, unable to know which foot to put forward. Her rapid tongue, quick mind, constant pose of knowing all and everything were a strong wall against the fear of both

present and future.

As the years passed her life became wrapped in her child. The wee baby grew into a remarkably intelligent and loving little girl who was bound to know a life which her mother, through circumstance and the trauma of the time, would be denied.

26

Beating the Devil and The Waters of Zam Zam

I WOKE ONE MORNING with a heavy head and that all-over feeling of disorder which announces the approach of some 'dreaded lurgy'. I can count on the fingers of one hand the times when I have felt even modestly ill in the Middle East, so I was surprised and annoyed at this boring beginning to the day. I knew that there had been yet another virus going around Al Ain. Everyone seemed to be either recovering from it or going down with it. Now it seemed to want to attack me.

I splashed some cold water on my face and went to breakfast, but that was the end. Back in my room I crawled into bed and pulled the blanket over my head. Baby was moved into the 'baby majlis' by my Zanzibari friend so that I could sleep. Some hours later, half awake, half asleep, I saw the Sheikha coming toward me across the bedroom floor.

'You are ill, Um Yusef?'

She sat beside me.

I dragged myself on to my elbow and said that I would be all right soon.

'Would you like to see the doctor? Would you like to go to the hospital?'

Seeing the doctor meant they would fetch some young Indian or Pakistani GP who would prescribe a vast number of pills and potions, plus an injection of some sort of penicillin derivative. As for the hospital out-patient department, this too would pump me full of every known drug. Both ideas were equally abhorrent. The cure was sure to be worse than the illness. Indeed, I felt ashamed to be in bed at all. My friends seldom gave in to illness and walked about dazed with fever rather than lie down.

'Say a prayer for me, Sheikha, that is much safer than the doctor,' I said.

She smiled and agreed. Then telling me to 'lie quiet', she went off to order fruit juice and, I hoped, to pray. Though she knew nothing of what Christians meant by the Christ, she knew a great deal about Jesus, who was one of their Qur'an prophets, and she worshipped as we worshipped the one God, Creator. I had confidence in her ability to speak to Allah, so I pulled an old black veil over my head to ward off a stray mosquito that kept droning around and around and fell asleep, a sleep which lasted most of the day and part of the night. I remember waking once in the night to hear the muezzin's call to prayer. I gulped some orange juice that had been left by the bed and dropped off again.

By the next morning I felt better except for the most thundering headache. A thermos of tea was beside me and as I sat up to pour myself a cup, Hussa came into the room, walking as always with her rolling gait.

'How are you?' she asked.

'Ashamed to have been ill.'

She touched my hands and forehead, announced I still had fever and then said she would give me something for my headache.

'To swallow?' I asked doubtfully.

'This would be good,' she answered, 'But you are not used to our ways. I will give you something to smell.'

I agreed to succumb for curiosity's sake. I couldn't resist new knowledge of their 'ways'.

After an hour or so she returned with a bit of black gauze torn from an old veil. Tied into the gauze were some hard, black chippings.

'Al aswad,' she announced and, settling her ample figure beside me, she showed me what they did. She took the little packet and rubbed it vigorously in the palm of her hand. Then she placed it against the nostril and breathed in. She handed it to me to do the same, and to her delight and amusement, I sat up spluttering. It was a cross between pepper and pine. I hadn't expected anything so powerful.

'You will be better now,' she said and went off, chuckling to herself.

It could have been the one sniff of aswad, the glasses of orange juice, the cups of hot camels' milk with sugar and ginger, but I believe it was my hostess's powerful praying along with some prayers of my own which put me on a fast road to recovery. I was soon quite fit again and went to look for Hussa to thank her for her care.

I found her in the big house of the Eldest Son's wife. Hussa and Shama and the Sheikha's daughter were all there, sitting in the little hall between the bedrooms, an area which had been adopted as a sort of on-the-carpet

living room. Another 'baby majlis' as we had begun to call them. It was the only cosy place in the outsized bungalow.

When we'd first met, the Eldest Son's wife had been painfully shy in her new family. Now she had settled down and gave promise of becoming a gracious and most hospitable hostess. She was already a fashion plate. Her clothes had a traditional elegance and she had chosen pearls as her particular jewel, simple, rich and rare pearls. With her beauty and gentleness she had already captured her husband's heart and he made the journey up from Abu Dhabi at every possible moment to be with her. It was a match that had worked well.

Like most young wives she did not wear her mask in the house, so it was easier to understand what she thought. The mask is a great concealer of emotion and reaction, but her husband, like most of the young husbands, found it tedious and encouraged her to abandon it, at least at home. This didn't alter the formality of her life, her adherence to tradition. She would never have allowed a strange man to see her face. My knock at the door and the creak of opening it sent her scurrying behind the heavy curtains of the 'baby majlis'. When she saw that it was only Um Yusef, she at once welcomed me. Her fine black eyes looked at me shyly, their long lashes carefully and heavily covered with kohl.

'You have been ill, Um Yusef?' she asked.

'Only a little,' I answered.

Hussa gave a good imitation of my shock when I smelt the aswad, much to everyone's amusement and, after settling down on the carpet, we launched into a long discussion about the merits and uses of herbs and spices.

As we sat talking and sipping orange juice from crystal glasses so new that the maker's seals were still on them, the young wife brought in a small brass tray with an odd collection of jars and packets. She put them on the floor in front of me and urged Hussa and Shama to tell me about them.

Just as the average Western family medicine chest will have packets of aspirin and milk of magnesia, so these families had their collections of medicinal herbs and spices, seeds and roots. They would call the doctor, use his pills and potions once or twice, then pile them in the refrigerator, where they'd stay until they were cleared out. A job I've done myself.

'See this,' said Hussa. 'I give you this *halool* and your stomach will be clean in one hour. Zip. Right through. You never leave the toilet.'

Roars of laughter were tempered with a consensus on how good halool was for purging. The young wife, losing her shyness at least a little, said that her 'sauce' was best. It was a 'sauce' of thyme, fenugreek, frankincense

and kheel. She said it was infallible. She had learned it from her mother. The women all had their own medicinal remedies or 'sauces'.

I learned that nutmeg mixed with cloves was good for the liver - 'good for anything - for everything', and that the smoke from African rue burned in an incense pot and held under the jaw would help toothache. The leaves of the sedr tree were used for sprains, as was a poultice of bread and camels' milk.

Hussa then said that they used myrrh for ulcerated sores and I told her that I remembered standing in my mother's bathroom when I was a child as she opened a medicine chest and took out a small bottle of tincture of myrrh. She soaked a piece of cotton with it and dabbed it on a canker sore in my mouth, its bitter puckering immediately allaying the annoying pain.

The young wife wrote down the names for me, a long list that I still have. There was black aloe, African rue, liquorice root, wild thyme, thymus serpyllum and fenugreek as well as the classic frankincense and myrrh with their inevitable prophetic symbolism. But two names were untranslatable and have remained a mystery. *Al aswad* - 'the black' which had sent the shaft of astringency up my head and a pain killer with the haunting name of *gheel* - 'the unreal'.

Shama picked up a packet of gheel from the tray and explained its power over pain. She eased her lame leg out from under her, rubbed it thoughtfully and said, 'Um Yusef, you mix this gheel with this kirkum,' - she picked up another packet and held the two in one of her hands - 'and you mix with tobacco and salt. This mixture is very good for the bullet wound and the knife wound. Very good. Heals in maybe five days or six.'

As always she threw me a thread of conversation which I longed to unravel. How many wars had she seen? How much killing between one tribe and another? How many invasions of territory? How many knife wounds and bullet wounds had she helped to heal?

She shifted her position, settled her long mask more comfortably on her face and looked directly at me. Her eyes were old, with impending cataracts, but they were straight and cool. She seemed to be making a decision. Then she said softly, 'Sometimes we use fire. You know this?'

A stillness settled over the conversation. The women sat quietly, impassively, expressionless, waiting for me to react. I did not answer. For one who is given to instant reactions, learning to wait, to think before speaking is very difficult. This time I waited, then said blandly, 'Yes, I know.'

Yes. I knew. I had seen it. Not here. Not in their place. I had seen it in North Africa. I had seen the children in hospital with infected burns on their necks, their backs, their legs. I had heard French, Lebanese, Egyptian

and Bulgarian doctors curse the parents for allowing such barbarism. It was a practice outside the law in most states, but it went on.

I remembered, too, a young Berber who believed he had been healed of a dislocated neck by 'the fire'. I can still see him dancing about, throwing his head around, see the round ring scars on his legs where he was branded. I remembered too, the story of the Eldest Son.

'I know about your husband,' I said to the Eldest Son's wife.

Hussa answered for her. 'Ah. She knows.' The atmosphere relaxed.

The Eldest Son had been branded when he was a boy. He had had a severely ulcerated lip which failed to respond to any of the known treatments of the women, so the fire healer was called.

'See, see. Look, you can see the place,' the Eldest Son said when he told me the story. He had lifted the hair on the back of his neck and I had looked for the mark of the circle but could see nothing. Apparently the ulcer had suppurated at once, discharging quantities of pus and blood. The healing was immediate, but there was no mark of the circle.

I told them the story of the Berber. The large rows of ring scars.

'We don't use that,' said Hussa. 'No, no, I've never seen that.' She said that their irons were long and pencil-thin. They can leave a scar about the size of a cigarette burn if used strongly, but sometimes they leave hardly any visible mark. They seem to operate in the same manner as acupuncture, though not in such a sophisticated or carefully defined system.

Hussa and Shama explained a few of the shock points. To heal an ulcer in the mouth or on the tongue the iron is placed on the centre of the back of the neck. For jaundice or trouble with the liver, the iron is put on the little fingers and little toes. Ringworm is healed by branding the top of the head, and so forth. Hussa said that the iron should be very hot and touched to the skin quickly and firmly. Needless to say, much prayer is offered both before, during and after the operation.

I have a deep-rooted fear of white hot metal. It is more fearful to me than fire itself. Listening to a discussion of fire healing, seeing its effects, was a lesson in self-control, for I ached for the patients and identified with pain.

Is it shock to the nervous system that in some cases seems to effect a healing? Or is it belief, faith in the power of sudden pain to purge the body of the evil within? There is a strong belief in the area that illness is a sign of the devil possessing the body. It's an ancient belief. Weren't Christians commanded by Jesus to cast out devils - evils?

'Do you believe you are burning out a devil?' I asked.

No-one replied for a moment. Then Hussa said, 'Devils can get inside

people. When they come in we beat them out sometimes, with God's help. Not the fire, though.'

I remembered the days in Europe and America when people believed in witches, in being possessed by the devil, and I shivered again at the thought of the innocents who were burned alive.

In Arabia, if a person becomes nervous, prone to shouting, crying, deep moods of depression, sleeplessness, over-excitement, boorishness, or a loss of manners, these can all be interpreted as signs of possession.

The young wife began to tell the story of a girl who lived near her own home in Al Ain. She had become possessed and her parents decided she should be cured in the prescribed manner.

'I can tell you, Um Yusef, it was a good way, for now she is well and as before. Calm, polite, good,' said the young wife. She explained the process of exorcism with corrections and encouragement from Hussa and Shama. Apparently the girl's family invited a well-known holy woman to the house, a woman who was well practised in such things and had a reputation for freeing from the devil. The hareem assembled in the women's majlis, sitting in a circle. Women slave descendants beat the drums, for no men could be part of a gathering of women.

They started by chanting appropriate verses from the Qur'an. The girl was brought into the circle and started to dance a slow, sad, undulating dance. The exorciser had a stick. She watched and followed the girl. They weaved around the circle in a seemingly endless pattern of movement, without beginning or end, the chanting and drumming becoming hypnotic. Eventually the girl fell into a sort of coma, swinging round and round, and then the healer began to beat her. She was beaten all over her body. She was beaten on and on, blow after blow, until she fell to her knees. Still the beating continued. The belief is that it is the devil which is being beaten and if the exorcism is successful, the devil will rush out of the big toe and the healing will take place.

'It was indeed the devil who was beaten, because there was no mark on the girl. No mark at all. She felt no pain,' said the young wife.

I wondered at the capacity of the human mind, that mysterious continent which is perhaps our last frontier. We stand on its fringes, terrified to look beyond. What is it within us that enters into a covenant with strange practices? Where does it begin?

'It is what a person believes,' I said to Hussa.

She spread her hands out on the floor in front of her.

'Perhaps. The English, they believe in what they have because they see it. We believe in what *we* have because we see it.'

'What of true faith? What of prayer? Surely this is better,' I said.

'It is the best of all means. It is the true way. Jesus, peace be with Him, he healed the blind and the leprous by God's permission. So says the Qur'an.'

Jesus, peace be with Him. They never mention his name without wishing him peace.

'Do you believe this?' I turned to the young wife.

Her reaction was one of amazement at my having to ask, coupled with the slightest hint of admonition. She lifted her languid, long-fingered hands and rocked back with a soft laugh, as though I had asked the most absurd question.

'Of course, naturally, prayer is the natural thing. I tell you, Um Yusef, it is the best way, thanks be to God. Praise God the Merciful. Now I will tell you, Um Yusef,' and she settled herself, called her maid to remove the tray of herbs and bring the coffee della. Once again I found myself feeling like a curious child, while the child - she was scarcely sixteen - was the teacher.

'If there is a bad illness, something that no-one can cure with our doctors or the new hospitals and their doctors, we will go far, very far to see a holy person. We will go across the border. My mother once went to Iran to see such a man. Such a holy man. Others have been to Egypt. But the most healing place of all is, of course, at Mecca.'

'Mecca?' I asked and then answered my own question with 'Of course.' How stupid I had been not to realise that attached to the Haj, the great pilgrimage to the Holy City which took place each year, there must have been an element of healing.

'I have myself seen someone leave their wheelchair after drinking the waters of the Zam Zam, praise God, thanks be to God.' She lifted her hands in an attitude of prayer. Then she went on, 'You know of these waters, Um Yusef, the waters of Zam Zam from the well of Hagar?'

I said that I knew of the well, because it had its place in the Bible.

'Truly?' asked the young wife.

'Truly,' I replied and began to tell the story as I knew it, of Hagar, the handmaid of Abraham's barren wife, Sarah.

'In her old age,' I said, 'Sarah begs Abraham to have a child by Hagar. In time Abraham agrees and Hagar gives birth to Abraham's first son, Ishmael.' They agreed that this was correct. I went on. 'After more than ten years Sarah gets a message from God that she will give birth to a son herself. When her son Isaac is born, Sarah demands in a jealous rage that Ishmael and Hagar be cast out. Abraham takes them into the desert and leaves them.'

In the Arab tradition, this was as much of a sacrifice for Abraham as the subsequent one demanded by God of his son Isaac. Both were redeemed through faith.

'In the Bible,' I continued, 'Hagar searches desperately for water. At the point of death, she finally finds it where God directs her to dig.'

'Ah,' said my young hostess as I finished the story, 'it is nearly correct. But in truth, Um Yusef, Hagar runs back and forth, back and forth between the mountains of Safa and Hurwah.' She made running motions with her hands and then added, 'Praise God. Thank God,' and continued. 'Then does she find the water where God directs her. These are the waters of Zam Zam. It is a bottomless well. No-one has found its source and it never dries.' She looked at me intently. 'And Ibrahim [Abraham] returns to look for them. He finds them. He builds a house for them where they live, die and are buried. This is the Kaba. You know of the Kaba in Mecca? Yes? So do you believe this, Um Yusef? And do you believe the waters of Zam Zam heal?' Again my doe-eyed hostess looked at me carefully. I answered her equally carefully.

'Yes. It is possible. We have many such things in Christianity. Surely Jesus told us to heal as he healed, love as he loved.'

'This is true,' said the young wife.

'It is surely so,' added Shama as she tucked her legs under her, bending over to rise. It was the accepted signal for the close of the evening. We all began to rise, murmuring the usual thanks, praises of God and thanking Him, wishing that His blessings were on all of us.

Thanking the young wife for her courtesy and lessons, I moved into the night with Hussa and Shama. It was fine and clear. The stars seemed so near that you felt you could pull them out of the sky with your hands. These were the same stars in the same sky that hung over Abraham, Sarah, Hagar, Ishmael and Isaac. Awesome thought. All those centuries were as nothing. What have we learned of ourselves in this arc of time? What's the good of invention without knowledge of ourselves?

Back in my room, the evening wouldn't leave me. The motor of my mind kept going round and round until I finally got up, opened my Bible and read the story of Hagar in Genesis. I found this seldom quoted verse: 'As for Ishmael, I have heard thee: behold I have blessed him and will make him fruitful, and will multiply him exceedingly; twelve princes shall he beget, and I will make him a great nation.'(Genesis 17:20)

As Isaac fathered the twelve tribes of the Hebrews through his son Jacob (Israel), so Ishmael fathered the twelve tribes of Arabia from which it is said that all true Arabians are descended. And yet ever since Sarah's jealous

rage, the descendants of Isaac have looked down on the descendants of Ishmael. Sarah's jealousy governs history still, but in both the Biblical and Arab tradition there was no such jealousy between Ishmael and Isaac themselves. They were together when their father, Abraham, died. They buried him together and lived in peace together. 'And his sons Isaac and Ishmael buried him in the cave Machpelah.' (Genesis 25:9) The same chapter goes on to give the names of Ishmael's twelve sons 'by their towns and by their castles; twelve princes according to their nations.' And then reveals that Isaac was with Ishmael when *he* died. '... and he [Ishmael] died in the presence of all his brethren.'

We still seem to accept Sarah's curse when both Ishmael and Isaac overcame it.

Questions wound round in my head. Thoughts became more jumbled as I drifted in and out of sleep. It was a restless night haunted by dreams of thirst, anger and cool, healing water. Is there a part of Hagar and Sarah in all women?

On the long flight home that winter, I thought of Ishmael and Isaac as the Gulf Air plane dog-legged around the Levant to avoid the air space of Israel. I stared out of the window straining to see the desert so many miles below. A small plane crossed far, far beneath us and I suddenly remembered those planes they use for spraying infected crops. Perhaps a plane could spray the waters of Zam Zam over that benighted area and the sons of Ishmael and Isaac would stand together again as their ancestors did. Perhaps. One day. One far-away day.

Part Six

27

New Dreams for Old

IT WAS OVER a year later that I made the journey to the desert which seemed to mark the end of one era and the beginning of another.

The plane touched down an hour and a half late, delayed in London by an onslaught of ice and snow. It was January and England had decided to have a cold winter. After seven hours in the air, we had landed in the Abu Dhabi warmth. The plane taxied slowly up to a new airport and I realised with a sudden loneliness that there would be no car at the foot of the steps, no young Sheikhs with their young friends to greet me, no-one to ease my way through customs. There would be nothing but cool efficiency. The informality of the past had given way to the technological present.

The plane moved heavily, as though exhausted after its long race from London. It docked near a suspended landing platform, which twisted its worm-like body towards us, sucking its mouth against the plane's exit. We gathered our belongings and walked through the immaculate tube, following a neatly uniformed Filipino girl whose high heels clickety-clacked as she walked.

'Follow me.' The words were crisp. I almost expected her to raise a rolled umbrella in the time-honoured way of a tourist guide. Trooping after her we eventually arrived at 'Immigration', where there was the internationally inevitable queue. It ended in a brief consultation with a voice whose body was hidden behind opaque glass. All was clinical, impersonal, efficient.

In the long reception hall I looked for a familiar face. There was none. It was past midnight. With a sense of weariness and overwhelming alone-

ness, I signalled to the porter to push his cart to one of the waiting taxis. Where to go? Had anyone arranged a hotel? One thing was certain. I knew the town well. I knew it very well indeed. I knew its good hotels, half good hotels and bad hotels, so I got in the cab and asked for the Sheraton. It took over half an hour to get there as the new airport is some thirty miles from the Corniche. Thirty miles of six lanes of cement which, at some point, went right over the spot where the boys and I had been almost sucked into a sand pit. Occasionally the road rose up on overpasses or ducked down through underpasses. An occasional car moved toward us on its opposite way to the airport. We passed an occasional lorry but there was no real traffic until we reached the outskirts of Abu Dhabi. There the Sheraton now punctuated the eastern end of the Corniche as the Hilton had once punctuated the western end. The Hilton now was dwarfed by a massive Abu Dhabi oil company complex.

I booked in with a sleepy-eyed Filipino receptionist, handed over my passport and went to bed.

At eight the next morning the phone rang.

'Mrs Tea Cup? Is that you? Thank God. We look for you. Where did you go?'

'Where did *you* go?'

'The man was there. He couldn't find you. It's the new airport. Too big. Never mind. I am coming now. We will have breakfast and then I will take you there.'

It was the Second Son. Within minutes another voice came on the phone, low, assured, full of charm.

'Welcome home,' he said. We talked easily, quietly. It was the Youngest Son, now a grown man. 'I made a room for you at the Hilton. It is nearer us. Never mind. I will see you there.'

I packed and waited. Then they came. My Arab 'sons' and their friends.

Thin, erect, neat, covered in white, crowned in black, these young gods of the Gulf came laughing quietly, jingling their car keys, joking with each other. They were as at home in the corridors of the Sheraton as their grandfathers had been in the desert. Hassan was with them, his black intelligent face alight with welcome. The two Omani brothers were there with their wide eyes and wide smiles.

My bags were shut, lifted like featherweights and we rode down in the lift with its stand of Asian orchids, always fresh.

'Breakfast?' I asked.

'If you like,' was the answer. That could mean, 'Only if you're hungry' or 'Yes, please, I'm hungry.' I weighed up the pros and cons and made a

decision based on what I knew. I decided on breakfast.

Leaving the bags in charge of the head porter we went to the coffee shop, found a remote corner and ordered a vast quantity of food, only half of which we ate. Over-ordering is a habit they've acquired. Unable to translate their own meal styles into Western customs, they order several main dishes and scarcely touch half of it.

At breakfast that day we had omelettes and fried eggs, pancakes and brioches, croissants and toast, orange juice and grapefruit, tea and coffee. The pancakes were pronounced 'not so good as yours', the maple syrup 'not like yours from Canada' - maple syrup connoisseurs already? But the coffee was hot and the juice 'fresh squeeze'.

They ate rapidly. They ate as though there was no tomorrow.

I knew the little group with me very well. Individually they might sit over their food, talk, savour what they were eating. Collectively it was a race. In half an hour the food had been ordered, eaten and paid for, and we rose from the table leaving behind enough for a second meal.

I walked through the lobby in my long skirts and dark glasses, the bags were collected and stowed in yet another big dark Mercedes and I was checked out.

'New?' I asked as I got in the car with the Second Son.

'Not so new,' was the enigmatic reply. 'Better for a family,' he added and we moved smoothly out into the Corniche traffic, the Youngest Son following in his own white Mercedes.

Abu Dhabi was growing visibly. The hibiscus bloomed, the lilies were white, the zinnias bright yellow, roses climbed over walls, hedges were clipped. It was new, glassy and glossy. Tons of concrete were poured each day for more and more tower blocks. New streets splayed out from the coast and there was the smell of trade everywhere. The smell of shuffling bills, of clinking coins. The sound of computers neatly adding columns of figures, the atmosphere of commission, of agency, of ten per cent.

The big car hummed in and out of the traffic. We passed the Hilton and turned left. Beyond the new ADNOC complex a hill was being pushed up by bulldozers. A new Intercontinental would stand above the rest of the city. It would observe Abu Dhabi from its own little mountain. It would provide, they said, every possible advantage.

We passed new villas, new schools, a new sports arena. The road widened into six lanes, lifting over a new six-lane bridge. Off to my left I could see the old cantilever bridge in the eastern distance, an antique at fifteen years.

We passed the airport, watching as a jet settled like a hen on the new runway. Then we turned toward Dubai. The desert spread around us. Signs

stood haphazardly here and there, announcing uncomfortably the merits of a cigarette, a fizzy drink or a battery. We passed a boy riding high on his camel, leading three other camels. They were perilously close to the road. We passed hillocks of sand being pushed in various directions by bulldozers. We passed the tents of workmen. Finally the car swung left towards an unmarked village, the tower of its mosque acting as a compass point. The rough tar road gave way to hard-packed sand and we were in the desert at last. I felt the tension slide off my muscles and leaned back to enjoy the rest of the journey.

The way was now marked by old tyres stuck upright in the sandy earth, supported by stones. Empty oil tins announced the edge of a soft sand verge and at an important change of direction a crashed car pointed the route. If this had been the old American West a new town might have risen there called 'Crashed Car Cross'.

The road to the 'camp' was outlined with more tyres and oil drums. I could probably have found the way myself. Certainly Range Rovers were no longer necessary.

As we drew nearer I felt a sudden wave of the old Irish second sight. Too many Irish ancestors. Too many to leave me in total peace. I knew at that moment, as surely as I knew my own name, that this would be the last time. This would be the last visit to this desert. I would not see it again.

As though he had felt the same wave pass over him, the young Sheikh turned to me briefly.

'What is it? Are you all right?'

It was my turn for the enigmatic reply.

In minutes we were there. I saw the familiar white tents, the cook fire, the Range Rovers, the saronged fishermen. I saw a large new water tower and a larger, newer, chain-link fence. As always the lights were there, battened to each fence post, continuing to ward off roaming camels, goats, sheep and the odd djinn.

It was the compound itself which had changed beyond recognition. Inside the fence were new pre-fabricated houses, low bungalows, hugging the sand. Only one of the old palm-frond huts still stood. It was now a weather-beaten centrepiece, its once neatly thatched roof sagging under the weight of a tarpaulin. This areesh, which had once housed the bride of the Eldest Son, was now a dejected reminder of another time, another age. She had moved into a new pre-fab, one of the dozen or so which ringed the square. With their chipboard walls, wooden porches and cement paths, they looked like a group of summer time-shares on the Mississippi Delta or the Florida Keys. Only the desert itself had refused to yield its character.

Its winter air was still clean and sweet and the wind blew steadily up from the Gulf.

The Sheikha was sitting on the porch of her new bungalow. She rose when she saw the car and we greeted each other with the affection of old friends.

'What happened to the lovely palm houses?' I asked. 'The Sheikh was so proud of them. Only this one left.' I pointed to the forlorn remnant in the centre.

'Ah, they were old and these are better for the bathroom. Especially for the grandmother. She needs to be comfortable,' said the Sheikha. 'It is good, Um Yusef?'

The statement was a question and there was only one answer.

'It is good.' What else could I say? But a large twinge of nostalgia wrenched my heart.

Children began to appear from everywhere. The two foster daughters of the Sheikha were now schoolgirls, not quite certain whether to act as children or young ladies. Then there was the beautiful baby boy of the Eldest Son's wife. A pensive, shy baby, never quite well in those days, he had the expression of a judge and I named him Al Hakim, the Wise. Their robust little daughter was all smiles and coquetry. As for baby, the tiny bundle I had first seen in an intensive care cot was now a toddler with a totally happy nature. She had a well-rounded head, short curly hair and a short upper lip, a face already full of character. An extrovert, she included everyone in her smiles and hugging arms.

Finally, there was the foundling. I had already heard the story of the child's arrival. It was an extraordinary tale, one worthy of a twopenny novel and a perfect example of the attitude toward orphans. Apparently the foundling had been discovered by a servant one afternoon during the rest period. Wrapped in a blanket, cradled in a cardboard box, this human parcel was left at the family gate of the Al Ain house. Left like a posted gift, by some silent, black-veiled figure who knew where to come and how to go.

The child, a baby girl, was only a few days old. How the mother missed being seen, God alone knows, but she did. What's more, she was wise. She must have known of the reputation of the Sheikha, known that her child would be cared for as a trust from God.

By great good fortune - or good planning - the Eldest Son's wife was still nursing her own baby boy. With profound generosity, the young mother shared her breasts with the strange baby and in so doing made her as close to a daughter as possible. The foundling would be able to come and go all

her life without having to cover for the men of the family. She was treated with much love and was much welcomed, as the Sheikha dearly loved children. A plethora of babies was her special delight. They personified regeneration, renewal. They were the heart of life to her, a promise of the future in the present. I watched her joy, her pleasure giving me pleasure. Indeed, I could share in it, for by now I had two grandchildren of my own and we often compared the progress of our respective progeny.

'How is Elizabeth?' she asked turning the 'th' into a 't'. 'And little Yusef?' And we began to talk about 'the apples that fall closest to the tree', as an Arabian saying describes grandchildren, for they are so close to the heart.

I gave her my news. The news of the grandchildren, of my children, my husband, my work. Coffee arrived, suitcases were despatched to the bungalow of the Second Son's wife and I sat watching the sky, the sand, the new bushes, the old palm house; watching the black veils, the masks, the sons in their kandoras, the daughters in their silks. I felt the hard cushion against my back, tasted the cardamom in the coffee, basked in the warmth of their welcome and in the peace of the place. I was back in their world.

The bungalow of the Second Son's wife would be my camp home. It was furthest away from the cooking fires and nearest to the Gulf itself. Although there were three bedrooms, baby and her nursemaid slept on palliasses in my room beside the wide double bed, as always.

That first night in the new bed in the new bungalow I slept fitfully. Dreams came and went. Strange dreams. Disorientated dreams. I struggled against the dark, against night visions. I was caught somewhere in the sky, tossed in the sea. I tried to wake up, knowing I was dreaming. Layer after layer of the subconscious had to be lifted. Finally I woke, gasping, and began to tremble. I was cold. The night was black. Groping along the bed I found a sweater, put it on, doubled the blanket and returned to my tossing and turning.

When dawn finally came I was more tired than when I'd gone to bed. The dreams haunted me. Dreams of faces weeping. Dreams of the dark. I had been told by an Egyptian friend that when you had nightmares you should spit over your shoulder three times and turn over. This would ward off the devil. I hated vivid dreams. As a child I had had many and several seemed prophetic. It was my grandfather who then declared that I had the Irish second sight. I didn't like the idea then and I don't much like it now. It disturbs me.

I knew that the Sheikha believed in dreams and decided not to share mine with her, as I was certain she would read some disaster into them. Reason declared they were a result of a long flight, a long drive and

unexpected changes. Nonetheless at breakfast everyone began to talk of dreams. Apparently it had been a restless night. My old friend Hussa began by saying that there was nothing irreligious in reading dreams. Indeed dreams were signs which one should heed. Her mother Shama added that some women could read them well and prepare themselves for good or bad, and some were reminders to contact a friend or relative. Listening to these black-veiled, masked women, smelling their musky perfumes, reading their eyes, I suddenly wished Freud was there. The man who made so much of dreams would have been swallowed up in this company, and I laughed aloud.

'What is it, Um Yusef?' asked a visitor of Sheikha Grandmother.

She was from Sharjah. She was old, she was rich and she was funny. No-one laughed more, derided the system more or 'took the mickey' more than the woman from Sharjah.

'What is it? Why do you laugh to yourself?'

There were few secrets. They saw much. But how could I explain Freud? He couldn't explain himself. So I said that I laughed at myself because I knew so little about anything. The Sheikha, who as usual had been listening to the conversation but saying little, looked at me knowingly. She knew I hadn't said all the truth but she smiled and then rose, announcing by her rising the end of breakfast. We all went with her to wash our hands at the row of basins in a back hall, and passed each other boxes of kleenex to dry them. Then we moved out into the sun.

After breakfast I began to feel better, lighter, less burdened by the night. Hussa and Shama were a comforting and comfortable sight and I was glad to see them.

Days in the desert had a pattern to them, just like days in Al Ain, Abu Dhabi or London. The pattern was less rigid but nonetheless there. After breakfast, after an hour of tidying rooms and clothes, we met again to walk. These walks were a ritual. Adventure would be discovered in the minutiae of life. We would gather together and troop off along the inlet; the children, the daughters-in-law, visiting friends and always Hussa and Shama. Hussa would invariably take the lead. We would let ourselves out of a small gate in the fence and walk through the dry, hot sand to the edge of the water. The sky was its eternal blue. The water lapped at the land quietly, almost affectionately. As we walked we bulldozed the homes of hundreds of those thousands of miniature molluscs, every tread making a massive rebuilding plan necessary. They would scurry into the sea dragging their conical shell houses with them in a flurry of confusion.

That day, the first day of that visit, I remember Hussa stopping after

some fifty yards and picking up a sliver of driftwood. Then she carefully dug a hole and buried a white plastic packet. It was the hair combings of the Eldest Son's wife. No man must see the combings or cuttings of a woman's hair or the trimmings of nails, so they are collected and buried beneath the desert.

We walked on, leaving the houses behind. There was nothing now but sun, sea and sand. All clean perfection. Sheikha Grandmother, who had decided to follow us with the woman from Sharjah, stopped for a moment and leaned on her tall staff. We all stopped, mindful of Grandmother's frail legs. I remember that the sun burnt mercilessly through my blouse and I begged a spare veil from the Sheikha's daughter. She gave me her abaya, carefully draping it over my head and shoulders. Immediately all was cool and protected. It was like entering a shaded room. They laughed to see me covered in black, but I vowed not to go out in the sun again without at least a veil.

Sitting down together on a hillock of sand among some dune grass, we watched Hussa and the children fishing. Hussa as usual had brought along a few lines in her pockets. The lines were wrapped around H-shaped holders, hooks carefully turned in to prevent their catching in her clothes. She always found some bit of bait, a worm, a lazy bug, a bit of bread or a hapless sand crab and cast lines, hooks and bait into the inlet while the children waited open-mouthed for something to happen. When a little fish was caught, she would unhook it and throw it back to the agonised cries of the children who wanted to eat it for lunch.

The Sheikha's daughter, who was now a teenaged young lady, but still more child than woman, gathered her veils and skirt about her, walked to the edge of the water and dropped on to the damp sand. She started to build sand castles, her diamond bracelets sparkling in the sun.

'Look, Mother of us all,' she called as she crushed the damp sand into balls or found some strange shell or caught a crab. 'Look at this,' or that or the other, and I would nod and smile as we do with all children on every beach everywhere. It was only the clothes that were different.

The following day Hussa and I, the Sheikha's daughter and foster daughters decided to walk to the sea on the opposite side of the peninsula beyond the inlet, that same inlet over which we had once dragged Maha. It had now been dredged and widened to allow power boats to come up the channel, but few ever made the effort as the sand silted up so quickly with the tide. A small harbour had had to be built on the far side of the island across the inlet, the same island where we'd once gathered flotsam and jetsam after a storm all those years ago. A bridge was built to connect the

compound to the island and the new marina. Made of four huge, round cement pipes, it allowed the inlet water to flow back and forth and permitted us to cross.

Hussa, the children and I crossed the bridge, stopping to look at the water rushing through the pipes. Hussa decided to cast a line for some fish she thought she saw, but she caught nothing and we walked on over the dunes to the Gulf. Here the waves were stronger. Not heavy. Not pounding and rolling. But firm and insistent. Hussa again cast her line into the water and stuck the 'H' holder into the sand in the vain hope that some sizeable fish would come near enough to the shore to grab at the small hook.

Impatient, she wound in the line, laid it on the sand and began to wade farther and farther into the sea, her brightly patterned cotton dress floating around her. Finally she caught up her veil in a turban on top of her head and, beckoning me to join her, launched her ample body into the water. I waded out. My own wool skirt was no match for her cottons, so I pulled it over my head, threw it back to one of the girls who had waded out to catch it and swam in my underwear and shirt. My own veil was wound up in an untidy jumble of a turban. My legs looked like two white eels in the transparent water. The children who stayed near the shore screamed with delight. Eventually we managed to pull the Sheikha's daughter into the water with us. Some of the maids had walked over the dunes, and in one grand jumble of wet dresses, shouts and screams we splashed, swam and paddled. We weren't long. A couple of hours perhaps. But it stays in my mind. Vivid. Clear.

Walking back, my woollen skirt felt wet and heavy, even though I'd tried to save it from a soaking, but my shirt dried quickly in the sun. We picked our way through stones and debris, scarcely noticing a carload of European men manoeuvring over the bridge with an Arab driver at the wheel. They got out and walked toward the small harbour the Sheikh had made. The men eyed me with total curiosity. I looked back blankly but was equally curious. Who were they? Why were they here? Were they going fishing? No. They weren't dressed for it. Were they visitors of the Sheikh? No. He was away. Who had brought them? Seeing them in that place was weird, as though someone had pressed the wrong button on the time machine. They had materialised in the wrong loop.

At lunch no one mentioned the men. It was as if they had never existed. Instead all the talk was of our swim, the sea, the fish, the food. The food was superb. Fish straight from the sea, fried and served crisp on the outside, soft and white on the inside. Fillets of hamour, fried saafi.

Just before lunch the Sheikha had taken me by the hand and led me to

the cook house where the morning's catch was spread out. Among the fish was a big hammer-head shark with its weird snout. It was a prehistoric nightmare dredged up from the ocean bed. What purpose was behind that wedge of fish flesh? Would we eat it? I asked.

'Oh no,' said the Sheikha. 'A bad taste, but sometimes good for the soup.'

That afternoon I slept. The swim, the sun, the lunch all combined and I slept. I slept too long, too hard and woke as the sun began to slide down the rim of the desert. I woke feeling restless and angry, knowing that it would not be easy to sleep that night. I shrugged off a feeling of self-pity with a conscious effort and washed and dressed for the evening.

No-one was about when I opened the door and stepped on to the wooden slats of the bungalow porch. The ring of lights was already on. I could hear the movement of the water in the stillness. No birds sang. No crickets whirred. No children's voices rang out on the air. The near silence was, in itself, audible, expectant, as though the earth was holding its breath before allowing life to continue.

'...stand in awe of Him. For He spoke and it was done.' It was a moment for prayer. Without recognising the ever presence of Life, of Principle, of Truth, I might have seen the tall, thin pillar of Boudariah rising from the sea. If I'd placed my feet on the sand a djinn might have pulled me beneath the earth. Anything was possible. Everything was possible. I lifted my arms in a puny effort to embrace creation.

A cricket began to sing. A child cried. The instant of union had passed.

28

The King Who
Listened Too Much

I WALKED ALONG the sand-silted cement path to the house of the Eldest
Son's wife. Children were gathering there to play with her daughter, to
gurgle over the baby son, to race their toy cars and do the important things
which children have to do. In the richly carpeted and heavily curtained
main room of the bungalow the ever-present square eye of the television
was watching and being watched.

The Eldest Son's wife soon walked into the room, buttoning her sleeves
as she came. It was a familiar sight after prayers were completed. Greeting
me with welcomes and her gentle smile, she settled on one of the couches,
ordered fruit juice and picked up a pile of uncut masks. She began to cut,
shape and stitch them. Like the Sheikha her fingers were always busy.

Hussa was there and she and I began to laugh once again about our
swimming expedition and teased the Sheikha's daughter for her lack of
knowledge about the sea.

'One day,' I said to them, 'one day in the far, far future, you will come
to see me in my country and I will show you places where the tide comes
in and out going up and down maybe twenty or thirty feet. Young people
stand on boards and ride on top of the waves as though they were riding a
horse. The water is so cold even in summer it makes your skin prickle. One
day you will come, God willing.'

'I have seen men standing like this on the water on the television,' said
Hussa. 'They do this with you?' She no longer doubted the authority of the
box.

241

We talked of the seas of the West, of oceans that pushed against cliffs urged on by prevailing westerly winds. We talked of the turning of the earth, the places of the stars, the moon pulling at the waters of the world.

'All this is told in the Qur'an,' said the Eldest Son's wife. 'Everything is in the Qur'an.'

'Three things will teach you most,' said Hussa. 'The Qur'an, life and keeping your ears open.'

It was dark now. The dark is always a surprise when you are not aware of its coming, when you are not near to fading light or are absorbed in talking, working or whatever. The dark brings its own atmosphere.

I told them of the moment of stillness as I left my bungalow, of the times in life when you seem rooted to the earth. I told them of lying on the lawn as a child and watching the clouds move, of the way the clouds suddenly seemed to be still and I could recognise the moving, turning earth. It was turning at such speed that I imagined I felt the very power of its engines.

'Perhaps the djinn are busy there as well,' laughed the Sheikha's daughter.

'You must not laugh at the djinn,' said the Eldest Son's wife with a smile and picked up her baby boy who had begun to be fretful. She arranged her veils about her, unbuttoned her dress and began to feed the child. 'You must respect them,' she said and held her child closer as if to protect him from the very thought of them.

'We do not know of the djinn there but there are others,' I said. 'In Cornwall they talk of piskies. Little men. Very, very small men who live in the woods among the trees and under the stones. Some are good and some are bad, as with djinn. But most are just naughty and do silly things like stealing milk or cheese. Some will place a spell on the cows to stop them giving milk. Those are the bad ones.'

'They are djinn and you must admit it,' said the Sheikha's daughter. 'It is all the same.'

'Ah, but you don't have great stone castles sitting on top of islands in the sea,' I replied. 'Castles you can walk to when the tide is out but when the tide is in you must reach them by boat.'

'We have castles. You know this very well,' said the Eldest Son's wife. 'They are cut off just the same. By those mountains.'

'This is true,' I said, remembering that I had told her about my unauthorised visit to Oman with the Second Son, as well as an 'official' visit I had recently made. I had seen a castle, high, high in the mountains, made of perfectly cut stone. Its walls were without cement or plaster. Just neatly, accurately cut stone.

'All is the same everywhere, I think,' said the nursing mother. 'It is only that we have lived in the past, while you have found much that is new. Soon we will have all this too and we will be as modern as you.'

'This is what I am afraid of,' I said half to myself.

'What? What is this?' She laughed and moved the baby off her breast, lifting him over her shoulder. 'Al Hakim must have all the new. He will talk on the telephone to me from his car just like Papa.'

'Well,' I said, 'I would rather the gallop into the future was slowed to a more comfortable trot.'

She told me that I was getting as bad as the old ones who always looked backwards instead of forwards. There was nothing so sweet about what had gone before. The life was hard and the sun was hot. The bones ached and the sickness killed many. Surely I could not wish for this.

Hussa looked at me as the gentle voice of this young mother spoke. We were both silent waiting for this bird to sing, for she seldom spoke out. Her thoughts remained sealed in the centre of her mind.

Handing Al Hakim to his waiting nurse, she buttoned her dress and ordered coffee.

'Um Yusef,' she said, 'you know I will never see these oceans and the castles of your place. You know that when we are in the West we cannot come and go as you come and go. It is not our tradition. But all things change and must change. Perhaps my daughter will know your place. Perhaps. But I will visit all those things which are possible. Why? Because now we have the oil. We have the gold. We can move. We can move a small way. We can learn. We have cars and roads and aeroplanes. These things. Is it not good and right? Surely it is.'

The Sheikha's daughter added, 'And I will not just marry. I will not. I will go to university.'

'Truly?' I exclaimed both with delight and incredulity.

'Surely,' she answered. 'For sure. The one they make in Al Ain.'

'Brave girl,' I said and clapped my hands. 'But you will marry too,' I added, knowing that this part of their lives was inevitable.

I turned back to the Eldest Son's wife. 'I wish all for you that you wish for yourself. All to make you happy. But I never hope to see you imitate the West. This is what happens to many. Be yourself. Carry your own life with you into this world of computers and robots. That is my true wish. Do you understand?'

The eyes of the young mother were like those of a young gazelle. Alert yet soft. The lashes were heavy with kohl. She laughed again quietly and poured coffee for us.

'Who knows what God has for us all?' she said.

'All is in God's hands,' said Hussa. 'Thanks be to God.'

'Thanks be to God,' said the young mother and ordered fresh juice.

'Um Yusef, since you like what is past, shall I tell you a story? A story of one of those castles?' she asked.

'Please,' I said.

It wasn't easy to catch them in a storytelling mood. Not any more. There were the babies, the households, the visitors. Even here life seemed ever busier, as though they had caught a slight case of our infection.

'It is a true story,' she said, 'but you will not believe. I know that you will not believe. You will not believe, but it is true. I will tell you and one day perhaps something will happen and you will believe. But it is in God's hands.'

Settling herself more comfortably, she smoothed her dress around her, saw that we were all properly served with coffee or juice, leaned back against the cushions, and began.

'In the mountains of Oman, deep in the mountains, there is a town where the houses are tall. The town sits on the side of this mountain and all around are the sides of other mountains. To go to the town you must have donkey or horse or walk. For camel it is too difficult. You must go over smooth black rocks to reach the streets. Very difficult. When you are within the town, the houses reach up and up. Some are cut from rock, some stone upon stone. There is water and many things grow. Many things. Lemons and mangoes and figs and fine dates. It is quiet but the people are rich because of the water.

'Not so very long ago, but quite a while ago, the king of this town, the Sheikh, he was a strong man. He lived in the tallest house. He was rich. His fields, his trees, drank the water first. His trees were the tallest and had the best fruit. Yes. He was a strong man but not so perfect. Why? I will tell you. He was curious. He wants to know everything from everyone. What they do. What they say. He listens. His ears are everywhere.'

She pointed to each child in the room and said the king would hear all their naughty secrets. They, in turn, began to tease and whisper until Hussa stopped them and ordered the story to continue.

'The people of the town are tired with this king, but he was so strong they can do nothing. The men of the town come together to talk. They ask one old, wise man of magic to come.'

She looked at me.

'You think magic is a trick. Like for children. This is not true magic. Magic is ... is ...' She stumbled over words, searching for the one which

could possibly explain such magic. She could not find it and said, 'It is a real thing. Not a trick. A real thing. Not a thing you can do or I can do. Magic people are special. The way some can sing and some cannot.'

Her explanation over, she went on.

'They ask this magic man to help them. They must meet when all are asleep. When the king is asleep. Asleep he cannot listen.

'They wait until the shutters of his tall house are shut. Then, they talk in the cool meeting place below the little musjid, the little mosque as you say, cut high in the rock. They feel safe in the shadow of the musjid. The magic man listens to the problem. He agrees it is difficult for them. Then he says to them, Come. We will walk together in the town and talk together.

'So they begin to walk up the steep road. Up and up they walk and talk. They reach that road beside the king's house. No-one hears them. So quiet were they. No-one except the king.'

She leaned back, raising her hands in horror.

'His shutters at the top of the house open with a crash. He leans his head out of the window.' She leaned forward. 'Further and further he leans with ears which are large with much listening. The magic man looks up. "Are you listening to all we say, Your Highness?" he said. "Do you think this is good in a king? Do you think, because you are king, the people should not talk as they wish? Such nonsense needs a lesson."

'Then suddenly,' she turned to me. 'It is true, Um Yusef, though you will not believe. Suddenly the king grows - grows these things which come from the sides of the gazelle's head.'

'Antlers,' I laughed.

'Yes, antlers.'

Her hands made delicate movements beside her head, creating antlers in the air.

'Yes, antlers. He could not move this way nor that way.'

She bent her head and turned it this way and that.

'He could not go in and he could not fall out for he would crash to the ground from his tall house. He sticks. And there he stays for a day and a night until all are certain he keeps his promise not to listen. The magic man takes away his - his antlers and from that day to this day the town is a good place to live. All can speak with safety. This is true. Though I know you will not believe.'

'Congratulations for this story,' said Hussa while the children made hands into antlers and began to run around the house.

I thanked the young mother for her perfect storytelling and felt strangely

comforted by her apparent belief in magic. Whether she believed or not was unimportant. It was her storytelling, her memory of their own beliefs, her delight in the wonder of her place that was important to me. Was this why she had told the story? To comfort me? Or was it to admonish me for listening too much to everyone and to the past?

Supper was announced and we rose to walk to Sheikha Grandmother's bungalow. The young mother held my hand and looked up at me. Such a little person.

'We will see. We will see what God has for us. And for you.' Calling for her burgah and abaya, she put them on with care and we walked out into the dark.

29

Halcyon Days

THE DAYS MELTED away, as days will when there is little to do but talk, eat and sleep. We walked and waded, collected shells, watched the maids carrying the cooking pots and trays down to the inlet to wash them, watched the fishermen row down channel to set nets for a catch. The sun rose and set, rose and set. Then suddenly it was over.

As always the decision to leave was made without preliminary. As always we were told one evening to have our cases ready before breakfast the next morning. I packed the now well-worn green tweed case that I had travelled with for so many years. Beside it was the snake-skin vanity box given me by a Sudanese friend. It too went with me everywhere. The two cases sat side by side with the bed rolls, Samsonite cases and carrier bags of odds and ends for baby, waiting for men to pack them into lorries.

Breakfast over, I returned to the house to find it empty of everything. Even the debris of rubbish had been cleared. It was an empty shell of a place, totally without character and I quickly turned my back on it.

At the gate of the compound fence, the whole 'caravan' was assembling. There were two trucks piled with bed rolls and an estate wagon full of cases.

The Sheikh was not with us this time. He was already off on one of his conference excursions. Without his entourage there would still be some twelve vehicles in all. The family went in six cars, the Youngest Son leading off in a Range Rover with the Sheikha and her daughter. He had proved to be an almost uncanny navigator and as excellent a driver as his father and elder brothers. The Eldest Son had arrived with his Mercedes the

previous night to drive his wife and family. Sheikha Grandmother went with them. I went with baby's father and mother, nurse and baby herself, and a new driver whom the young father had the responsibility to train. The rest of the family and guests were dispersed in other Mercedes with drivers. There were two Range Rovers with servants and two trucks with luggage which brought up the rear.

The cars strung out along the desert, dust flying, wheels spinning. It still took considerable skill to get over some of the sand hillocks and drivers still raced up one side in one way or another and skidded down the other. The road had remained in parts quite a soft track which grew softer according to which way the wind blew. Baby's father talked our new driver over the hills. 'Now left, quick right, low gear here before we go. Go.'

It always amazed me how they got those rear wheel drive cars over the sand. But they did and after an hour or so we pulled up *en masse* at a petrol station on the main Abu Dhabi road. Coffee dellas and water bottles were pulled out. Petrol was bought. The men and servants got out to stretch their legs, to laugh at each other's driving problems, to drink Pepsi Cola out of tins. Then we were off again, a modern caravan.

The women were still masked and veiled as they had been five hundred years ago, fifty years ago, fifteen years ago. The men were still in their white kandoras, white head dresses and black circlets. The coffee had the same flavour, the desert the same dust, but now the only camels were bloodstock for racing, or fat stock for eating. The caravan routes were roads which had been constructed, then widened, then extended. We set out with stereos blaring the latest tunes from Cairo or Beirut, children shouting or sleeping, maids gossiping and the steady hum of tyres on hot paving. We were in Al Ain in under two hours.

'Come, Um Yusef, we will make a visit to my mother.'

The Sheikha and I were walking down the long porch. We had been in Al Ain for two days. These were the halcyon days of the place. The winter storms were over. The heat had not begun. The air was cool and sweet and the prospect of visiting the Sheikha's mother particularly alluring.

I liked her. She was old now and bent almost double, but her once strong body gave an air of objection, perhaps disdain, to the crippling of her back. Her long face and bright eyes expressed strength of mind and a once structured beauty. Though she moved with great difficulty, she still sat with grace. Thin, angular, old-fashioned and affectionate, she waited in her large, old-fashioned room in her large, old-fashioned house to welcome us.

It was a house that I loved. Built like an old fort around a large square,

its rooms all opened on to a covered porch which was more like a cloister than a terrace. The court was hard-packed earth and gravel punctuated with date palms. Her high-ceilinged room had windows at floor level, small windows with wrought iron grills and wooden shutters. They were just the right height to look out when you sat on the floor. The walls of the room were thick, and wide - wide enough for a window seat if such a thing were needed. Here a cushion or mat on the floor would do.

In the centre of the ceiling was one of those large rotating fans which remind you of Kipling's India. It went gently round and round on its old motor, stirring the air just enough to keep the flies moving and the heat from overpowering you in the summer. There was no sign of air condition-ing.

The floor was covered in fine old carpets and her four poster bed stood in the corner piled high with palliasses and bundles of various sorts, the embroidered valance circling the top like a crown. There were the hard cushions with their frilled covers, the incense pots, brass coffee pots and smiling young servants padding in and out on their bare young feet, careful of each expression of their mistress.

Her voice was remarkably deep and strong but with a gentle control, as if she knew it could ring out too powerfully. It was the voice of a contralto and had just enough resonance to add certainty to the knowledge that she could sing, or had once been able to sing. For whom and where would remain most private information.

Yes, I liked her. I liked her house. I liked to go there, driving up to the old wooden gates, stepping through the postern door, over a high lintel and into that particular moment of maintained history.

We sat sipping coffee and commenting on the weather, the family, the news of the travels of various Sheikhs, the impending marriage of some young cousin.

A tray of fruit was brought riding high on the head of a servant. A conical 'hat' covered it. The 'hat' was set aside as soon as the tray was settled on the floor in front of us and there on the tray among bowls of grapes, apples and oranges was one of red pomegranate seeds.

There is something so ancient and luxurious about a bowl full of sweet, red pomegranate seeds. It is as though you were living out a Greek myth or a Persian poem. Besides, I like them. To crush or crunch your way through sweet mouthful after mouthful without worrying about their bitter pith is a delight.

The Sheikha's mother laughed at my pleasure and asked whether we had pomegranates in the West, and bananas and oranges. So began a long

discussion of what grew here and grew there, the snow of the winter and the green of our fields compared to heat of the desert and their harvest of dates. Like Um Hamed, she thought that we lived in a Paradise and did not know it, that we did not truly understand the blessings God had given us.

We spoke of the past, of the simplicity of the life, of the work in the date groves. We spoke of the old boundaries and who went where. Their knowledge of their own history is phenomenal. It is as though the men relied on them to be living books. Every war, every battle, every birth, every event that had affected the lives of the tribes was catalogued in their minds. Their memory cells were sharpened and honed from birth.

The fan whirred round and round, the coffee was passed again and again and I began to ask questions as it seemed a moment for sharing and learning. I asked about the mask. The whys, the wherefores, the how-comes.

'These?' said the Sheikha. 'You have never asked this before. Surely you know this is our tradition. It is not in the Qur'an. This you know. Women can be uncovered. Good and faithful women walk with their face uncovered, but we do not.'

'But why?' I asked, not willing this time to walk away without an answer. 'If it is not in the Qur'an, when did it come and why?'

'There are many stories. Some say one thing, some say another,' said the Sheikha's mother in her rich contralto.

'What do they say, then?' It was hard to know whether I was being rude or they were being diffident. The mask is a tender point as they know what the world thinks of them. They know it cannot last, they know it is incongruous and yet they cling to its security, its proclamation of exclusivity.

'We do not know for sure,' said the Sheikha, 'but it is said that there was once a king who searched all the country, all the desert, everywhere. He searched for beautiful girls. He sent his men everywhere. He took them back to his castle and raped them and made them slaves. So our men said we should wear the burgah. This way he would not know who was beautiful and who was not. This way the women were cared for and it has gone on till this day. This is one story I have heard.'

'They say, I tell you,' said the Sheikha's mother, 'this king was Allesander.' I knew she meant Alexander the Great. 'The boy Allesander. Or perhaps it was the men from Turkey or the Portuguese. You have seen some of our women with blue eyes, you have seen this? These are from the Portuguese.'

Yes, I had seen startling, almost hypnotic and certainly fascinating

blue-green eyes and wondered where and why they had come and I had not thought of the Portuguese. I had seen the ruins of look-out forts said to have been built by Allesander's troops, high in the Oman mountains, but I had forgotten the invasion of the Portuguese some centuries ago.

'Others say that the burgah was to make us separate from the slave,' said the Sheikha's mother. 'The slave always had a naked face for all to see and sometimes a naked body when selling. Wives and daughters must separate themselves from this.'

No doubt there were germs of truth in each story but whatever the origin, it is the women themselves who perpetuate the custom and, consciously or unconsciously, maintain it for those ancient reasons of segregation. If you see a woman with the burgah, you know her to be a native of some part of the Gulf, a woman of tradition. Though many slave descendants adopted the custom as they were drawn more closely into the tribes, it is still a mark of identity in an area which is drowning in immigrant populations and struggling through the traumas of a material bonanza, a cultural implosion.

There was one other reason for the burgah which had not been mentioned, the one which had always seemed obvious to me.

'Surely the burgah, the old burgah, kept the skin protected from wind and sun. Especially when you travelled? Is not this so?' I asked.

The Sheikha and her mother agreed that this was so, but had never heard of it as a reason. It was plausible. Arabs admire light skin. Their prejudice against dark skin is different from ours. It has nothing to do with the fears of the unknown, the dark fears with which Northerners have burdened themselves from the days when we wore wode. The Arab prejudice is on the basis of beauty. One brother will say of another, 'Look at him. He is too black. Look at this hand,' and he will compare his hand to his darker skinned brother, just as two Northern sisters will argue about hair that is too fine or ears that stick out. Yes, they like light skin. Where Western women spend their time baking on the beaches of at least five continents to achieve a fine shade of *café au lait*, Arab women cover up against their common enemy - the sun.

I spoke then of Shama. She had blue-grey eyes. I once thought she had cataracts, not realising that she had the ancient gift of the Portuguese. I had thought of her as wrinkled and withered. Her hands were like paper, strong paper. Strong, dry hands. Dry as though moisture had left them years before. Then I went to visit her when she was ill.

The house of Hussa and Shama was built around a square, like the one in which we were sitting, but on a small scale. It was an inside-out house. Carpets were outside. Clothes were hung over a line in the centre of the

court and there was an air of 'just about to leave' everywhere. Of course there was a television - outside - a television which threw out pictures of overdressed, overblown women singing or dancing in a mockery of their tradition and history. Hussa soon turned it over to someone reading the Qur'an.

Shama was sitting on her bed, a sort of raised platform with a palliasse. It was nearing twilight, nearing time for prayers and I decided to wait until their prayers were over. Perhaps that is why it happened, why she took off her mask and sat there without it. Her face was startling. From behind that long, old-fashioned mask the full person revealed itself. She sat without her burgah, without her veil, an old woman of perhaps seventy or seventy-five, but her face - what an amazing face, a face of unimaginable fascination. Every feature was still perfect. The skin, protected over the years by the long mask, moistened by its own sweat, was almost unwrinkled. A high, wide forehead, prominent cheek bones, a long, straight Arab nose, a mouth still generous, still with its own teeth.

But it was the eyes that held you, hypnotised you. Carefully lined with a rim of kohl, they shone turquoise in the night. They were almost luminescent, like the grey-blue-green of the Gulf preparing to storm. She herself was completely Arab and there was no Berber legend here. Yet there they were. Those opalescent eyes.

Now I knew. The Portuguese invader. The Portuguese pirate. What ancestor of hers had been loved or raped by a Portuguese sailor? Or was it further back? Far away in some thread of history woven by a blue-eyed man of the Caucasus or the Urals who had joined the troops of the boy Allesander.

Whatever the gene that had weaved its way forward, Shama presented a face of haunting fascination, a fascination multiplied by smooth skin.

'Yes. It is so,' said the Sheikha's mother when I confided what I had seen, 'but not for everyone, Um Yusef. Not for everyone. Some do not have such a face.'

She did not seem at all alarmed that I had seen a face supposedly seen only by husband or children. It was a confidence which we now all shared and I felt closer to them. Drawn, inevitably drawn nearer to the centre of their lives. Bound by their cloister. Free, certainly, to come and to go, but never free to speak all that I knew outside those invisible veils.

That same afternoon I sat in the Sheikha's doorway thinking of our morning visit. The children were chattering behind me while watching some Canadian nature programme with subtitles. The maids called to each other in their own languages. The long, beautiful porch extended past the

coffee house, past the guest rooms towards the dining majlis and the great women's majlis which was rarely opened. Beyond the porch, beyond the drive, the carefully nurtured grass grew green. Bright green. Pool table green. Mammoth zinnias sprouted from their new beds and jasmine wound its way over new hedges and up new poles for the driveway lights. The pigeons were still there, rising and tumbling like white feather fans tossed in the sky.

I sat cross-legged against a hard pillow. There was a breeze coming through the door. It was pleasant. Soporific. Beyond the walls the folds of the desert barred us from any feeling of involvement with the world's problems. We were held in some pocket of largesse. All that mattered was the politesse of entertaining, of marriage, of birth, of death, the interweaving of the families, the state of the larder, the quality of the cloth. I was observing a society which had suddenly, after great deprivation, materialised every material dream. Here was the full flower. When would its petals begin to brown and fall?

'Shall we walk, Um Yusef?' It was the Youngest Son, whose company I cherished. I rose and we walked wordlessly around the court, through the new grass, avoiding the spray of multiple sprinklers which had been evenly spaced throughout. We walked under an acacia tree, around the back of the new great house, then on to the farm, hopping over the cement falaj, bending low to avoid the palm fronds of young date trees.

'See the new dates,' he said, 'They are inside this pod. When they burst they are like the golden hair of a woman.' He looked up at me, his dark eyes full of thoughts he wouldn't share.

When the date pods burst in the late spring, the golden hair becomes strong and tiny yellow fruit begins to grow. Now the pods were tucked well inside the long, spiky fronds of the trees. These trees and their fruit had been the life of this place for thousands of years. Even now when we eat, the dates are carefully taken at the end of the meal, covered and placed in Sheikha Grandmother's cupboard.

'The hair of a woman,' the boy repeated almost to himself. Then said, 'There are men trees and women trees. Did you know that, Um Yusef?'

I said that I had known that and we walked on.

Between the palms were the mango trees, lime trees and lemon trees and we looked for the budding fruit. I said how big the lemons would be. Like grapefruit when they are ripe. He laughed and said he would grow a grapefruit/lemon for the market.

We walked through the alfalfa growing succulently for the animals, through newly planted patches of onions, cabbages and potatoes. We

walked under fig trees and past the sheep pens with the woolly animals waiting for slaughter, past a goat on a tether and on to the cow pens. Their yield was small but rich. Butter, yoghurt, butter milk and milk were all to be found in the dairy behind the coffee house.

The boy said little, laughed often, watched me and wondered as I wondered what would happen next year, the year after that and the year after that.

I turned to him. 'It cannot last. It will all change.' I said.

He stopped and looked at me. 'I know,' he said. His eyes were expressionless. We walked back to the house.

Epilogue

Epilogue

In Limbo

FOR FIVE YEARS I never saw Al Ain. I never drove down the long highway and through the red dunes. I never set foot on the long porch with its fine balustrade. I never slept in my room in the bride house. Why? The Sheikha and her hareem had followed the other great hareems and moved down to the coast. They had packed their masks and veils and traditions and moved to Abu Dhabi.

Al Ain had become a memory. A memory of peace and laughter, of bougainvillaea vines and fresh dates, of masks and veils and time to talk, to write, to think. A memory of children and grandmothers, of feasts and fashions, of acacias and jasmine and pomegranate seeds. Al Ain had become a memory stored well in the mind.

Abu Dhabi is another world. Now a city of over quarter of a million foreigners, it is ruled by less than ten thousand Arabs whose roots grow out of that dry, salt-silted island. It is a city where wide streets are lined with hedges and palm trees, where the shops of Hamdan Street sell silk from Thailand, crystal from Italy, perfume from Paris and porcelain from Japan, where banks of zinnias and beds of petunias surround roundabouts and the traffic builds up at rush hour in a perfect imitation of London, New York, Tokyo or Rome.

Was it the lure of the shops that tempted the hareems out of their gardens in the desert, out of Al Ain? Certainly not. It was the men in their tall glass and concrete office blocks who couldn't get home to Al Ain more than one day in a week, the men who had become prey to a demi-monde

and a *sous monde* which had grown like a fungus. It had grown to such proportions that it became unacceptable to the respectable hareems, so the women packed and left for Abu Dhabi for the new 'palaces' which their husbands prepared for them. Bait? Perhaps, because the husbands knew they needed the cushion of their wives and families. They needed havens against the storms created by their own wealth.

The Al Ain compounds were kept, of course. They were kept as summer houses or holiday homes or week-end retreats to be used when the families weren't in residence in their new small palaces along the Gulf coast or their new great palaces in Abu Dhabi city.

My premonition came true. The camp is no more. It has disappeared under the concrete of a new desalination plant, a new cement factory, a new chemical factory or some such project. It is no more and I have never been to that part of the desert again. I have never seen their new small palace on the coast.

Instead I have stayed in Abu Dhabi in the new great palace.

The Sheikha is usually there with Sheikha Grandmother, who aged twenty years when they brought her down to Abu Dhabi. The distance from her beloved Al Ain was too far. The humidity of the coast seeped into her already arthritic bones. The pain of walking became too great. She withdrew into a self-made shell of age from which she rarely emerges.

Sheikha Grandmother lives in a comfortable bedroom next to a fine women's majlis. Her furniture is inevitably too new, too modern for such a traditional lady. The mirrors of the big new wardrobe are covered in brown paper as Grandmother makes one last stand against the encroaching maggots of modernity. There are nurses to care for her, maids to wash and iron her few dresses, to sweep and resweep her carpets, to listen for commands she no longer gives.

'She won't know you,' says the Eldest Son.

'She will,' I answer and I sit in front of her, take her hands and look into her near blind eyes.

'Sheikha?' I ask. 'Sheikha. I am here again. I have come again. The English one.'

She grips my fingers for a moment. 'Um Yusef?' she whispers and I kiss her hands. Then she is gone again, exhausted by my demand that she look out of her shell. It is enough. She knew me. My eyes well with tears for all the days behind her, behind me.

It is autumn. November. The days are cool. The ever-present sun is still high, still brilliant, but without its accompanying furnace heat. I have learned to loathe the Arabian sun, to hide from it as they do, but I have

not come to terms with it as they have. My skin is too white, too dangerous in this ozone-shattered world. I have learned to bask in the shade walking from house to house in the compound with a parasol over my greying head.

Every year I visit. There used to be six or seven visits in a year. Then slowly they became less. There was less need on their part, less travelling needed on ours. My youngest Arab 'grandchildren' scarcely know me now. Only the older ones recognise the English grandmother and run with wide arms for me to catch them and swing them round and round. The little ones stand back shyly. It takes hours or days to win them.

I feel somewhere inside that time will pass and it will all be a dream. I will sit in our Cornish garden with its primroses and bluebells and columbine and I'll remember the jasmine and bougainvillaea and the Sheikha and Um Hamed and it will all be unreal, a vision of the mind.

Um Hamed is already a dream. She has gone. She is dead. Suddenly, shockingly, she is dead. That beautiful creature has already passed into the realms of the mind where she lives with an eternal grace, her alluring voice calling to you over some impassable divide.

The Sheikha never speaks of her, as though the pain of the loss is too great to allow. Um Hamed was her confidante. She was the ear to her voice, the reflection of her mind's eye, her sounding board. She misses Um Hamed as she would miss her alter ego.

As for Shamza, Um Hamed's beautiful daughter, she was rushed into an early marriage after the death of her mother. She married her first cousin, both of them stunned into agreeing with forceful adults. Surrounded by the same large and powerful hareem, she now lives in strict purdah, rarely seen, rarely emerging from her cloister of grief.

The pain of Um Hamed's death overlay the move to Abu Dhabi. The Sheikha used the move as an unconscious therapy and every complication was a disguised blessing. Even today she would not admit that she missed Al Ain. She could never admit that the pattern of her life had a disappointment, for that would mean that she dishonoured God. All is in His hands and if it is His will that Um Hamed be called to Paradise and that she herself be in Abu Dhabi, then that is as it should be. She is His willing servant.

Moving was a long, involved affair. It happened slowly over months, if not a year, as the palace never seemed quite ready. It is a vast place, architecturally uninspired and with the multiple flaws which bedevil buildings in a city where too much construction is undertaken with too few overseers and is completed by too few craftsmen. Drains crack, unseasoned wood warps, windows are carelessly fitted and roofs leak. These are common problems in every villa, mansion, office building or palace on the Gulf.

None of it would have mattered too much except for the rain. With every passing year there seems to be more rain. Deluges flood the new streets without gutters. Downpours drive through leaking windows and roofs, overburdening household drains, bursting sewage pipes and soak-aways. Umbrellas are now household necessities. If I forget my parasol I can always borrow an umbrella.

'It is the trees that brought the rain,' some say. Millions of trees have been planted on the command of Sheikh Zayed.

'It is God's blessing. A blessing. We cannot have oil without water,' say others.

Whatever the cause, the effect is the same. The mini monsoon may drain away in days, but it leaves its mark. It leaves damp, festering spots on newly painted ceilings and walls. It leaves cracked pavements and streets caked in drying mud.

The rains had not begun when I arrived in November. November is a dry, pleasant, quiet month, as though a rest was needed after the exhaustion of the summer heat. I was met at the airport by a driver. The sons are now too busy with their businesses, and the drivers know me well. I got in the back of the Sheikha's Mercedes and leaned my head wearily against the cushioned seat. Travelling overnight has never suited me, but the day planes from London land too late for the early-to-bed routine of the hareem.

We drove down the broad highway, now well signposted in both English and Arabic, turned off for the 'Sheikh' section of Abu Dhabi and headed for the palace.

'You are tired,' said the smiling Omani driver.

'It is a long way,' I answered. 'How is your wife and the children?'

'They are well, thanks be to God, and your family? Your husband and children?'

'Well, thanks be to God,' I answered.

'You will make a long visit, God willing?'

'God willing. But Christmas is coming.'

'Ah, Christmas.'

So we drove on until I saw the wall around the great palace. The wall is, as always, mounted with lights, but the gate is different. Now the gate-man sits in a little house from which he operates a red and white pole which bars the way just like the barriers of car parks. The gate-man lifts it automatically when he sees the car and waves when he sees its English passenger. He knows me. They all know me and greet me with the warmth of years of knowing or years of reputation.

Once inside the gates we pass the great men's majlis with its long, long dining room and its many, many guest rooms all for male guests. We pass the family mosque and the men's informal majlis with its billiard room and its adjacent swimming pool. We pass the servants' houses and the main kitchen which inside is a look-a-like for a steel-cupboarded modern hotel kitchen, a look-a-like with the exception of the adjoining barbecue pits which had been forgotten and then built into a too small walled area. Here the wraith-like bodies of cooking genies preside over blazing fires even in summer, their bodies sweated down to muscle and bone, their eyes wide with blank staring. I wonder what cruelty in a past life condemned them to this or what future sainthood awaits them.

We drive through more gates and there in a garden park are the houses; the great family house for the Sheikha with the women's majlis and the rooms of Sheikha Grandmother beside it. There are the sons' houses, three in a row. All the same on the outside, all different on the inside, like bonbons with different centres.

We pull up in front of the Second Son's house. I will stay here for a day or two, then spend a day or two with the Youngest Son. I go back and forth, visiting, visiting.

Inside, the rooms of the Second Son's house are very big and very quiet. There is an air of not quite finished, not quite furnished. He is a 'poor' man compared to his brothers, a professional man who has made a long-term investment in life. Though he may have the income of a top British executive he is poor in money by Abu Dhabi 'Sheikh' standards. But he is rich in reputation.

His wife rises to greet me from a couch in a small area beside the stairs. All the wives have chosen this little area to 'live' in. The television is always there, always on. The telephone is there, the tape machines, the book shelves and coffee tables with magazines. They live in the stairwell, the only central, small area of the big house.

Their youngest daughter, born within three days of my youngest grandson, is tied by her ankle to a marble pillar near the staircase itself. She is tied with a long lead of torn black veiling. Eighteen months old, she sits with her toys all around her, shrugging her shoulders up and down, up and down to music from a tape.

Seeing me she scrambles to her feet and brings me her Teddy, her English Teddy sent out from London. She laughs doubling over, eyes dancing, hands held to her mouth. She is her father's image. Thin and wiry, she is shy of no-one. I kneel down, undo her lead and lift her high.

'If you let her she will go up the stairs,' says her mother.

'I must send you a gate,' I answer and we greet each other with kisses.

Another baby is in a walker. A boy. The pride of the house. The eldest daughter, once our baby, is in school, private school where she learns English as a second language from teachers 'out from England'.

'Come. Mali will bring your case to your room.'

It is the same maid. The one who shakes her head when she means yes. We are old friends now. There are new maids too and a new ayah for the baby boy. But there is still the paucity of furniture, the barren look of rooms and walls.

My room is enormous. Its double bed seems to float on a sea of carpet. The windows overlook the garden square, which is very like a London square with its surround of hedge and drive, but the trees are young orange and lemon, mango and date instead of plane or oak or ash.

The room is airy and orderly and once my cases are unpacked, I lie down to absorb the quiet, drifting off into a jet-lagged nap. When I wake I listen to the near silence and wonder why stillness means so much to me now, why I drink it in like a thirsty animal. It is as though my mind can no longer function without being first refreshed by silence. Have I seen too much, done too much, been too far, too fast, too many times? Have I leapt from world to world to world once too often?

I shake off the thinking and rise and dress for this world. I now have a larger wardrobe for Abu Dhabi than I have for London. My long silk dresses hang in rows in the wardrobe. The traditional ones have all been given to me by the sons' wives. I take down a red one and slide it over my head. I never thought I could wear red but to the delight of the Youngest Son's wife it is flattering.

Yes, he is married. The handsome, charming, self-confident boy is now a married man with a small son of some two years.

He was married in Abu Dhabi. I was there. Yes, of course I was there, but I had nothing to do with his house. Nothing whatever. It was all furnished by a decorator from the town. I have no idea who the man was but he knew how to impress. The ceilings are heavily picked out in gold. The furniture is gilt, ornate, Italian. The carpets are thick, the curtains rich. Only one area reflects the real taste and life of the Youngest Son. The stairwell. Here a white modern couch without an ounce of decoration faces a bank of computerised equipment. Television, tape recorders, video, telephones, clocks, computers are all inset like the panel of a submarine. Here the poet cum mathematician cum engineer cum businessman lives out his dreams and relaxes.

Three days before his marriage we sat there together, his eyes heavy with

exhaustion. He leaned back against the couch and said, 'My God, what have I done? Why did I agree?'

I said nothing as I poured his tea. English tea in English cups. Then he began again. 'What is she like? What do you really think? She is arrogant I think. She doesn't like me to joke about my mother. You know how I like to joke.'

I had visited his prospective bride at his specific request. I would have visited in any event, but he particularly asked me, so I had paid a formal visit with the Sheikha. Though I had never met her, I'd heard about her for years. She had refused to marry until she completed her university correspondence course. Yes. She was the girl who had refused the Eldest Son.

A favourite of her father, when we finally met I realised why. Tall, my own height, thin, with fine features, she had an easy grace and her eyes spoke with particular intelligence. She spoke English with scarcely an accent and her grammar was neat. Arrogant? Never. Independent of mind and spirit? Yes. Traditional? Absolutely.

The Abu Dhabi wedding was totally different from that of the Second Son six years earlier. Invitations, silver-embossed invitations, were sent to the Sheikhas of the area and their hareems. As for the maksar, there was no procession to collect the guests. Instead the hareems drove in separate splendour to an enormous tent erected near one of the homes of the bride's father. The carpets were covered with chairs, rows and rows of chairs making it quite impossible to sit on the floor. At the front were two rows of couches for the 'important guests'. The elite were now very elite.

A woman singer entertained us before our breakfast feast which was laid in a second tent. The gifts of jewels were in steel cases with bullet-proof glass. Women police were everywhere.

All this had been preceded by an authorised three days of celebrations. Anything longer was against the law, as was the carrying of guns and shooting them off. The three days ended for the men in an enormous dinner in the ballroom of the Hilton. It could have been the Meridian, the Intercontinental, the Sheraton or any other large and famous hotel.

When the Youngest Son's bride came home, she wore white from a couture house of Europe. Her hands were exquisitely hennaed, but the henna had come from some commercial preparation already mixed into a tube. It gave her a tormenting allergy. There was no gold cap, no gold bib, no gold entwined in her hair. Instead there were magnificent modern jewels. She paraded up and down the great palace majlis in front of hundreds of richly dressed women. She paraded like a European princess

in European white and wearing her own *savoir faire*.

As I settled into the red dress which she had chosen for me, I remembered a brief meeting I had had with the new bride and her father shortly after her marriage. Her father was the uncle who had put us on the ruler's plane when the Youngest Son had been so ill. The Sheikha's brother.

'I am glad you were here for the wedding,' said the uncle. 'It was good of you to come so far.'

'But he is like a son to me,' I answered. 'Of course I had to come.'

'And I hope my daughter will be a daughter to you,' he said gravely.

'I am sure she will,' I answered.

I didn't know then how close we would become. I didn't know how often they would be in London, how often we would be together and how I would long to show her our way of life, knowing at the same time that to show her much was impossible. It was impossible to take her to concerts or the theatre, impossible to take her to lunch anywhere other than my home. She was caught in that limbo between two worlds, but with a sublime innocence she didn't even know it.

She was not like the Second Son's wife. She was not at all like our kitten with the bell-like laugh. The arrogance of that child-woman had long since worn off. Her air of knowing all had given way to a desire to know more and we spent long hours together exchanging the knowledge we each had. She shared her knowledge of the area. I told her of life 'outside' for, unlike her sisters-in-law, she never travelled. Trips to Al Ain and to her mother's hareem were like cups of cold water in a parched land. With a mercurial temperament, she had often made wrong decisions which her husband and children suffered, but I felt that the temper was only a reflection of her shuttered life. She thrashed around mentally looking for some way out. On the other hand, I knew that had she been given a way out, she would have run back to her purdah like a frightened child. She too was in limbo.

I went to look for her. She was sitting in the stairwell playing with her baby boy.

'Come,' she said. 'They call us for lunch. I think you sleep. Come.'

She arranged her mask and veils, I fetched my parasol and we walked into the sun. It was a five-minute walk to the dining majlis, especially at their pace, which is slow to meandering. On the way we discussed my plans to go to Al Ain.

'I must go this time,' I said. 'I must go to compare, to make notes. You will speak to Sheikha for me? She won't want me to go, but you girls must help me get there.'

'It is difficult because no-one is there,' she answered. No-one meant a

complement of some eight workers and servants.

'I must go,' I repeated, as we walked up the two or three steps into the dining majlis.

Hussa and Shama were there, sitting on the couches that lined the majlis walls. Hussa was as strong, as welcoming as ever. Shama was as ageless as ever.

Little Miriam and Amina were there. They had grown into teenagers. Amina was on the telephone. She was always on the telephone. She rose to greet me, dragging the long cord behind her. Amina was all coquetry, Miriam all devotion.

The Sheikha's daughter was there, her eyes laughing and eager when she saw me. She was a grown woman now, continually reading, continually learning. She had tucked one degree under her belt with the aid of tutors and a library of books, but had not married, which was a constant worry to her mother. No doubt something would be arranged within the year as the girl was well past the marrying age, which was usually between sixteen to twenty these days. I loved her dearly. She could always see the funny side of life. Indeed, if you asked her, I think she would say that God made man as His own private joke.

'Everything is crazy, Mrs Tea Cup, everyone is crazy,' she'd say, but behind her eyes were tears. She was a Pagliacci.

Lunch was laid on the floor along with a stack of plates. These days we each had our own plates, as there was such a variety of food that the constant passing of platters around the table had become a nonsense. Plates were the only answer, but we still ate with our hands.

We didn't wait for Sheikha Grandmother. She ate in her room. We didn't wait for the Sheikha. There were now so many of us that one or the other of the young daughters-in-law would start the meal. We sat round the table and peeled off the silver foil which covered each dish. There were no more conical hats.

No one knew when the Sheikha arrived. She stood quietly in the door, silhouetted against the sun, holding her adopted daughter by the hand. I think no-one heard her or saw her. It was the child who broke the moment. She ran to greet me and as I hugged her, we all stood to welcome her mother. She was welcomed as friend, mother, mother-in-law. She was still the centre of this wheel of women.

Looked at through the lens of time, the Sheikha was the same but not the same. We were both older. She was a bit thinner, I was a bit fatter. But oh, how glad I was to see her. After the usual tumble of words in two languages, we held each other's hands for a moment in that wordless way

of greeting we had both accepted. Our eyes spoke everything that was necessary. We had known each other through too many years, too many crises, too many joys to need to struggle with language.

The Eldest Son's wife joined us, lifting her veils off her face, speaking to a waiting servant and welcoming me all in one moment of arrival. What a confident, competent person that shy little bird had become. For some inexplicable reason, she was the only person in Abu Dhabi or Al Ain who greeted me with a nose kiss. She always greeted me nose to nose, as though I had been born one of them. She and the Sheikha and I sat together at the 'table', exchanging news while they both heaped more and more food on my plate.

The last person to arrive was the Youngest Son's wife. She had the farthest to walk. I rose again and she smiled at the sight of my red kandora.

'It is your colour. You should always wear it,' she said, kissing me on both cheeks, French fashion.

During lunch, the Second Son's wife told the Sheikha that I wanted to go to Al Ain.

'Al Ain? Why? We are all here. Why go there? No-one is there. It is empty. No. You must be with us.'

The Second Son's wife explained that I wanted to see Al Ain to compare, to see the changes, to see it for my writing. They all knew that I was always writing, always making notes, and they always helped me 'to make all correct', but I think they doubted whether it would ever be fruitful.

'I want my people to know the truth, Sheikha,' I said, watching her eyes behind her mask. 'To know that you are not as they think you are, masked creatures from some other world. I want them to know your life, its charm and the way you are so welcoming and caring. Help me in this.'

She sat for a moment. The Youngest Son's wife translated the words again for her, carefully explaining.

Then the Sheikha said, 'Um Yusef, it is we who must understand you. Somehow we must begin to understand.' Her eyes looked beyond me into some blank darkness which she couldn't fathom. Then, turning to the Second Son's wife, she said, 'Your husband will take her when he goes? Only the farmer is there and a few others. He must take a servant. He must be responsible.'

'Yes, tawil omrich,' said the Second Son's wife, smiling like a conspirator in a grand plot.

All was now approved. I would go to Al Ain.

Two days later the Second Son and I left for the Buraimi. The sun was already dropping behind the horizon when our mini-caravan of three cars

slipped quietly out of the main gate and on to the highway. The young Sheikh and I were in his new black Mercedes. An escort of friends followed in a white Mercedes and the servants tailed behind in a blue Buick. The Buick would be left for my use in Al Ain. Now it was loaded with some of the young Sheikh's desert equipment, for he was going on a four-day expedition. While he was away, I would stay in the Al Ain compound in the care of one of his escorts, a driver and a house servant. The farmer and his family were in their house on the farm, the gardener was there along with a few house boys, as well as an old woman servant called Mosa who had stayed on in her box of a house, overseeing the kitchens and roaming around the houses. I would be anything but alone.

We drove steadily up the road toward the new bridge, then over it and on to the Al Ain highway. Its six lanes crack over the sand like a whiplash. Wordlessly the Second Son reached for his seat belt. It was the first time I had ever seen him wear one. Immediately I, too, buckled in, guessing at the speeds we would travel. His car was a superb piece of machinery, computerised, quiet and capable of cruising at well over 100 mph. At night there would be heavy traffic as new villages and work centres spotted almost the entire length of the way. The threat of crashing into a camel had given way to the threat of crashing into poorly trained immigrant drivers. Hibiscus bushes planted years ago in the traffic islands had now reached a height of eight feet or more, protecting eyes from the headlights of oncoming cars and trucks.

The Second Son was silent as he drove, his mind deep in plans for his expedition. Suddenly he spoke. 'You will be all right. I will leave Ahmed with you to take you wherever you want to go. Omer will stay as driver and Abdullah will care for you in the house.'

I knew them all well. Ahmed had assumed Hassan's place as close friend and escort, Hassan having left the service of the family. He had completed his education as an electrical engineer and joined a major company in the area. Omer and Abdullah had been with the Second Son for over five years, one as driver to the family, the other as manservant.

'It is not as you left it,' the young Sheikh went on. 'Nothing is as you left it. The house is a problem with no-one to watch over it every day.'

'Never mind,' I answered. 'I'll see to it. I'll fix it up enough to stay in it.'

'I know,' he laughed. 'I know you.'

In fact his wife had warned me that there were problems with her house as she rarely went to Al Ain.

We drove on in silence again. There was no need to speak. We knew each other too well.

I watched for landmarks, but it was already dark and we were travelling fast. Estirahat Khalifa was just a blip along the way, its shade trees and flower beds sacrificed to the ever widening road. Even the great red sand dunes which once acted as bastion for the Buraimi seemed to have diminished in height.

Beyond the dunes we came to a broad clover-leaf junction. Swinging right in order to join the crossroad, we met the north-eastern approach to Al Ain.

On and on we went round roundabout after roundabout, past the new university, past the new government buildings, past hedges and trees and villas with lights burning bright. With the wide, clean streets, flowers in winter, warm, soft air and palm trees we could have been in Florida's Palm Beach or California's Palm Springs.

At last we reached the area I knew. Swinging right, then left, we drove through the familiar compound gates. Lights were on along the compound wall. Lights were burning on the porches and in the farmer's house, but the rest was dark. No-one was at home. We passed a new house which had been built for the Youngest Son and his wife and finally pulled up in front of what had once been the bride house. The drive from the Abu Dhabi palace to the Al Ain compound had taken an hour and a quarter. It would be another twenty minutes before the other two cars caught up with us.

The young Sheikh got out, went up the porch steps and unlocked the double doors. I followed him and, as the doors swung open, I felt and smelt that awful dank wave of decaying house.

The place was a disaster. Unkempt, dusty, soiled, suffering from the rama, the wood-eating termites, and suffering equally from the minute creatures that eat cement. Chew, chew, chew. You could almost hear them at their work.

My room was a sad echo. The dressing table was gone, eaten by the rama. The wardrobe was broken by the rama. I pulled up my mattress and my bed fell to the floor. Rama, rama, rama. The curtains had years of dust clinging to them and the hot-water pipe in the bathroom was broken.

We dragged the mattress on to the floor and made it up with new sheets which the Second Son had bought for me in Abu Dhabi. There were new pillows and a new blanket, perfume, soap, a toothbrush, all bought for me in Abu Dhabi before we left. Bought with care. An apology? Or just prior knowledge of the situation?

That night I slept amazingly well considering the chewing of the rama. I woke early, made tea and shared it with the Second Son who was already up. He had planned an early start. Abdullah was packing up his things,

checking out a long list.

'I will be far away for four days,' he said as he kissed me goodbye. He looked fresh and eager and ready to be off with his men to places and work that he loved, but there was a dark glint in his eye which meant he was concerned about me.

'God be with you,' he said.

'And with you,' I answered. 'Don't worry, I am well cared for. Go and God go with you.'

As soon as the cars turned out of the gate, I called Abdullah. An orgy of cleaning began. Curtains were taken down, slip covers stripped, carpets beaten and swept, a plumber called for the hot-water system. We threw out the rama-devoured beds. I would have thrown out the wardrobe but felt I was being too ambitious. Shelves were dusted, ornaments washed, windows and doors opened to let in the sun and air. Bathrooms were scrubbed and re-scrubbed. Mosa came to greet me and to cluck-cluck like a mother hen over the flying dust. By the end of the day we were all exhausted, but I went to bed feeling clean and content.

Throughout the day the Youngest Son had been continually on the phone. 'I feel guilty that you are there alone. You can work here. Come back here. I will send a driver.'

I told him that I had a driver. I had Ahmed to escort me. 'Leave me. Let me work,' I said. But he called again. And then again just before I went to sleep. 'I am fine,' I said. 'I'm just going to sleep.'

'Where? On the floor?'

'Yes,' I answered.

'It won't do. He should look after his house,' he said.

'He's busy.'

'He's always busy.'

I made all the necessary soothing sounds of reassurance, said goodnight, hung up and went to sleep.

I slept that night deeply and peacefully, dreaming dreams of gardens and light and joy. In the morning I woke to the dawn call of the muezzin from the family mosque and then slept again. I was at home.

When sleep would come no more, I rose, showered with the now hot water and dressed. My breakfast was waiting for me in the baby majlis. Egg, toast, orange juice and tea. Abdullah, who was just recovering from the shock of the previous day's work, was standing by for further orders. He had folded the freshly laundered curtains, waiting for me to put them up, but before I'd finished my breakfast, Ahmed arrived with Omer and the gleaming Buick.

269

'Shall we go today? Have you finished your work here?' he asked.

'Finished? It will never be finished,' I said. 'But we will go.' The decision seemed to please him. Ahmed was not like Hassan. I knew that once he'd fulfilled his duty to escort me around the town, he'd be off back to Abu Dhabi.

Leaving instructions for Abdullah to continue the housework, I picked up my glasses, parasol and notebook and we set off.

'Where?' asked Ahmed. 'Where do you go?'

'To the Jebel Hafeet,' I said.

I had some sort of nebulous plan in mind to try to retrace the steps of my first visit to the Buraimi, when Abed had acted as guide and we'd climbed the rock mountain. Poor Abed. He had divorced his faithful Palestinian wife to marry again and then again. I had heard that he'd sold his antique shop and left for Bulgaria with his Bulgarian third wife. All had changed.

All had changed on the way to the Hafeet as well. A fountain of huge, gaping, metal shells marked the entrance to what was once the valley for collecting petrified shells and fossils. It was now a 'way' for garages, repair sheds, tyre shops and wheel dealers. It was a quarter of a mile of spare parts for Datsun, Nissan, Honda and Mercedes. Electricity pylons and tall streetlamps lined the road. Humps of tarmac to slow down the traffic erupted continually. All this covered that ancient shell valley.

We moved ever closer to the mountain until it stood above us, until its great rock mass stood glowering over us. The road wound through the jagged rock piles which serve as foothills and we began to climb. It was a new road, a perfect road. Six miles of sleek black tarmac creeping up and up, higher and higher. A man-made snake.

Near the top an area had been levelled as a viewpoint. It was surrounded by steel fencing to keep visitors from tipping off into the desert below. I got out to look down at the way I'd once climbed. Had I done that? Had I really climbed up that precipitous mountainside? It hardly seemed possible, and yet I knew that I had. Below, the green jewel, the Buraimi, was now the centre of a web of highways.

It was cold up there. The steel railings moaned as the wind went through them. It was the same cold wind that had bitten into my soul a dozen years ago, but now there was resignation with it. The mountain was invaded. It would never be the same. They were building a cafeteria up there, for God's sake. The razor back was levelled. The Hafeet had been conquered.

I had seen what I wanted to see, more than I wanted to see. We started down, winding slowly, passing one car on its way up and one lorry on its

way down.

As we neared the foothills, Ahmed decided that I should see the new hotel, the Intercontinental.

'You remember Abed?' he said as we started off.

'How could I forget?' I answered. How could I forget Abed with whom I'd climbed the Hafeet, who had first shown me the falaj, who had introduced me to a slave?

'Well, he is now security chief at the Intercontinental,' said Ahmed.

'Abed? Truly? I thought he'd gone to Bulgaria or some such place. We must go and find him.'

'Perhaps he only works at night,' said Ahmed.

'Then I'll leave him a note.'

We pulled into a parking space in front of the Al Ain Intercontinental and I walked out of the sun into the hotel shade. At the desk a neatly dressed Filipino answered my queries about Abed. Would I like to speak to him, she asked. Yes, I would and within minutes he was in the lobby. A little heavier. A little greyer. But the same Abed.

We had lunch together. I ate too much. Abed ate nothing. We talked. He was disillusioned as much with himself as with the place. He had married for the fourth time. A young Singapore girl. But he missed his first wife who had remarried and lived in Jordan. He missed his daughter. He had been a long time in Al Ain, known too many sadnesses, watched too much money corrupt too many people, watched young Sheikhs founder in their fortunes and old Sheikhs lose their dreams. A bitter edge ravelled Abed's once total devotion.

'I will take you tomorrow on the old tour and some other places,' he said and we arranged to meet the following morning. He drove me back to the compound, Ahmed and Omer having long since returned to their more familiar food.

As I opened the door to the house I was greeted by the comforting smell of polish. Abdullah was waiting both for my approval and with the news that the Youngest Son and his wife had arrived and were in their house next door. Without changing or washing I walked the few steps to the Youngest Son's Al Ain home. It was as unpretentious as his Abu Dhabi house was elaborate.

'We could not let you stay alone, so we came,' said the Youngest Son as I walked in breathlessly. 'I would come in a few days all the same. We just came early, that's all. You are surprised, eh? We surprise you.' The idea seemed to delight him.

I knew that the Youngest Son had considerable business interests in Al

Ain. I knew too that he was trying to make me feel less guilty for bringing him away from his work in Abu Dhabi.

'You will stay here with us, Um Yusef,' said the Youngest Son's wife. 'Everything is ready for you.' She took my hand and showed me to their guest room where everything was indeed ready for me. My suitcases were there. My dresses had been hung in the wardrobe. In the bathroom new towels hung on the towel rails and a beautiful new green kandora was waiting for me. On either side of the bed the Youngest Son had placed two new lamps so that I could read at night. You turned them on and off just by touching the metal.

'I know you like to read and work in bed,' he said, as he tested each lamp.

What could I say? How could I refuse? I accepted and relaxed. The Youngest Son's wife made us a cool fruit drink in her electric blender - one of her specialities - and we sat reminiscing, laughing, enjoying our time together.

Their house was charming and comfortable. Pale blue carpets met white walls, glass doors curtained with long, fine, white curtains opened on to the porch, photographs in silver frames sat on round tables which were in turn covered to the floor in blue silk. Everything was immaculate and the larder was full.

It was obvious that this house was now the centre of life in the compound. Mosa sat in their tahat majlis with the farmer's wife, the maid rustled about in the kitchen and the door was open for all to come and go for news or instructions. The Youngest Son and his wife were in Al Ain often and the Sheikha relied on them for news of her houses and farm. They had made the place their own and I was as relieved to see the condition of their home as I had been saddened to see the Second Son's. I told them about seeing Abed again, about the ride up the Hafeet.

'Everything has changed,' I said. 'How it has changed!'

'Of course it has changed,' he answered quietly. 'Much is different. You knew and I knew it couldn't stay the same. Some of the change you will like, some you will not. I know you. I know what you will smile to see and what you will frown to see. We have to grow, Mrs Tea Cup. We cannot just sit down on the money.'

'It is how you grow that matters, not that you grow,' I said and he shrugged his shoulders in that way that means 'What can I do about it?'

Abed arrived at nine the next morning with a Range Rover and his fourth wife Annie, the pretty girl from Singapore. We set off towards 'Main Street' Al Ain.

Al Ain? That one-time village with a general store, a shade tree, a camel market? Al Ain is a town, a busy town with a flyover flying over a roundabout, a flyover which dwarfs the great mosque with its crystal chandelier. Shops are everywhere. Small shops. Big shops. New markets with tall cement arches. Everything is clean due perhaps in part to lorries marked 'Municipality' which grind slowly through the town, loudspeakers blaring, 'Do not throw litter on the ground. The fine is 500 dirhams (around £90).'

We started down the old road out of Al Ain. I wanted to see that great white fort again. The Al Jahili which once defended the Buraimi from raiders and marauders. The Al Jahili has been restored, but it no longer stands proud on its sandy hill. It is surrounded by a pretty park with a fancy garden wall. It reminds me of an old soldier dressed up for a children's party.

We drove to the edge of town, to Masoudi, where Abed turned off the road. Some tracks lay in front of us. Strange how sudden the change was. There the road, the hedges, the gardens. Here the desert. So much desert. An ocean of desert. They say it moves at two feet a year. What an effort to keep it back. What a Herculean effort. On the way I'd noticed that one stretch of road had a complete lane covered in sand. One week, one month without the army of workers and it would be finished.

We drove until the red desert became beige and the sun stood high. Then we left the car to walk through the sand, letting it slide through our sandals. We sat under a thorn tree drinking Cokes and watching the neat tracks of birds and lizards on the untouched sand. Here nothing had changed. Nothing would change. Like the sky, the desert was immortal.

Unhurried, we returned to the car and drove out of the desert and back into the Buraimi to the Oman side. We drove to the old market. It was now a new market with vegetables and fruits piled high, pick-up trucks honking in and out and no sign of the ancient Nubian and his miniature pipe. We bought some water melons and set out again toward the Oman mountains, driving mile after mile across a pebble-strewn landscape. Desert, yes, but a desert of stones, sharp and unyielding.

When we returned to the bride house that evening, tired and thirsty and sun-smitten, I thanked my old friend and his new wife for another unforgettable day which would be stored in the mind's bank. Abed. I wondered if the echelons of the Intercontinental knew that their security chief was an archaeologist, antiquities expert and guide not only to the area but to the life of the place, to the Sheikhs themselves. I doubted it.

Now there was only one day left. One day before the Second Son returned from the desert. One day to savour the peace of this place. I asked

whether a carpet could be placed for me in front of the Sheikha's house.

'Like the old times?' asked the Youngest Son.

'Like the old times,' I answered.

'But no-one will be there.'

'I will be there,' I said.

They indulged me as always. A carpet was pulled out on to the Sheikha's porch. Two white cushions, immaculately clean, were placed against the side of the house. I settled down with a sigh of content and sat listening to the sounds of the day. Birds flew in and out of the pergola. Thin, small, hardy little birds always looking for water, bathing in dust. Bedu birds.

A blossom fell from the bougainvillaea vine and blew toward my feet. I remembered Um Hamed walking through the pergola, blossoms showering on to her black veils. She is dead, but the blossoms are there, falling and drifting towards me.

Mosa came with coffee sent over by the Youngest Son's wife. She sat pouring cup after cup, talking in her heavy patois, asking me about my children and grandchildren. My eyes turned toward the majlis. I thought I saw a black-veiled figure coming down the porch, but there was no-one there.

This is a ghost house. There are no black veils, no smell of incense, no children playing, no voices laughing, no silks rustling. Only the sound of the birds and the trees moving in the autumn wind. It is over. The days have passed.

I sat there all morning. I sat there until the noon call for prayers, the muezzin's voice calling from the family mosque. God, the one God, the creator, and Mohamed his prophet. The chant continued high and penetrating. I could see the tower of the mosque rising like the handle of a sword in front of me. The sword of Islam has been plunged deep into the centre of the earth here. It is a declaration of sovereignty.

I love this place. I love the grace of it, the space of it, the way the autumn wind blows not too hot, not too cold. I love the peace of it. Prayer and praise seem to seep out of the very ground here. Will that protect it? Will that keep the sand barricaded? Will it stop the rama of the spirit, the rama of the soul? If not, nothing will.

The Second Son arrived before dusk. He came out of the desert, tired, satisfied, his smile lighting his face before it reached his mouth.

'I need a shower and a sleep,' he said. 'It was rocky where we were and my back is all bruises.'

'It was good?' I asked.

'Yes, good.'

I explained that I was sleeping in the house of his brother. 'You can entertain all your Al Ain friends.'

'No, thank you,' he laughed. 'I will sleep and tomorrow we'll go.'

Abdullah took his kit, his escort said their goodbyes and the young Sheikh went off to his room to sleep the night around.

I have no idea what he does in the desert. Sometimes I think he goes out there to get away from us all. Sometimes he refines maps, he says. Sometimes he surveys the land. Sometimes he is with geologists, sometimes without. But he tells me that he feels alive out there with his men. Alive as in no other place, and I understand.

In the morning we all met, the Youngest Son's wife covering her mask with her veils because the Second Son was there. We all talked together. The Youngest Son and his wife decided to stay on for a few days. I would go down with the Second Son.

As my case was packed into the car, I looked around the compound and wondered when or if I would see it again. Who knows what is in store for us? As the car turned out of the gate, I didn't turn round. I didn't look back.

Postscript

IN ABU DHABI that evening, the Sheikha and the young wives and daughters and I set out on our usual evening walk after supper. It was a nightly exercise. A ritual. The Sheikha changed to an incongruous pair of plimsolls while the rest of us made do with our sandals. We walked round and round the centre garden as though perambulating around a London square. We talked and joked and told the news of the day. The children followed us. That night the stars were hanging above us clear and bright and close. Suddenly I saw a shooting star.

'Look. Look,' I called and took the hand of the Sheikha's adopted daughter to show her the star.

'Look. Look,' I said. 'It's a shooting star. A shooting star.'

The Sheikha stopped, and putting an arm around the shoulders of her daughter, she pointed to the sky.

'No, no,' she said. 'That is not a star that shoots. No. Not at all. You must understand, my daughter. You must understand the truth. When a devil rises from the earth and tries to reach heaven, God throws a star to knock him down. This is the truth. It is written.'

She turned to me, 'This is the truth, Um Yusef. You will not believe, but this is the truth. It is written. We see many of these stars in these days. Many devils are trying to reach heaven.'

I too believed that many devils were trying to reach heaven. What did it matter whether her definitions of devils and mine differed? I understood what she meant. I had crossed the bridge to her world.

The question now was whether she would be caught in limbo trying to cross to mine.

Glossary

Note: It is difficult to write Arabic words in English as the sounds are entirely different. These words are as used in the Abu Dhabi area.

abaya	:	long coats made of a very finely woven natural fibre; sometimes trimmed with gold
areesh	:	house made of palm fronds
bedu	:	those who live a nomadic life in the desert and adhere to certain ancient principles of survival, particularly hospitality
bibi	:	mistress (Urdu)
bilaleet	:	sweet vermicelli occasionally presented with a thin omlette on top
della	:	coffee pot
falaj	:	irrigation channel or canal
ghee	:	clarified butter (Hindu)
Hadith	:	sayings of the prophet Mohamed
harees	:	mortared cracked wheat and lamb
helawa	:	Arabian sweets
kandora	:	dress; refers to men's costumes as well as women's dresses
kohl	:	mascara made of a finely powdered type of coal
majlis	:	principal meeting room; drawing room
maksar	:	literally a large tent; colloquially, the women's wedding party
mashwi lamb	:	whole lamb marinated in lemon juice and spices, baked slowly in a pit over and under sand heated by fire
Qur'an	:	Holy book of the Muslims containing revelations as heard by the Prophet Mohamed
rama	:	local termite
sandook	:	chest

serwal	:	women's under-pantaloons, usually cut like jodhpurs fastening at the waist and at the ankle. Adults' serwal have several inches of embroidery at the ankle
shayla	:	veil
sheikh	:	leader of a tribe; (modern usage) a leading figure in the tribe and his sons. Also applied to certain respected religious men
sheika	:	daughter of a sheikh; (modern usage) also wife of a sheikh
suffra	:	white or white checked head-dress worn by men
tahat	:	down
tawil omrak (m)	:	untranslatable phrase of respect (literally 'long life yours');
tawil omrich(f)		used in the same context as 'sir' or 'ma'am'/'my lady'
thareed	:	bread and mildly spiced stewed lamb covered in tomato-based soup in which the lamb has been cooked
thoab	:	finely woven over-dress worn by women; usually embroidered with silver or gold thread
ummi	:	my mother
wezaar	:	sarong of fine cotton used by men under the kandora; used as pyjamas

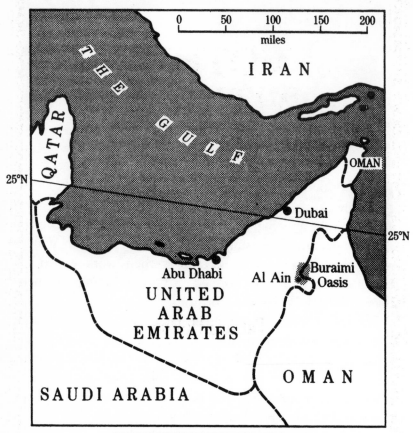

MOTHER WITHOUT A MASK

P ATRICIA Holton was born in Westchester County, New York, and educated at the Madeira School in Virginia and Sarah Lawrence College. She married a Cornishman and they established a business in South Wales, where they had three children. As their work expanded throughout Britain, they moved to London, retaining their links with both Wales and Cornwall.

Through a series of unforeseen circumstances, they found themselves travelling to and working in the Arab world. Patricia has travelled extensively in the Middle East; she knew the Lebanon before it was torn apart by war and subsequently rebuilt. She has made frequent visits to Egypt, Libya and Oman, but her greatest love is Al Ain in the United Arab Emirates, the setting for this book.